MER   APR 2 7 2016

35444002567500

362.29092 LAN

Lansky, Sam

The gilded razor a memoir

WITHDRAWN

D0349754

the
Gilded Razor

the
Gilded Razor

A Memoir

Sam Lansky

Thompson-Nicola Regional District
Library System
300 - 465 VICTORIA STREET
KAMLOOPS, B.C. V2C 2A9

GALLERY BOOKS
New York   London   Toronto   Sydney   New Delhi

G

Gallery Books
An Imprint of Simon & Schuster, Inc.
1230 Avenue of the Americas
New York, NY 10020

Copyright © 2016 by Sam Lansky

All rights reserved, including the right to reproduce this book or portions thereof in any form whatsoever. For information address Gallery Books Subsidiary Rights Department,
1230 Avenue of the Americas, New York, NY 10020.

Some names, locations, and identifying details have been changed.

First Gallery Books hardcover edition January 2016

GALLERY BOOKS and colophon are registered trademarks of Simon & Schuster, Inc.

For information about special discounts for bulk purchases, please contact Simon & Schuster Special Sales at 1-866-506-1949 or business@simonandschuster.com.

The Simon & Schuster Speakers Bureau can bring authors to your live event. For more information or to book an event, contact the Simon & Schuster Speakers Bureau at 1-866-248-3049 or visit our website at www.simonspeakers.com.

Interior design by Jaime Putorti

Manufactured in the United States of America

10 9 8 7 6 5 4 3 2 1

Library of Congress Cataloging-in-Publication Data

Lansky, Sam.
    The gilded razor : a memoir / Sam Lansky.
          pages cm
        1.   Lansky, Sam—Childhood and youth. 2.   Teenagers—Substance use—United States — Biography. 3.   Drug addiction—Treatment—United States. 4.   Gay teenagers—United States—Biography. 5.   Authors, American — 21st century—Biography.   I. Title.
      HV5805.L36A3 2016
      362.29092 — dc23
      [B]
                                                                      2015015092

ISBN 978-1-4767-7614-9
ISBN 978-1-4767-7616-3 (ebook)

3 5444 00256750 0

the

Gilded Razor

Prologue

*F*or many years after it was over, there were songs I could not listen to, for fear they would take me back there; certain photographs that made me clench my jaw in a particular way; and street corners where, crossing from a subway exit to reach an appointment or a restaurant, I would flash back momentarily to a long-forgotten winter night years earlier and see myself, seventeen years old and spectral in the lamplight, stumbling out of a brownstone with a runny nose and my fly unzipped. My hair would have been too long, probably, from always taking the money my father gave me for a haircut and using it to buy drugs. ("What do you mean, 'It doesn't look any different'?" I'd ask, always doe-eyed.) My hands would have been wedged into my pockets because I always forgot to wear gloves. And I would have been walking briskly back to my father's apartment, eager to get into bed and pretend it never happened.

I say that I would have done so because so often I did, but if I could, I would do it differently. Memory is a funny type of haunting. The subconscious keeps chewing away at sins atoned for long ago. Even after everything has been set right, the body doesn't forget the places it's been.

Stockholm. I sleep badly, tossing and turning in my hotel room. In the night, I awake from strange, listless dreams. The furniture turns to gold when I touch it, then crumbles into dust, silken as ash. I'm just tired, I tell myself; it's just jet lag—the foreignness of a new place. One morning I wake up and the bed is full of glitter. I fall back asleep, and when I awake again, the sheets are crisp and white as fresh snow.

At a fancy party, there's a champagne toast; I hold my glass up to the light, watching the bubbles fizzle and break as they meet the surface. I set it down on the table unsipped. I am used to that by now. It may not always get better, but it will always get different. That was the promise—the only promise.

There are ghosts around every corner. At a cocktail bar in Södermalm: I am alone at a table, writing in a notebook, when I see a man I recognize, although I can't say from where. He smiles at me—he knows me, too, and more intimately than I know him. He has a handsome, doleful face. Faces like that all blur together for me now. His name could be Jim, or Steve. He could be an investment banker or a surgeon or a congressman.

He approaches me. Slowly, he reaches out to touch my face and presses a finger against my cheek. I want to ask what he's doing, but instead I just sit there, frozen. He raises his hand to show me. On the tip of his thumb, there is a speck of glitter.

"Where did that come from?" I ask. We both begin to laugh.

I don't go home with him because things are different now.

But that night, alone in my room, I dream of falling down the stairs in a town house in Boston. I dream that I'm running through the ruddy desert of Utah, with no shoes on, under a silver moon.

I dream that my apartment is full of snow, and there are wolves at the foot of the bed, nipping at my ankles.

One

I was seventeen years old and had been subsisting on a diet of cigarettes and Adderall for months. Now, on a sunny fall morning, I was on my way to visit Princeton.

My father was waiting downstairs, on Eighty-eighth Street off West End Avenue, in front of our apartment building. He had rented a nondescript blue sedan—no frills, with upholstery that smelled faintly medicinal, talk radio pontificating from the tinny speakers—and now stood with one hand on the hood of the car, making small talk with the doorman. On his hand, his wedding ring was conspicuously absent.

As I watched him, I convinced myself that I could see a trace of a tan line on his ring finger, a thin band of flesh paler than the natural olive of his skin—but then I blinked, and it was only a trick of the light. I shook my head. It was a stupid, sentimental thought.

I usually tried not to think about my parents' divorce: its once-prominent space in my consciousness had descended into the shadows of everyday normalcy, and now sometimes it even seemed as if they had never been together at all. In the same way that I watched people milling about in midtown Manhattan, so inoculated to the city's mammoth scale that they no longer realized how strange and spectacular a sight it was—the skyscrapers, the crowds, concrete and steel—the emptiness left by my parents' separation was so enormous that I had forgotten how it once felt extraordinary. And when I was in midtown, I, too, looked straight ahead like a native New Yorker. Only a tourist would look up. Only someone embarrassing would still be haunted by the collapse of his parents' marriage a full year after it had happened.

I stood on the sidewalk for a moment, nursing a sickly sweet cup of bodega coffee and sucking down my first cigarette of the morning. In a paper bag at my feet was a lemon poppy seed muffin, glazed with a sugary sheen, which I had bought not to eat but to prove to myself that I could keep from eating. I wasn't about to ruin my diet by eating solid food now, especially on the day I was to visit Princeton, which I had recently decided was probably my dream school.

I was dressed in preppy staples—a V-neck sweater in a warm autumnal scarlet, the ivory collar of a dress shirt starched and collegiate around my throat, a rep tie knotted in a loose four-in-hand. My father wore a long-sleeved thermal shirt and jeans, the self-effacing functionality of which annoyed me. Whenever he came home from work, he always seemed eager to shed the markers of his professional life—the cuff links, the wool slacks—and change into something comfortable and utilitarian. I preferred to keep my tie on until I went to bed, not wanting to lose the power I pretended it gave me, aligning me with the pedigreed prep school boys whose cravats were always effortlessly askew. There were even nights when I slept in my blue blazer—a security blanket, I told myself, to remind me who I was supposed to be. (Mostly, though, I did this so I could tell people I'd done it—I hoped it would make me seem more interesting, somehow.)

Earlier that summer, my father had told me he would take me on a trip to visit the colleges that interested me, but I'd been wary. My prospects for college were dim. I was already certain that no school that met my impossibly high standards would accept me as a student, and no school that accepted me as a student could possibly be worth attending. Princeton, a bastion of privilege—even the name sounded rich in my mouth, *Princeton*—seemed like the institution most beyond my reach, which was exactly what made it attractive.

But the actual process of applying felt so tedious. I preferred to spend my time in self-aggrandizing fantasy or its darker counterpart, neurotic dread; it was much easier obsessing than actually *doing* anything.

Most of all, the whole thing seemed implausible: Would my father really make the time to chauffeur me up and down the Northeast Corridor to check out colleges that he and I both knew were too good for me? His travel schedule for business was unrelenting, and even when he was in the city, he often stayed at the Upper East Side apartment of his girlfriend, Jennifer.

So now that we were finally leaving on this road trip, any flickering enthusiasm I might have felt for this next chapter of my life was smothered by what I perceived as the emptiness of my father's gesture. Surely this college tour had nothing to do with where I would actually end up going to school. It was about maintaining the lie that I was a happy and successful teenager with a bright future before me. I had to keep going through the motions, because if I didn't, my father might start to pay closer attention to me. *That* was the last thing I needed.

Yet even though I hustled my father constantly, lying and manipulating him to keep him at arm's length, I was devastated by the fact that he couldn't see through it. I wanted him to know me deeply enough to recognize that I was struggling. Not that I would have admitted it at the time.

My mood grew foul as I lingered on the sidewalk, smoking the cigarette down to the filter. My father called my name and I extinguished the butt with the toe of my loafer, then stalked over to the car. As usual, he had not realized that I was upset—but then, I hadn't realized I was upset yet, either, let alone why—and I was unwilling to tell him. Instead, and also as usual, I was determined to punish him for not understanding this thing that even I didn't understand by being as sullen as possible.

I slid into the passenger seat. The mood in the car felt heavy. To most seventeen-year-olds, I imagined, college represented liberation, a period of endless possibility, but for me, the idea of being shackled to academia for another four years was exhausting.

I was what I liked to call myself in fits of self-description a "lazy overachiever" or a "failed perfectionist"—a deadly combination of ambition and sloth. College would just be the next place where I would strive and fail in the pursuit of excellence, and subsequently loathe myself for it. As I sat in the passenger seat and considered this line of thought, I couldn't help but feel a thrill of smug superiority: To be already so bitter as I toured one of the nation's most prestigious colleges felt like the ultimate mark of how very adult I had become. Certainly it elevated me above the ranks of naively optimistic high school seniors who were genuinely excited about college—those kids weren't as sophisticated as I was. It took years for me to learn that there was a difference between cynicism and maturity. In that car that day, they seemed to be one.

My father looked over at me with a sort of friendly disdain. "You know that everything you own smells like smoke, right?" he said.

"I know, Dad," I said.

"Just checking."

As he turned the key in the ignition, I took out my iPod and put on my father's noise-canceling headphones. We cruised onto the highway. I rolled down my window and let my arm drape lazily on the frame of the car door, feeling the chill of the wind erecting the downy hairs on my arm. It was still early in the morning, and daybreak was crisp and clear. The trees on Riverside Drive were beginning to turn. Autumn was a welcome respite from the steaming heat of the New York summer—my first full New York summer, the brutality of which had astonished me. The city festered and stank, hot mist rising in a scalding cloud from the subway grates where, below, I could hear the shrill whistle of trains piercing the muggy night. Even my cigarettes had wilted.

My father hated the summer heat as much as I did, although we both had spent much of the season away—I went to Oregon to see my now-single mother, while he took frequent business trips punctuated by weekends away with Jennifer. On the rare occasions that we were both in the city at the same time, we sprawled across the living room couch, saturated with perspiration, panting like wounded animals while the air conditioner clicked and whirred, straining against the sauna that was the city.

Strangely, I loved those sweaty moments with my father, those instances of shared suffering, though I lacked the emotional intelligence to ever tell him so. On some level I must have recognized the significance of those times because I locked them away in my mind as evidence that there was a bond between us more meaningful than blood. I could see it, but I couldn't quite access it; I couldn't translate it into actual affection.

On those days, which I could have spent lolling around in the heat, my father would quickly grow restless, needing to busy himself with shuffling paperwork at his desk or leaving to take a jog through Central Park. He always seemed most comfortable in motion—like me, he had been chubby as a child, and he exercised religiously.

Now, behind the wheel, he was cool and controlled even as the chaos of rush hour exploded on the street outside. Back in Oregon, my mother would speed and brake breathlessly, muttering expletives under her breath and, on one memorable occasion, careening the wrong way up a one-way street, past a well-marked DO NOT ENTER sign. I missed that recklessness—

especially here, gliding so smoothly through the city with my father.

We approached the mouth of the Lincoln Tunnel, the lanes clotted with underslept commuters. With my headphones on, I could see my father's mouth working, but I pretended not to notice. He tapped me on the shoulder and I took off the headphones. Symphonies of honking horns suddenly screamed around me, making my shoulders clench.

"What?" I said, sighing loudly in a performance of agitation.

"I said, 'First stop, Princeton!' " he said. I could tell how hard he was trying.

"I know, Dad," I said. I wanted to connect with him, but I put the headphones back on instead.

I had never really felt that close to my father. He was the executive director of a nonprofit foundation headquartered at Rockefeller Center. We had moved to New York from my native Oregon a year earlier, after the divorce, when I was sixteen, under the pretense that, based in New York, he would travel less. That didn't happen. It still seemed to me that he was always en route to Dulles, Heathrow, Logan: places I had heard mentioned throughout my childhood, shrouded in mystery, abstract proper nouns muttered across the dinner table while my mother's frustration filled the room, invisible but toxic like carbon monoxide.

But as I got older, those names began to acquire meaning, so that when my father called to tell me that he was stuck on a layover at O'Hare, I could almost feel the steady thrumming of the moving walkways underfoot, a kaleidoscope of multicol-

ored lights overhead in that tacky rainbow tunnel. I felt then as
if I understood him a little better. On the occasions when we
traveled together, I marveled at how he could doze off shortly
after takeoff, with a studied grace born from spending decades
practicing transcontinental commutes. The melting ice in his
half-consumed cranberry juice would fill the plastic cup with
rosewater while he slept peacefully through the screams of apo-
plectic babies. He was unflappable, aloof; on those flights, I
always wanted to wake him and bid for his attention, ask him
to play a card game with me, but that would have been childish.
Instead, I watched him sleep.

He always remained a cipher to me. Even when he told me he
was proud of me, it still felt like I had embarrassed him, somehow.

Or maybe he was always trying to please me. Maybe I was
the one who withheld approval. When we first came to New
York together, a year earlier, he had already been subletting a one-
bedroom, second-floor walk-up in a brownstone on Eighty-first
Street and Columbus, for several months while he commuted
between Portland and New York. Its primary tenant was a real
estate broker who traveled often; he vacated the apartment when
my father was coming to town. It wasn't bad, by New York standards—small and well maintained, with hardwood floors and a
bachelor-like sterility—but I had been sleeping on the couch in
the living room for the past several nights since arriving from Oregon, and I felt claustrophobic, pinned, starved for light.

I came home to that apartment from school and sat at the
kitchen counter, listening to the honking horns on the street out-

side. The noise grew louder until it felt like I was inside a horn, the blast and the blare, my nerves fraying. I was going to boil over. A one-bedroom in a brownstone was a far cry from where the kids at school lived. My father stepped out of the bedroom, freshly showered, with a towel wrapped around his waist. "Oh, Sam," he said. "How was school?"

The noise outside grew distant, then faded away into the clicking of a radiator.

"I can't stay here," I said. "I need to go somewhere else."

He looked at me, studying me as though I were a specimen, then softened. "Okay," he said.

"Can we go to a hotel?" I said.

He nodded. "Okay," he said again.

That night, we walked—each of us wheeling a suitcase like displaced tourists—a few blocks south to a little boutique hotel on Seventy-seventh and Broadway. I liked the glamour of this ("We lived in a hotel when I first got to the city . . . ," I imagined myself telling a throng of rapt if as-yet-nonexistent friends), but it turned out that it was better in theory than in practice. That hotel room was cramped, too, like everything in New York—two queen beds separated by a nightstand, and a desk too small to write at comfortably. I complained that there was nowhere for me to sit and do my homework. My father looked disappointed, as if he had let me down yet again. The next day at school, a girl in study hall, curious about me, asked me where I was living. I told her the name of the hotel.

"Oh," she said. "I haven't heard of it."

Eventually we found a sublet on Eighty-eighth between Broadway and West End, not far from my school. But my father wasn't there very often. A few weeks after he and I arrived in New York, he met Jennifer through mutual friends who took them bicycle riding in Central Park. That was the story, at least, although I entertained a paranoid fantasy that they had met before he split from my mother. My parents ended their marriage after twenty-seven years, and my father began dating Jennifer just a couple months later. Could it really have been so easy for him to say good-bye to my mother and resolve any grief over the dissolution of their marriage all in the space of a few short weeks? I wondered this some nights as I lay awake in bed. My teenage heart was still bruised over wounds inflicted in flings that lasted only a month or two. Was he callous, or just capable of accessing a type of tidy emotional resolution that I, too, would learn someday?

Jennifer lived in Yorkville, in a stately one-bedroom in a pre-war building; my father quickly began spending his evenings with her there, except for the nights that she spent at our apartment.

Jennifer was an executive at a technology company; she reverse commuted to Westchester every day in an old taupe sedan. "I used to drive this fabulous sports car," she said. "But what's the point if you're parking on the street? It's just going to get trashed!" I disliked this, especially since my father frequently borrowed her car. How glorious it could have been to zip all over the city in a fashionable little coupe, the way my friends did in their parents' cars, parked in Upper East Side garages at exorbitant rates.

When she came over, she sat at our kitchen table, drinking from a lipstick-stained glass of red wine and talking about "the corporate culture." She was nice to me, but she often seemed uneasy, too eager to win my approval. She was in her midforties and she had never been married or had children, and I suspected that she saw me as an irritation, an impediment to her ability to hold my father's uninterrupted attention.

She talked to me as if I were her peer, which annoyed me. There was nothing maternal about her, which I was grateful for. She was blond, which I liked, and athletic, which also annoyed me, with half-moon glasses and a smile that split her face sideways into a dozen crinkles. She had grown up in the Southwest and had the sort of style that I associated roughly with a childhood trip to Sedona: turquoise jewelry, velvet blazers, clogs, a shimmery purple leather handbag in the shape of a ruched butterfly. I gave her compliments when she wore something classic, trying to reinforce how I thought she should dress. She fretted about her weight, she trained for and ran marathons, and she drank too much. When she did, she would talk endlessly about her early twenties, when she had lived in Germany, and all the dear friends she had made overseas.

She didn't seem to have many friends in New York, dear or otherwise, I thought—but then, who was I to judge? I was too hard on her, but I couldn't help myself—it *bothered* me. I should have been kinder but I didn't know how.

My father never told me exactly what drew him to Jennifer, but often they giggled like children together, in a way that I found unbecoming. With me, my father was the same as ever, endlessly pacific and perpetually detached. But with Jennifer, he seemed suddenly vitalized, leonine, coming home in his bike shorts on a hazy summer day, shaking sweat from his hair, boyishly besotted. There was something about her that electrified him, and I hated her for invigorating him in a way that neither my mother nor I could.

It took me a long time to fully realize how I experienced his happiness: as a betrayal, an abandonment, the creation of a new family. One that didn't include me.

Jennifer was exactly what a second wife should be, even before they married. There was a levity, an ease to her, that my mother never had. I had inherited my mother's emotional intensity—maybe that was why, like her, I couldn't fully connect with my father. I believed that I should like Jennifer, and pretended to myself that I did. "I'm happy to see my dad so happy," I would say when anyone asked me about her. This was untrue, but it seemed like the mature, adult thing to say, and people nodded appropriately.

I hurt Jennifer's feelings one time, not long after they began dating. I was standing on the corner of our block finishing a smoke when I saw her crossing the street toward me, her gait slightly lopsided. She spotted me as I extinguished my cigarette.

"You shouldn't be smoking!" she said. I shrugged in response, smelling the wine on her breath. She reached on a mailbox to steady herself. The wind had blown her hair askew. She was sloppy, I thought snidely. I *never* let myself get that sloppy. (In truth, I got that sloppy pretty regularly.)

"Are you going to see my dad?" I said.

"Yes," she said. "I was just in the neighborhood and thought I'd stop by. Is he home?"

I nodded.

"All right," she said, hesitating. I resented her for monopolizing his attention. Not that I wanted to spend time with him, frankly, but I wanted him to *want* to spend time with me, and when she was around, he didn't.

"Well, be careful," I said. "It looks like you've had a few. Don't want your new boyfriend to think you're a drunk." Our rapport up till then had always been friendly, but it came out sounding nastier than I had intended. She looked as though she had been slapped.

"That was so mean," she said.

"I'm sorry," I said, backpedaling. "I didn't mean it like that." *Like what?* I didn't know. I could feel that amity between us, the amity I had been working so hard to cultivate, evaporating.

"It's fine," she said. "I'm going upstairs." She didn't speak to me for the rest of the night, glowering at me from across the room.

Later, my father asked me whether I liked Jennifer.

"Of course I do," I lied.

"You do?" he said, searching my face for honesty. He looked eager, suddenly, as though my approval meant so much to both of them—more, I thought, than my opinion on anything else ever had. "It's very important to her that you do."

"I'm really happy for both of you," I said. Partly this was because I wanted him to see me as grown-up and reasoned, but also I knew that if he thought I approved of her, he would spend even more time at her apartment, and less time monitoring me.

Jennifer kept an African parrot as a pet; she had bought the bird in her youth, not realizing (or perhaps realizing fully—I never knew for sure) that this particular breed had a typical life span of fifty years. The bird seemed to think of Jennifer as a mate, and quickly came to see my father as a threat, screaming a bracing caw and beating its wings whenever he approached. Soon his hands were covered with cuts from the animal's sharp, demonic little beak.

A handful of times she left the bird in our apartment while she traveled. It shrieked through my phone calls with friends, which mortified me. "This bird," I muttered into the phone. "This *fucking* bird."

My friend Daphne came over one afternoon when we were hosting the bird. It began screaming like a siren as she walked through the door. "What is that terrible noise?" she said, pulling off her oversize sunglasses. "Is that the smoke detector?"

"Bird," I said flatly.

"How awful," she said.

"It's Jennifer's," I said, "which should tell you everything you need to know about her. I mean, look, there are two kinds of people in the world: people who have pet birds and people who aren't completely fucking insane. Like, you know they're tiny feathered dinosaurs, right? What is the psychology of someone who has a bird? The people who keep birds as pets—well, *people*, more like women and gay men, I guess; strange, lonely women who have resigned themselves to lives of solitude and aging Florida show queens and Arizona hypoglycemics; who has an exotic pet in the Northeast?—must want to hold captive an animal with no humanoid qualities at all. Except, I guess, mimicry. How creepy is that? There's nothing warm or cuddly about them. Like, get a puppy. You know? Honestly, if I become one of those mottled old gays with a pet bird, please kill me. That life is not worth living."

"You're horrible," Daphne said fondly. She considered it for a moment longer. "But so is that animal. In fact, I don't know who's more of a monster—you or the bird."

She had a point—we were both preening beasts. Yet what chilled me most was how, on some level, I empathized with the need for companionship that had prompted Jennifer to adopt the bird in the first place. It was the very same willingness to accept affection from inappropriate sources that I saw, and hated most, in myself.

I liked that my father wasn't around. He left his credit card sitting in a leather valet on his bedroom dresser, as well as envelopes of cash on the kitchen counter. He also left me preloaded subway cards, an implicit invitation to take public transportation, which I tried to avoid. ("Dad, you know as well as I do that the crosstown doesn't stop on Park!"—I was fond of saying things like this, with what I considered a rarefied wit, although everyone around me must have found it very tiresome.)

My father always returned to New York with unlikely souvenirs for me, like a boarding pass emblazoned with the autograph of the celebrity next to whom he had been seated, or novelty T-shirts that I would never dream of wearing. Once, he came home from a conference organized by a well-funded think tank with a gift bag that included three different brands of expensive anti-aging facial moisturizer. I was vain and obsessive, so I used all three of them each morning, inadvertently turning my face a glistening pink, shiny as a gutted salmon.

For my benefit, my father wrote his travel itinerary in cursive scrawl on an oversize calendar, which hung in the hallway of our apartment. I never checked it, though. Most of the time, both of us slipped in and out of the apartment like ghosts, communicating via phone and email.

He was, I thought, waiting for me to graduate from high school so he could turn his attention to Jennifer full-time, and I was trying to stay exactly where I was, unparented enough that I could do whatever I wanted, whenever I wanted.

As we sped along the New Jersey Turnpike, the panoramic New York skyline disappeared into the rearview mirror. I always thought it was peculiar to think of Manhattan as an island since it always felt to me like a mainland, the only place that had ever mattered.

After an hour of stop-and-go traffic, my father needed a bathroom break. So did I, but for other reasons.

We pulled over at a rest stop outside of Edison. I circled the hallways until I found a handicapped-accessible restroom, single-occupancy. I locked the door, then jiggled the handle as I always did, to make sure that the door was really locked. I turned the spigot in the sink, letting the water gurgle noisily, then unfastened the changing table. From my back pocket, I removed a small leather pouch and emptied its contents onto the smooth grooved plastic of the table: a pocket mirror, a golden razor blade (I'd bought it at a head shop in the East Village, thinking it very edgy), a straw about two inches in length, a travel-size bottle of nasal spray, and a few dusty orange tabs of dextroamphetamine, trade name Dexedrine.

Dexedrine was increasingly hard to come by; I had prescriptions for methylphenidate, trade name Ritalin, in both standard and extended-release formulations, and I could always find amphetamine salt, trade name Adderall, but dextroamphetamine was the best. If someone had asked me, I would have explained, patiently and clearly, that methylphenidate is a less potent analogue of amphetamine salt, which itself was composed of two separate and distinct molecules of amphetamine: the levorotatory and dextrorotatory stereoisomers.

I would run through the medical terms in my mind frequently as I prepared the drug. The levorotatory amphetamine, or levoamphetamine, acts primarily on the neurotransmitter norepinephrine, producing a feeling of clarity and focus—whereas the dextrorotatory amphetamine, or dextroamphetamine, induces release of another neurotransmitter, dopamine, producing a feeling of pleasure and satisfaction.

Ritalin made me feel good, and Adderall made me feel great, but Dexedrine made me feel amazing.

Dexedrine elicited none of the twitchy, breathless anxiety that Adderall and Ritalin tended to induce; it didn't make me want to study, because I didn't need to study; it didn't make me want to clean my room, because suddenly, my clothes were strewn about the floor for a very good reason. Dexedrine was just pure, clean euphoria, the thrill of acing a test without even trying, the vertiginous rush of getting everything I had always wanted all at once.

I took a card from my wallet and crushed the two tablets of dextroamphetamine into small chunks. Then, with the razor blade, I cut them into a coarse powder—thinking, as I always did, that the powder looked like the flavoring packet that came inside a blue box of macaroni and cheese. The gilded blade shone in the light. It had come attached to a chain, meant to be worn as a necklace, so its edge had been dulled just enough—not sharp enough to cut myself on, exactly right for chopping up pills. It screeched conspicuously across the surface of the mirror as I ground the powder into a chalky dust, then combed it into four choppy lines. In two quick breaths, I snorted it.

One, two.

Three, four.

Finely pressed fireworks exploded in my septum, then dripped down my throat: a welcome bitterness. Insufflating the drug, I repeated to myself, as opposed to taking it orally, potentiated its effect and expedited its impact. I knew all this very well because I had stayed up many nights in fevered highs, reading about it online. I knew it also because I carried a pocket-size prescription drug reference in my book bag. I knew it mostly because everyone I knew was snorting pills, too.

I wiped down the mirror with a moistened paper towel, then took several hits of nasal spray to irrigate my sinuses. I checked my reflection for those telltale orange granules that could so easily betray me. A dribble of snot, the sunshine yellow of an egg yolk, pooled in my philtrum. My pupils were pinpricks in the gray-green sea of my irises. One vein at my right temple throbbed cartoonishly. I wiped my nose, put on my sunglasses, and exited the bathroom.

My father was idling in the convenience store, and I watched him through a pane of glass for what felt like a long moment. It had only been one year since he had left my mother, who had never cared much about how he dressed, and started dating Jennifer, who—if nothing else—had upgraded my father's once-Spartan style. Gone were the saggy chinos and old cork Birkenstocks, grimly waxy from wear; in their place were overdyed indigo designer jeans, buttery leather loafers, cashmere sweaters. Even today, dressed so casually, he looked tall and handsome, with a prominent nose and a dark beard that masked his weak chin. He looked more virile, somehow, than he had before, emasculated by his marriage to my mother. I had inherited his sturdy build, thick hair, and full lips, and I was glad that he had passed this genetic inheritance on to me.

In that moment, I was glad that I was his son.

He looked up as I approached.

"Everything all right, Sam?" he asked.

"Oh, yeah. I'm fantastic," I said, now meaning it.

"You want anything?"

I looked down the aisles of candy bars and potato chips. Coolers of brightly packaged soft drinks. Grinning celebrities on magazine covers. Suddenly, the lights were glaring, but that didn't bother me. I was joyfully, blissfully happy.

Amphetamines! You, only better.

I smiled at my father. "Let's hit the road," I said. He beamed back.

And in the car, the daylight was shining through the window a little bit brighter, and I plugged my iPod into the auxiliary jack so we could listen to Arcade Fire together, and my father drummed his fingers on the steering wheel to the beat in that way he always did, and the bitterness I had felt at the beginning of the trip melted away to reveal the smooth, sun-warmed surface of my sentimental self-regard.

When I was high, I could be kind and engaged, cracking jokes and smiling warmly. Like the son I thought he wanted.

"Thanks for taking me on this trip, Dad," I said.

He glanced at me, surprised. His eyes crinkled, like he knew he'd gotten it right and he was pleased with himself. "Of course," he said.

In that moment, it seemed that the future that awaited me, the future that had felt leviathan only an hour earlier, was now as airy and attainable as a dandelion wish floating out of reach just slowly enough to grasp before it disappeared forever.

I could do this. It would be easy. I was sure of it. I would get through this year, and I would go to a great college, and I would be a successful, functional adult.

I was wrong.

The streets in Princeton were lush and lined with grand old oak trees, dignified colonials on picturesque cul-de-sacs. As we circled through the neighborhood surrounding the university, it reminded me of the area where I had grown up in Portland, on a quiet street in a white house with a little fenced-in side yard and grand stone steps that led up to the front door, which was painted a bright cherry red. The street was arched with birch trees, and it smelled like anise after it rained. My family had felt whole there.

In early childhood, I had shared a bedroom with my brother, Ben, who was two years my senior, down the hall from the French doors that led to my parents' bedroom, which was always streaked in beams of golden sunlight. In the hallway, a laundry chute trapdoor led to the basement two floors below; I imagined there was an underwater lair of detergent bubbles for a villain who clanged in the night. My brother loved animals, and so my mother painted a jungle mural on the wall of our bedroom, a verdant green rain forest with monkeys swinging from high-up branches, the round dark spots of a giraffe.

And there were pets—so many pets. A kitten for Christmas one year who grew up into a surly, sedate cat who only purred when she wasn't being touched. A Jack Russell terrier who was returned after a disastrous month or two. A black rabbit named

Midnight and a white one named Snowflake kept outside in a hutch that made the whole backyard smell faintly of urine.

Lizards and salamanders in a large glass terrarium—they fed on live crickets that had to be retrieved from the local pet store every week. On one such occasion, while my mother was driving home from the pet store, my brother accidentally punctured the plastic bag in which the crickets were transported; out came several dozen of them, hissing and circling, and my mother screamed and swerved, maneuvering the station wagon to the side of the road, then jumping out and patting down her body as insects streamed out of the car like some kind of biblical plague, my brother and I screaming with perverse laughter.

Guinea pigs and mice and hamsters in little cages, spinning on their plastic wheels. If the mural was anything, it was a concession; my mother couldn't give my brother the tropical menagerie he wanted, so she settled on an imitation.

She was fiercely devoted to both of us. There were cookies baking in the oven when I came home from school, and hot chocolate on snowy winter mornings, and unless she was away, she came in to my bedroom to tuck me in and kiss me good night.

It wasn't perfect—I had to remind myself of that to keep reality from stinging too badly. For weeks at a time my father was away on business, which I assumed he preferred to spending time with us, and my mother was frequently in bed with migraines, which I assumed were fictional. Ben tormented me as older brothers do, and I, in turn, delighted in playing the victim. We were cared for by a string of nannies, and when each inevitably moved on (to other families, I imagined, boys who were nicer and smarter than I was), I was inconsolable until I had attached myself to the next one.

I was awkward. I had no natural athleticism. I didn't want to go outside—I wanted to stay indoors and read. I fantasized about being kidnapped, held captive by the brawny protagonist in whatever book I was reading. I liked to alphabetize my books and grow my coin collection, the latter of which my parents happily indulged. I subscribed to a trade publication for numismatists and ordered bags of old Lincoln pennies by the thousand and fished through them, looking for rare dates.

Eventually I moved into my own bedroom. As my stockpile of coins grew, I began to worry that this would make us a target for neighborhood thieves. I envisioned armed gunmen padding silently up the stairs to my room, wanting to steal a valuable century-old penny. For my eighth birthday, to placate my anxiety, my parents purchased a large fireproof safe, which was installed in my bedroom closet. I was ecstatic. Hours flew by as I obsessively organized my coins into durable leather books. On blithe sunny afternoons while children laughed and played in the street, I closed the venetian blinds over the bay window that looked out onto the neighborhood and sat on the floor of my bedroom, counting my money.

That was the same year I became friends with a boy who lived in the neighborhood, Brooks. He was a little overweight, like me, but built of stronger stock; I was malleable and too keen to please. One night, after my parents had gone to sleep, he wanted to sneak into the hot tub that had just been installed in the backyard; I said yes, not knowing how to say no. It was there that he put his hands, and then his mouth, on my groin. He was aggressive, and I was afraid but aroused, too, some fumbled fight-or-flight impulse turned erotic. His mauve nipples were buoyant on the sea of his suntanned chest, and he dipped beneath the water, grabbing my wrist, twisting and snickering. My hands scrabbled at the pebbled shelf of the hot tub, and he held my head down in the chlorinated depths, the slippery surface of a hairless thigh, and I came up from below to stare at a canopy of browning leaves and papery twigs swaying beneath a spooky-bright moon, gasping for air, his fingers like sea snakes.

Maybe I yelped or my mother heard the splashing of water, but suddenly, I heard her voice calling to me from across the yard as she stood at the side door.

"You boys okay out there?" she called sleepily. It was late.

Brooks gripped my thigh.

"Yes!" I called back in a high, strange voice that didn't sound like mine. "We're fine!"

He let go.

The next night, my mother came to tuck me in for bed. She tried to give me an Eskimo kiss, as she always did, but the secret burned in my chest, hot and shameful. I couldn't look at her. I tucked my chin against my chest.

"I'm too old for that," I said. Something flashed through her eyes—some quick pain, as though I'd cut her—then faded to a lower-frequency sadness. Surely she had studied childhood development enough to know it was normal.

Only it wasn't normal. Brooks came over one more time that I recall, and my parents weren't home; we were downstairs in the basement, where there was a side closet that housed my toys. We were in the closet together, Brooks and I, and I had fallen to my knees in front of him, and I wanted it to happen again, although I didn't know why. Maybe it was the physical pleasure, even though it made me feel ashamed, or the attention—the thrill of being desired. I was telling him that I would give him anything, any of my Lego castles, any of my Disney movies, even *this*—anything from my coin collection—anything he wanted, he could have. I just wanted him to do it again—to violate me again, to validate me again. He looked at me. He was confused, disgusted. So was I, with myself.

I had night terrors. When I closed my eyes I saw dark, murky tides of amorphous gray water. I sweated through my sheets. I wet the bed. I stayed up until dawn reading under the covers. One night, I heard my father returning home late from a business trip; I ran to the top of the stairs and asked him to come read to me until I fell asleep. I could see the weariness in his eyes, the exasperation.

"Just go to sleep, Sam," he said. I couldn't trust him, either.

My mother took me to a doctor; she didn't understand why I couldn't sleep. They pestered and prodded me, but I believed instinctively that this thing was too private to share, that neither of them would understand.

My mother saw that I had changed, even if she didn't know how to identify it. One afternoon, we sat together on the teal sofa in the living room. There was an art deco painting I always liked hanging on the wall, women depicted in rigid geometric lines. On the other side of the room, an unplayed grand piano sat beneath a window that framed a view of a pair of trees. She faced me while I sat cross-legged. She took my small hand and held it up to hers, and I felt the pressure of her slender fingers against mine, the cool gold of her wedding ring. Her skin was soft, and she smelled like lavender from the bath she had taken.

"Sam," she said, "I want you to remember this moment for the rest of your life. I want you to remember how small your hand is against mine."

I did remember, still, but the memory had grown more difficult to access over time. There were moments where I wasn't entirely sure if it had ever happened at all.

Quickly, it felt like there were so many secrets. I could feel what had happened with Brooks growing in my belly, rotting and tumescent; I had not known that I could have a secret life from my mother, experiences to which she was not privy, and it exhilarated and horrified me in equal measures to learn that this was possible. There were moments of thrilling joy in this newfound autonomy—the winter afternoon when there was a blizzard and I was walking home from a friend's house and the streets glowed white and empty and I stopped on the lawn of a nearby church and made a snow angel, alone, laughing, just because I wanted to and because I could.

And then there were secret moments that chilled me in another way, felt connected to the Brooks thing through some imperceptible webbing of dark matter that lurked just beyond my field of vision. Another day, after school, by that same church, when I was nine or ten, I walked past a parked car with the passenger-side window rolled down. Inside, I could see a man, his hand in his pants.

"Hey," he called to me. "Come here." I had read a novel where something like this happened; the main character (a bright young boy—*like me*, I thought) was kidnapped and held as the sexual captive of a charismatic pedophile. It had sounded thrilling, but the unglamorous reality of this sad old exhibitionist was much less so. The idea of having a man's undivided attention for that long *was* appealing. But not appealing enough.

"Come here," he hissed, exposing himself to me. "*Come here.*"

I kept on walking.

If I'd had fantasies about being kidnapped as a child, by the time I was seventeen, equipped with a fake but convincing New York State ID, I had no trouble finding men who would play along. With girlfriends or alone I would go to gay bars in Chelsea or Hell's Kitchen. I flashed my ID to the bouncer, already spun out on painkillers and uppers. My rangy frame was compressed in skinny jeans, my face gaunt, my eyes gritty with sleep deprivation and hunger. *What could be sexier than looking sick?* I thought, sickly.

I felt safe there, in the dim light of the glittering club, against the glossy backdrop of sinewy oiled men gyrating in G-strings, getting accidentally-on-purpose groped by men in white patent leather heels who gave names like Elvis or Stealth, deafened by the thundering clatter of trance music. One night, a suit—dusky blond, in his thirties, with Wall Street hair—clasped my shoulder.

"Are you a model?" he asked.

I laughed theatrically. "No," I said, smiling, fawning, flirting. I looked at my reflection in the mirror above the bar. I got higher off the fantasy. *I could be a model*, I thought. (I couldn't.) But my clavicle jutted from my chest, emerging from the V of a too-small button-up. My head teetered disproportionately atop my blue-veined neck, rosy cheeks pinched taut against my jaw. I was tall enough, over six feet. And this particular pickup line was so banal that it had transcended its own banality—he had to be using it in earnest.

He couldn't possibly think that I was stupid enough to fall for a line like that.

"You should be," he said. "You have that face."

This is the single greatest moment of my life, I thought. *It's all downhill from here.*

I held my clammy hand against his cheek.

"You're so sweet," I said. "Buy me a drink?" And he did, and so I went back to his hotel, and it would not have occurred to me that there was any other option.

I met men in bars. I met men at the gym. I met men through friends. But more than anything, I met men online.

I had tired, by early in my senior year, of going through my own doctor for my prescriptions—I wanted a doctor who would prescribe me anything I wanted. One ad on an online hookup message board was titled "In Search of a Deviant Doctor." In it, I wrote:

> *I'd like to emphasize the fact that I'm not interested in engaging in a fantasy relationship predicated upon a weary doctor/patient cliché. I want a real doctor: Can I be the Rimbaud to your Verlaine? Smart, sensual Manhattan private school senior looking for a sexy doctor. Note "sexy," which to me means no older than, say, 45, preferably clean-shaven, fit, charismatic, etc. I'm not into fetishistic role-playing, per se—but there is something indelibly attractive about a doctor, especially a doctor with a perversely sexual streak. Maybe it appeals to the repressed, idealistic Jewish girl in me.*

I concluded, "I live in Manhattan and so should you—preferably close to the park."

I was disappointed when this message didn't field many responses.

Had I been too glib? I wondered.

Maybe it had just been too subtle. I needed to be more specific. The crystal meth epidemic ravaging the gay community was in full force, but "T," as it was euphemistically called, didn't really interest me. I'd run across enough tweakers to know to steer clear, and more importantly, I was abusing enough Adderall that even on the handful of occasions where I had taken a toot from the freebase pipe—the first time when I was fifteen, with a guy I'd met online, red-eyed and skeletal, and then a handful of other times when I was too drunk to say no—I hardly felt anything. Never mind all the hand-wringing about how addictive it was. Prescription amphetamines were a cleaner high. "Skiing," or partying with cocaine, was risky, too—it often made me impotent. Increasingly, I was fascinated by the effects I could produce with cocktails of more obscure drugs: amphetamines and benzodiazepines, imidazopyridines and opioids.

In a later ad, I wrote:

> *I know everyone's all crazed about T and hitting the slopes but you know, I've got more than enough energy to fuck all night—what I'm looking for are pills. Barbiturates, Valium, Xanax, Klonopin, Ativan, Halcion, Ambien, 'ludes (rare as they are), Darvocet, codeine, Vicodin, Tramadol, Percocet— not looking for anything specific, not looking to develop an addiction, just looking to experiment with all of those funny colorful pills. Am I the only one who just loves a safe night of off-label fun?*

It was this ad that produced a fling with a skinny artist in his midthirties who lived in Hell's Kitchen and introduced me to the uniquely euphoric cocktail of cocaine and Ambien. The two synthesized to produce almost complete retrograde amnesia: a state of perfect, regretless bliss. Over a period of several months I saw him four or five times that I remember, which means that I probably saw him at least five more times in blackout.

In our last encounter, I have foggy memories of falling down a flight of stairs at Grand Central Terminal and coming to in the elevator of an Upper East Side building in which I didn't live.

I told that story to my friends the next day and nobody but me thought it was funny.

That should have been a bad omen.

But still, I needed more drugs. Walking home after posting that ad looking for pills, I checked my email from my phone, awaiting more responses. Eagerly, I opened a new message.

"I am a doctor if you care to chat, but I won't supply any pills," it read. "Just talk to you about addiction if you want."

I bristled. *How presumptuous*, I thought.

There was a much more promising reply, though—from a guy who didn't identify himself by name but wrote that he was a psychiatrist. "I know you said you didn't like role-play," he said, "but that really turns me on."

"I am many things," I wrote. "Difficult to persuade is not one of them."

The next day, after school, I went to his office, in a brownstone on an Upper West Side street. He was fortysomething, stocky, with a reddish beard. I locked the door behind me and stripped down to my briefs, standing before him.

"Get on all fours," he said.

I dropped to my knees and put my hands on the area rug, gripping its fibers in my fingers. He sat down on the couch and unbuckled his belt, then slid his hands in his trousers. Behind him, there were walls of bookshelves. I recognized a few of the titles from my mother's library. She had been a mental health professional, too, but that felt like a very long time ago.

I crawled across the floor toward him.

"Just tell me," I whispered. I put my hands on his knees. Suddenly, inexplicably, my eyes welled up with tears. I blinked them back.

It didn't feel good, this situation, but it felt necessary, for some reason I couldn't yet identify.

He looked down at me. "Tell you what, baby?" he said.

"Tell me," I said, gazing up at him. "Tell me who you want me to be."

By the time we left Princeton that evening, the drugs had worn off. A headache was beginning to pulsate behind my eyes. I felt weak and weary. I had buckled to the pressure and eaten a slice of pizza at a pub, some hole-in-the-wall my father had thought would be fun. I wanted the pizza out of my body, urgently, but I couldn't get away from him for long enough to throw it up. It was too late, now, anyway.

"Have we been here before?" I asked, standing with him at the check-in desk of a roadside hotel, a midscale chain where my father always had points. I had a feeling of dizzying familiarity, some déjà vu—the plastic wood paneling, an all-glass elevator overlooking a courtyard viridian with artificial plant life, perimeters of identical doors stacked on top of one another. I steadied myself on the countertop. My father looked at me funny.

"No," he said. "Not with me, at least. All these hotels just look the same. We stayed at one in Chicago last year, remember?"

But the feeling was so powerful. Had it been Chicago? Or had I been in one of these hotels in the Financial District a week before with a guy I'd met online? I remembered the dimly lit lobby, the musculature of his back, his hands around my waist.

Everything was starting to look the same; everyone was interchangeable lately.

I shook it off.

In the hotel bathroom, I changed into a T-shirt and the shorts I'd bought at the Princeton gift shop, black and orange and made of mesh, hitting just above the knee. I swallowed two Ritalin, then slipped a Xanax under my tongue, letting it dissolve slowly. My father was at the desk, working on his laptop.

"I'm going to go work out," I said.

"Oh," he said, excited. "Is there a gym?"

"No," I said. "But there's a pool."

"That's nice," he said. His eyes were glazed. Away from work all day, he had the look of a gambler returning to the slots after a too-long hiatus. He turned back to the computer. "I'm glad you're making your physical fitness a priority."

I forced my face into a smile. My stomach gurgled.

The pool was empty, solarium windows and an inky sky overhead. I swam a few laps halfheartedly, but I was exhausted. As I bobbed my head back up to the surface, I heard a noise coming from the steam room. I wiped my eyes and squinted. I could see an outline through the misted glass.

I pulled myself up the ladder, spitting chlorine, and walked in that direction, leaving a trail of wet footprints on the cement. My heart was pounding. I opened the door.

There was a man inside, a towel wrapped around his waist. He eyed me. I sat down next to him.

"Water's nice," I said. He didn't say anything. I smiled at him. My body temperature was rising. Suddenly, I felt liquefied, smooth and flirtatious. The drugs were hitting in exactly the right way. My heart was a hummingbird, its wings vibrating in my chest. I was not the boy I had been sitting in that car with my father, a petulant teenage waste—nor was I the overeager aspirant I had been on the Princeton campus. I was not myself. I was someone who surged with confidence, someone fearless and bold. I pulled off my wet shorts and stretched out, naked, extending my limbs like a cat awakening from a nap. He was probably forty, brunet, a broad freckled chest dewy with perspiration. He met my gaze.

He opened his towel.

My feet squished in my shoes as I walked quickly down the hallway leading back to the elevator. The Princeton shorts, after being wadded up in a sweaty ball on the floor, felt dank around my thighs. I rubbed my neck; he had put his hands around my throat at one point and choked me, not so much that it scared me but enough that I was gasping when he let go.

Too rough. I knew my limits.

I stepped outside from a side door and fumbled in my gym bag for a pack of cigarettes. It still amazed me that I could get away with this—that the kinetic escape of sex was so available, so ubiquitous. I lit a cigarette. My whole body felt tender. There was something running down my leg—was it water or blood? I checked. Water. He didn't finish inside me. I had to go get tested, stop being so irresponsible. I had more Xanax upstairs, right? Sure. The night was too cold to be outside, sopping wet in just a T-shirt and shorts, the cherry of my cigarette glowing. I could see my breath. It all hurt.

I shouldn't have done that.

Back upstairs, I slid my keycard into the door of our hotel room and entered. The room was darkened, my father reading by lamplight.

"You were gone a while," he said. There was no judgment—it was just an observation. He closed his eyes and inhaled through his nose. "You smell like smoke."

"I'm sorry," I said, although I didn't quite know for what.

After he fell asleep, I stayed up staring at the ceiling, listening to the wheeze of his breath. I ran my fingers over the grooved pendant lettering on the shorts, picking at it with a fingernail, then realized what I was doing. I pulled back the covers and looked at the damage—I'd scratched off half the letters. They were ruined now.

It all felt ruined.

I rose. Stealing through the moon-shot room, I changed into boxers, then stuffed the shorts into a drawer, where nobody would find them until I was long gone. It felt like I was hiding the evidence, hiding a piece of myself.

Maybe tomorrow I wouldn't take so many pills. Maybe I wouldn't sleep with any strangers. It wasn't too late to change, right? I made myself a solemn promise: *When morning comes, I'll be someone else. Someone different.*

Someone better.

Two

---

*T*he day after I got back from my college tour, Daphne and I skipped French class to sit outside at a French restaurant on the Upper West Side—which could almost, I thought, be considered a field trip. I ordered a bottle of wine. Daphne ordered a Caesar salad with dressing on the side and a black iced coffee. She was a platinum blonde with a droll wit; I liked performing for her, but I could be honest with her, too. Like me, she was a recent transplant, having moved from London with her family one year earlier. Since her father was an advertising executive and her mother was a psychoanalyst, she was clever and inquisitive—a perfect foil for all my glib posturing.

"Can you take this bread away, please?" Daphne said to the waitress. She took a drag from a Parliament Light and looked at me skeptically.

"Here's the thing, Daphne," I said, lighting my own cigarette. I was jittery. I had been up for the first half of the night studying; then I'd gone to the apartment of a guy on Riverside Drive just past midnight and stayed there until four, sniffing poppers and fooling around; then I'd had a 7:00 a.m. detention in the dean's office, which I had nearly every morning; the upper-school dean doled them out to students a week at a time if he caught them smoking, which happened to me virtually every week. I was so hungry that morning that I'd gnashed two tablets of Adderall with my teeth just to have something to chew on.

"I just feel like—okay, so, ever since I was a little boy, I have known that deep inside me there is a door, and that door leads to a room, and inside that room, there is a table, and on that table is a locked box that contains the meaning of life—like, all of the happiness that I could ever wish for or want or dream of having, you know?—and I've always wondered what the key is to open that box because it's always been locked to me, impenetrable. And this week, when I went to Princeton, it just felt like—I don't know, like I finally realized what that key is, Daphne, because that key is Princeton. It's *Princeton*. It's Princeton, and their grand, grand architecture, and their Nobel Prize–winning faculty, and these expanses of green lawn that go on forever, and benches, like, wrapped in tendrils of ivy—fucking *tendrils*, I swear to God. And you know how, like—remember walking around Columbia before our SATs, and how, like, there just really wasn't anyone cute around? It was a lot of stocky girls in hoodies and basketball shorts and UGGs—I don't even *know* how that happens—but Princeton was, like, the *opposite* of that. And I know that, like, if I went to Columbia, I'd still be in the city so at least I could still have a social life—I mean, I could go down to NYU to party since that's basically a trade school for attractive people with family money, right?—and if I went to Princeton I'd be in New Jersey, which is so *ugh*, but like—would

I even want to come back to the city when everyone there is so fucking beautiful? And I don't mean normal beautiful, I mean Hamptons beautiful, Saint-Tropez beautiful, beautiful in that *rich* way—you know what I mean—and this *privilege* that's so thick in the air you can taste it. And I want to be one of those people, those privileged few. So I guess, then, the question is, like, *could* I be one of them, Daphne? I could just—I could feel it as soon as I set foot on campus, that it was the only place I could ever really be happy, that I belonged there. I mean, I *have* to get in, right? I'll do anything to get in. Like, literally anything. Except, you know, studying and extracurriculars."

Daphne impaled a ribbon of lettuce with her fork, as unimpressed with me as she was with the salad. "You'd better apply, then," she said. She chewed for a bit. "Do you really think you can get into Princeton, Sam? I mean, you know I love you, but—fucking hell—you're a mess."

I ground my teeth anxiously.

"I could do it if I really set my mind to it, don't you think? I just have to quit doing all the bullshit that I've been doing. No more cutting class to blaze on the Great Lawn. No more sneaking out at midnight to go sit at Marquee, which sucks now, anyway—how many hours have we clocked, like, watching Lindsay Lohan text and scowl?—just waiting for some probably-married dickbag to buy me a Red Bull–vodka and take me back to his hotel room for completely unfulfilling sex. Honestly, Daphne, I'm so sick of that, aren't you? No more showing up for morning detention still drunk from the night before—and this is going to be hard, I mean, I'm *really* going to need your support if we're going to pull this off, but I mean, like, if I can curb all those bad habits, I could probably do it, right?"

I sipped my wine.

"I could get into Princeton, couldn't I?"

I didn't want to say good-bye to those nights—catching a cab uptown with girlfriends as they changed out of slinky cocktail dresses into dress shirts and ties, replacing their stilettos with suede boots, emptying out of the taxi in a cloud of smoke, fragrance, and tousled hair, popping pills and blinking Visine tears and sucking on breath mints. Huddling outside the Gothic wooden doors of our school, waiting for Willie, the hobbled old security guard, to let us inside.

More than the buzz and stomp of Meatpacking District night-clubs with my friends, though, I lived for the nights I spent with strangers. By midnight, with the rush of the evening's amphet-amines surging through me, I could go online, find an older guy with a nice apartment and some blow, and lose myself in that euphoric lust daze for a few hours. I would tell him my name was Brock or Cory and that I was a junior at Indiana State just visiting New York City; or I would tell him that I had a girlfriend and that I'd "never done this before." And then there would be quickening pulses, some itch that I couldn't quite name being scratched—and for a few hours, I would be wholly present in my body and also somehow able to exit it entirely. And then it would be over, a bleary comedown, two strangers, naked in a cold apartment somewhere on Central Park West. I would say I needed money for a taxi home; he would fish out some cash—often, and to which I did not object, several twenties or hundreds—and then I would walk home through that desolate predawn hour, use the money to buy painkillers or cocaine for myself or just to go out with my friends the next night. Yet I rarely spoke about it with my friends. There was socially acceptable wildness—the typical antics of bored, indolent, private school kids—and then there was what *I* did.

Surely, I reasoned, there had to be some way I could keep doing *that* while also becoming a more serious, motivated student. Someone purposeful and civic-minded, with a commitment to service. It seemed in that moment unjust that they should be mutually exclusive.

"Well, it's ambitious," Daphne said. "You know. A leap. And, like, you're sort of the worst." She shook out her hair, as though trying to rid herself of some stress, real or imagined. "Not to mention that Princeton doesn't even *matter*—it's just a tangible embodiment of this unattainable version of yourself. It's practically Jungian, really. Symbols or whatever."

I was caught off guard. "No," I said. "I'm pretty sure it's about going to Princeton."

She shrugged. "Thank God I'm going back home for university. The ways they torture you Americans. It's shit, really." She looked at me with pity and sighed. "Aren't you supposed to have safety schools?"

"I mean," I said slowly, knowing she was right and disliking it, "there are Wesleyan and Hampshire—but I'm not that liberal or lazy. And Harvard and Yale. They're both, like . . . kind of overwhelming and underwhelming at the same time, you know?"

I kept talking but avoided her eyes. "Like, as an undergraduate at those places, you don't have a lot of options to take, you know, like, small, intimate classes with professors, because it's mostly lectures, and you have to cycle through, like, nineteen TAs before you can get a word in with the professor, if ever, and, like, I'm sorry, but I'm not going to bust my ass and spend fifty thousand dollars a year—well, it's my parents' money, but whatever—to go to a school where I can't even develop a relationship with my instructor. I'll buy a fucking book on tape, thank you very much. You know what I mean? It's just, like, whatever. And my adviser says I should apply to Connecticut College, but, like, what is that even? I mean, okay, there's Sarah Lawrence, and the academics there are great, but it's kind of a dump, you know? It just looks run-down. And it's *so* close to the city that I'd probably come down all the time and just, like, end up living here, which defeats the whole purpose of this holy residential college experience everyone keeps talking about. Also, I mean, not that this is a reason not to go, but you know I've been really trying not to do coke and, like, when I went up there and I saw that girl Eleanor, do you remember her? Like, I was staying overnight at her place and she wanted to get a gram and so I just went for it, which, like, was stupid because it had been so long since I'd done it but it just seemed so harmless and, like, do I really want to be around a bunch of cokeheads all the time? If I wanted that, I could just go to Vassar, right? I mean,

Amherst and Swarthmore are both gorgeous—at least they *look* like Ivies, even if they're not, but I just kind of feel like, I dunno, like, there's only so much foliage that a person can take in before their head explodes. I mean, am I being elitist here? I don't think I am. That's why it's Princeton. It *has* to be Princeton."

I chewed on my fingernails. I ran my fingers through my hair. I lit another cigarette.

"You take too much Adderall," Daphne said.

If someone had asked me why I was like this, I would have snapped back, "Like *what?*"—yet, if pressed, I could point to a dozen little threads of dysfunction that I'd teased out over the course of years in therapy. The monstrousness in me had crystallized in New York, but it had its roots in Oregon, where, by the time I was fifteen, I had already begun to disappear down the rabbit hole of addiction. I blamed it on my parents because that was convenient, but it was a tougher knot than just that.

Still, as I told myself often to excuse my bad behavior, my parents probably hadn't helped. As their marriage had slowly disintegrated, my mother unraveled. We fought constantly. After she figured out that I was using drugs, she began administering drug tests. I worked around them: Nothing could keep me from my beloved pills. I could sense a drug test coming a mile away, and neither of my parents was around often enough for it to be consistent, anyway. They were too distracted to effectively parent a child as precocious and strong-willed as I was, and I had grown skilled at manipulating them into looking past what should have been obvious red flags.

A few days before my sixteenth birthday, my mother surprised me with a urinalysis test, and I came up positive for cocaine; after consulting with my father, they grounded me for a few days.

Neither of them brought up rehab—at least not to me.

My mother pursued her spirituality, trying to unlock the secrets of her happiness. She returned to the house at odd hours with red eyes, reeking of burnt sage. ("I'm going out on a dream quest," she'd say, her eyes daring me to laugh. "I'll be back in three days.") Shortly before my parents separated, my mother described my father as "the most emotionally and sexually repressed individual I've ever met." I loved how cinematic this was—how withering.

Several weeks later, my father and mother sat me down in the kitchen.

"We're separating," my mother said.

"I've taken a job in New York," my father said.

"You can stay here with me," my mother said. "Or you can go to New York with your father. It's up to you."

I told them that I thought it was for the best, and I did.

"Maybe now we can all be happy," I said, although it didn't seem like that was in the cards. But I thought I would gladly trade my mother's more watchful eye for my unerringly unavailable father—and a fabulous new life in New York.

Later that night, the house blanketed in silence, I slipped

out the front door and jogged along the gravel that paved our cul-de-sac, down to the DEAD END sign where my best friend Kat's SUV was parked. All summer, Kat and I had been doing blow—too much blow, if there was such a thing—but Kat was two years older than I was and much more experienced, and I trusted her judgment implicitly. Even on the nights when she drove seventy mph along the perilous curves of Skyline Boulevard, her lipsticked mouth working animatedly, my teeth chattering, charring my fingertips trying to kill the roach of a joint—even then, I always felt safe with her. We had become friends not long after we had both been unceremoniously dumped by our first loves—me by my boyfriend, Jerick, a charismatic theater kid, and her by Rob, an aspiring rapper from a bad neighborhood. At first, we medicated our loneliness with fast food and bad movies, but it didn't take long for us to graduate to harder vices.

Kat was behind the wheel, looking fidgety, ambient pop bleating on the stereo. She was a bombshell, blond and curvy, but—perpetually self-conscious—she hid in formless sweatshirts zipped up to her throat, hood pulled up moodily to hide her long, wavy hair. I sat in the passenger seat and began chopping up a gram bag of nacreous blue-white cocaine on my pocket mirror.

"Well, it's not like you didn't see it coming, right?" Kat said.

"I really think it's the first thing they've ever done, like, for themselves," I said.

Kat shrugged. "I hope you're right."

I snorted a line.

She turned up the music and drove down Vista Drive, her car hugging the curves, filling up with smoke from my cigarette, my spine tingling. At an underdeveloped industrial neighborhood by the train tracks, a corporate park was dead by night, save for the scratching of Kat's razor blade against a jewel case. She stopped the car and we got out, circling the perimeter of the parking garage in search of the stairs. The summer had been a blur of nights like this: although I'd dabbled in drugs the year before, that had mostly been taking a hit from a joint on the way to a party; only over the last few months had things started to feel dangerous. Parties where I blacked out and found out the next day that I'd made out with some straight boy from school. Mixing barbiturates I'd bought off an upperclassman with alcohol and feeling my breathing slow to a frightening sluggishness, picking up the phone to call 911 and thinking better of it.

I will be fine, I would think, and in the morning I always was. And then there were the nights I stayed out with Kat until the sun rose, driving across Portland, doing blow and taking long walks along the river. Early in the morning, searching for an empty public bathroom or abandoned parking garage, we promised each other that we would "kill this bag and not do this anymore." But then, a day or two later, we would be back at it.

We climbed several flights up the stairs, then crossed the roof and hopped over onto the next building, emboldened by the drugs and adrenaline. We were high enough to see the whole city, a panoramic view of the valley, all those glimmering lights. I followed her up to the base of a water tower, which cast its looming shadow over the roof. A slender ladder mounted to its side looked rickety and treacherous, but we climbed up that, too, stopping at ledges along the way to survey the view, to feel the fear, to congratulate each other on how brave we were being. *How far can we get? Can we make it to the top tonight?* We scaled those heights, dizzy, queasy. My sweaty palms slipped on the rungs. Gravity tugged at me. My limbs felt featherweight, then heavy as lead with each step.

"Don't look down," Kat whispered. "Don't look down."

Up there, at whatever peak to which we'd ascended, cold and high with the summer air prickling at the nape of my neck, I looked up at the sky. It was shot through with stars, in the way Oregon nights always were, bright lights so eerily lucent. I hung from the ladder with one arm and reached one out toward the sky.

I felt my grip starting to loosen. In a moment, I would fall. Or maybe, I thought, I would just fly.

The next week, I went to New York with my father to interview at prep schools. I vetoed a Jesuit academy on the Upper East Side—too staid, too Christian—and a day school in quaint Park Slope—too unpretentious, too dressed-down.

Finally, we reached the Dwight School. In the art classroom, panoramic windows framed a view of Central Park. The boys were doe-eyed and rumple-headed, in wrinkled chinos and blue blazers, their ties sloppy. The girls were inscrutable behind opaque Jackie O sunglasses, wearing oversize men's dress shirts and leggings. Their nimble feet were silent in ballet flats. I yearned to belong. *Could this be my life now?* I wondered. *Please.* It felt like a dream.

That evening, the last of our visit, I arranged to see my friend Aria. We'd met several years earlier at an academic camp I attended each summer and kept up with each other via email. Aria lived just outside of the city in New Jersey; she took the train in, and we met two of her friends, scrubby-bearded prep school trustafarians who went to St. Ann's and kept talking about some book called *Finnegans Wake*. I had never heard of it, and it didn't sound very good, but I pretended to be interested. One of them, I was told, lived in a town house in the East Eighties that had previously housed a Latin American embassy, and the other had just bought a penthouse on Central Park West from a famous singer. We bought an eight ball of cocaine, splayed it out in thick lines on the grand silver music stand in the closet, and casually, as if it were a perfectly normal thing for fifteen-year-olds to do, had a foursome.

While attempting to penetrate one of the boys on the balcony overlooking the park at about 5:00 a.m., so dizzy from all the blow that I could barely see, I lost my erection; I was mortified, although he was really nice about it. Nevertheless, every time I ran into him over the next two years I was unable to look him in the eye.

Back for my last few weeks in Portland, I skipped class to sit outside a local coffee shop, smoking cigarettes and telling anyone who would listen that I was moving on to greener pastures.

"Yeah, Paris Hilton went to school there," I said smugly. "So, you know. It's whatever."

I did not hesitate to leave, not knowing how I would later ache for Portland. In the car on the way to the airport, the trunk stuffed with suitcases, my mother sobbed as she maneuvered the steering wheel, fingering the pendant of Saint Bridget that hung around her neck. I gazed out the window at the white Oregon sky, loathing its emptiness, dreaming of cityscapes clotted with skyscrapers.

My father found an apartment a short walk from Dwight. I did not feel displaced, only the curious sensation of returning home to a place I hadn't been. I concluded that I had always been a New Yorker; I just hadn't ever lived in New York.

I didn't come to New York to be the same person I had been in Portland. No, I had big dreams: of transformation, of glamour, of becoming the urbane prep school sophisticate I had always wanted to be. Later, when it was time to apply to colleges, I chose Princeton not because I wanted to go to Princeton but because I wanted to be the kind of person who *could* go to Princeton. It was the final, essential component of the persona I had created for myself.

Dwight maintained its community prestige as an interna-
tional school that was a popular destination for the children of
ambassadors and members of the United Nations Secretariat,
despite its reputation in the internal prep school circuit as a
"school for rich fuck-ups," as a rock-star alumnus once described
it in an interview. (I sent that home to all my friends in Portland,
as evidence of how cool I'd become, though mostly I was trying to
prove it to myself.) Students were fond of saying that Dwight was
an acronym for "Dumb White Idiots Getting High Together," the
redundancy of which, sadly, proved their point. I heard reports,
whether true or not, that the year before I arrived, students would
simply put their bags up on their desks and snort cocaine in the
middle of class, an act of brazen rebellion that I found hypnoti-
cally compelling.

What I hadn't heard was that a crackdown on the trade of street
narcotics in the school had shifted the focus to prescription
drugs. It was harder to find cocaine than it had been before, I
was told—at least, to the extent that it used to be easy to pick
up in school. But when abused properly, I was learning, phar-
maceuticals were just as effective. I began snorting prescription
amphetamines for breakfast, which put me in a state of perpet-
ual but frantic euphoria. It was like having my coke and eating
it, too.

Sahara, an Italian heiress with a lissome frame and a tangle
of wild, dark hair, remained undeterred by the threat of random

urinalysis. She single-handedly buoyed a thriving underground market for clean urine.

"Do another line, baby," Sahara said, scratching at her nostril. "Where's the bag? Baby, I wanna do another line. Let's do this shit."

My assimilation was rapid, even if it was mostly just an act. I went to fancy restaurants—private school kids went to dinner as a form of recreation, which I found very curious—and picked at Kobe tartare, trying to look bored. I kissed my female acquaintances on the cheek—twice, in the European style—and assumed the drifting vernacular of my new friends, who spoke in an odd sort of rarefied Ebonics, urban slang peppered with preternaturally savvy references that only those born rich would understand.

"Yo, Daisy, that dress is mad dope," my new friend Jesse said. "Is that shit Ralph Lauren Purple Label? He summers on Shelter Island with my parents, yo." I knew how ridiculous he sounded, but I much preferred to imitate it than to challenge it.

Jesse's bedroom looked like a Mexican pharmacy. He didn't sell any pills, but gave them to me freely in small plastic bags of twenty, appearing thrilled to find a peer who shared his geeky fascination with psychopharmacology. Jesse introduced me to modafinil, trade name Provigil, a narcolepsy medication that, he said, was being tested by the U.S. military as their new "go pill," enabling the user to stay awake for up to six consecutive days without any deterioration of mental acuity. The paranoia and bloating were a small price to pay for hundred-hour days that were rapidly filling up with social commitments, drunken one-night stands, and detentions in the chancellor's office. Someone told me once that in New York, trade-offs exist among academic excellence, social fluency, and sleep. You could really only have two out of the three. Jesse and I both chose to forgo the last, neither of us realizing that going without sleep wasn't realistic.

"I need to get in to see your doctor, yo," I said one afternoon. The pockets of my cashmere topcoat were stuffed with sacks of assorted pills, but I was already counting them in my head, thinking about how fast they would go.

"Yo, it's just Chester," Jesse said. "Dwight referred me to him."

The next day, I took a cab across the park to the office of Dr. Walter Chester, who, it turned out, treated many of my friends. They referred to him universally as "Chester"; you could hear his name, sotto in hallway asides. "Yo, Chester wrote me a script for thirty days of Tramadol, but I don't even know what the fuck it does." What *did* Tramadol do? I didn't know, but I wanted some.

The doctor saw patients in the funereal cloisters of a Park Avenue ground-floor co-op. In the waiting room, I idled through a tabloid. The door to an adjacent room opened and a boy I recognized from school—whose father, I knew, was the president of a massive media conglomerate—exited and crossed through the lobby. He shot me a knowing glance, and radials of pleasure, the stuck-throat feeling of a shared secret, coursed through me.

Chester had owlish spectacles and a mustache that he stroked in a performance of erudition. I explained that I was having difficulty paying attention, that my sleep was troubled, that debilitating panic attacks tormented me through the night. I went on that it was tough adjusting to the "frenetic pace of the city," a phrase that I used often in lieu of original thought. ("How do you like living in New York?" "Oh, you know, the pace is just so frenetic." "What did you do this weekend, Sam?" "Just got carried away by the frenetic pace of the city, I guess.") I was restless and unhappy, I said, and I knew that it wouldn't be possible for me to realize my full potential in my current condition.

Although I lied often, generally with the bristly indignation of the unfairly maligned ("Come *on*, Dad, do you *really* think I'd do something like that?"), I was a cautious, calculating liar. Preparing the alibis and excuses was half the fun. But these fabrications to Chester came automatically and without premeditation, as charged with authenticity as if they were true. I could almost convince myself that I really did have generalized-anxiety-major-depressive-attention-deficit-disorder. (It would not have occurred to me then that formulating such diagnoses should be the responsibility of a doctor.)

As I exited Chester's office, the autumn wind whipping my cheeks redder than they already were from three days of running only on cigarettes and amphetamines, I fingered those delicate slips of paper in my pocket, acknowledging their power. At any moment I could turn them into little orange bottles that would jangle in the pocket of my blue blazer, rhythmic as the shaking of maracas. They weren't prescriptions; they were keys, they were lovers, they were shoes, they were new friends I had known forever. They were magic.

"I'm living in Manhattan now," I wrote to a friend in Port-land, "surrounded by Upper East Side sophisto-puppies who spend the majority of their lives getting in and out of taxis. If you saw my life you would immediately vomit up your bean sprouts and acai onto your mandals . . . I'm incredibly busy, constantly overcaffeinated and exhausted, always broke, utterly cantanker-ous, lungs filled with tar and blood filled with chemicals, and happier than I've ever been—just thriving, thriving, thriving on the excess and intensity of this city."

I had been so rapidly subsumed by the mundane glamour of life in Manhattan, a breathless circus of coke lines at Bunga-low, white-gloved doormen in funny hats, tiny dogs in quilted coats. But stepping onto Park outside of Chester's office, raising my arm to hail a cab, I saw a pair of girls standing on the adja-cent corner—two, and then three, clustered together. Plumes of cigarette smoke circled around their bellies, charcoal and chalky white, and the sunlight percolating in auburn beams through the spaces between buildings made the smoke look almost opaque. The girls were thin as the leafless trees along Riverside Drive, their legs bony in black leggings, iridescent as coal. One of the girls was crying, and shouting into her mobile phone. "Mom," she was saying. "*Mom.*"

For an instant, it occurred to me that there was something sort of strange and sad about my life in New York. I had a nig-gling fear that I wasn't really happy in it. But the thought that I hated most of all was that despite outward appearances, I still found it hard to assimilate to the city. I would never be anything but a tourist. I was an outsider, a spectator, a dilettante. That terrified me.

That night, I went up to the roof of my apartment building and called Kat.

"Kat," I said, "I miss you."

Looking at the sky, I couldn't see the stars in the city, everything so clouded by smog and pollution. I stepped up onto the squared railing and felt the autumn wind against my body as I looked out over Broadway. I remembered the sky in Portland, the silence of the cool night. I thought about how it had felt to climb, how I'd been so sure that I would fly, the way that ladder had soared majestically toward the sky. Here, there was only the endless whirring of taxicabs below, all of them spinning their wheels, just like me.

"I'm lonely," I said.

It was the first true thing I'd said in a long time.

The week after I visited Princeton, I met with my college adviser, Ms. Sharma, a stout Indian woman who spoke in hushed conspiratorial tones. Meeting with her usually gave me a tension headache, which, fortunately, could be remedied with the Vicodin that Jesse was giving me.

She leafed through my paperwork, sending a stack of white paper sailing across her desk. "What did you think of Princeton?"

"It's my top choice," I said.

"Early decision, then?"

I nodded. She leaned forward.

"Sam," she whispered, "Princeton is the most competitive school in the country. Their acceptance rate dropped to eight percent last year. Your class rank and your SATs are good but not exceptional. Your extracurriculars are lacking. Your personal essay is strong and I'll write you a glowing recommendation—I know your instructors will as well—and I trust that you can deliver during the interview, but that's not secure. You look like a dabbler, Sam. Are you a dabbler?"

I shook my head.

"No. You need a passion. You like to write, yes?"

I nodded.

"You need to strengthen that element of your identity. Princeton rejects well-rounded students; that's not what they want. They want a well-rounded student body consisting entirely of students who excel spectacularly in one specific area. So you need to become . . ."

She paused for dramatic effect. The wait was excruciating. I hung on her ellipsis.

"*The writer.*"

I set my hands on the table. Both of us had bitten our fingernails raw. Ms. Sharma saw me looking at her hands and folded them in her lap. She was an outsider, too, I thought, dealing with the petty problems of lazy rich kids all day. It must have been miserable for her.

"What else can I do?" I asked.

"Keep those grades up. Strengthen your extracurriculars. And find someone to advocate for you during the admissions process. Do you know anyone who went to Princeton?"

A familiar sharp pressing began to form behind my eyes. In a moment I would cry. I didn't know how to explain to Ms. Sharma that I didn't come from this rarefied Upper East Side milieu, that here was where my middle-class Pacific Northwest trappings would betray me—here, because my father couldn't put in a phone call or donate a building. He went to *Berkeley*, for God's sake.

"I don't know," I said.

"Well, see what you can find, Sam."

Outside her office, I slumped against the wall, feeling sorry for myself. Becoming "the writer" was easy—I had already begun that process by moving to New York. The city (also, I suspect, the amphetamines, but that seemed irrelevant at the time) had sharpened my identity as a writer; I knew that I was not the first young writer to draw inspiration from the gritty song of the city, a song that I thought I could hear if I listened closely enough. The streets slippery with cab filth and rainwater outside the scuff-toed chaos of Lower East Side dive bars; daytime drunks on Upper East Side terraces; the cloying richness of grilled ostrich and polenta at Butter, where bony actresses clustered against a mural of painted birches. It was the realest forest in the city, and I loved it.

I was always writing this narcissistic little book in my head. Each moment was a potential vignette, every conversation mined for a savory snippet. Friends formed composite characters in my mind. At first, I had written to lend reason and meaning to a life that had grown chaotic, but the balance had reversed; I began living chaotically simply so that I would have something to write about. But my quest for drama had its own price: I had become so self-absorbed that even my most beautiful paragraphs were repellent. Even in English class, after returning a personal essay, a teacher told me, "This is very well written, but your protagonist is unlikable."

"It's about me," I said, genuinely dismayed.

I convinced myself that he was jealous of my youth and my talent. Only if I stayed in crisis, I thought, would my life retain its narrative viability. Still, I knew on some level that the damage had begun to exceed what was necessary for compelling storytelling. This was one difference between writing and drugs: with cocaine, after the first line, other lines followed whether I wanted them or not. When I wrote, I could control exactly how many lines there were, and when it all stopped.

I smoked a joint with Sahara in the garden of her parents' apartment off Fifth Avenue.

"What do I wear to my Princeton interview?" I asked. "I need something that says, 'I was up all night teaching quantum physics to Somalian orphans with cleft palates.'"

Sahara extinguished the roach with the toe of her metallic pump and considered this for a moment. She flipped her hair to one side. "Helmut Lang?" she said.

"You're no fucking help," I said.

"You'll be fine," she said. "It's just Princeton."

It's just Princeton, I repeated to myself as we groped down the darkened stairwell, back to the ordered earth tones of the living room. Stoned, my feet felt heavy and club-like, my palms sweat-slick against the banister, an indistinct buzzing in the back of my head. We paused in the vestibule outside the door to her apartment, a tasteful bouquet of dried flowers in a vase on the end table, a paisley umbrella hooked on the coatrack in the corner, and I caught a glimpse of myself in a mirror. I looked rosy-cheeked and glamorously exhausted. To my eyes, then, I looked like someone who really might belong there.

It's just Princeton, I said to my reflection. *It's just Princeton.*

My Princeton interviewer asked to meet me at a coffee shop on Eighth Avenue, near his office in midtown west. I wasn't nervous, I told myself. Not one bit.

I went home from school early and took an hour to dress myself with fastidious attention to detail: pressed khakis, a black Helmut Lang sweater I'd taken from Sahara's dad's closet. ("He'll never miss it," she'd said.) Did it look effortlessly chic or just contrived? Probably contrived. Was it possible to decontrive something that I'd already spent so much time contriving? I spent a lot of time asking myself questions like this instead of actually doing anything productive. I snorted two lines of Adderall off my dresser. I talked myself up in the mirror.

You're hot shit. He will find you irresistible.

In the bathroom, I applied tinted moisturizer and studied my face in the vanity, working different muscles, practicing a casual-yet-cool smile.

I wet a hand towel and wiped off the moisturizer. Suddenly I was blotchy. I opened the cabinet to expose the neat rows of orange prescription bottles. I took a Dexedrine, then a Xanax. I put another Xanax in the breast pocket of my shirt for good measure. It seemed likely that I'd need it later.

I closed the medicine cabinet and took the elevator downstairs. I waved to the doorman. I got in a cab. There were traffic lights. My cabdriver murmured incomprehensibly into his hands-free phone. I removed the second Xanax from my breast pocket and held it in my hand until it was almost beginning to melt. I popped it into my mouth and rotated it around until it found a neat space underneath my tongue. (Dr. Chester had advised me that taking pills sublingually made them hit faster—"great if you need an extra Ritalin during, say, your SATs," he'd said, and I had nodded thoughtfully; it sounded like great advice.) As it began to dissolve, I imagined that my inhibitions were being swept away by the gunmetal tides of the Hudson River. There was no traffic on the West Side Highway. I was young and free. Anxiety bubbled somewhere in my belly, then popped like a balloon, yielding to serenity.

Who cares, anyway? It's just Princeton.

"It's just Princeton!" I yelled to the cabdriver.

"What?" he said.

"I said, 'Can I smoke?' " I said, flashing a big-tip smile.

He waved a dismissive hand and rolled down the window. The interview was a cigarette, I thought. I had to get enough spark to light it up, but after it was lit, I could just let the words drift from me in ephemeral plumes, warm and aromatic.

I exited the cab and walked to the coffee shop on the northwest corner. My stomach was somersaulting. I ordered a large iced sugar-free nonfat vanilla latte, took a sip, then promptly threw it away at the risk of appearing too effete. I bought a bottle of water and let it dribble down my throat. My mouth was dry.

My interviewer, Paul, was country-club blond and faultlessly polite.

Paul had majored in economics and was captain of the lacrosse team.

Paul worked for an investment bank.

Paul was married last May.

Dread pitted in my stomach. I would never be Paul.

"What is it that interests you, Sam?" he asked. He was cheery, fraternal; I hated him for the effortlessness of his success as I imagined it. I realize now that Paul probably worked pretty hard in high school to get into Princeton and probably didn't spend his evenings doing blow with older men, but in the moment, I was outraged by his grace, his charisma. It must have been so easy for him, I thought.

The writer.

"English," I said. "And writing. Creative writing." It was convenient, I thought, not only because it was true but also because I was fairly certain that the legitimacy of an interest in creative writing was difficult to investigate; surely it was the discipline with the least rigorous associated extracurriculars. If anyone asked, that was why I didn't have many activities on my résumé. It had nothing to do with staying out all night on drugs, fucking strangers. I'd just been too busy *writing*. Internally, I bristled, preparing to fight for my identity.

"Interesting," Paul said. "Who are some writers you like to read?"

"Edmund White," I said. "Joyce Carol Oates. Jeffrey Eugenides. They're all great."

Paul laughed. "They're all on the faculty, right?"

I licked my lips. I could feel myself starting to perspire.

I asked him about the English department. He didn't know too much about it. I told him that I loved Edmund White, that I loved his triptych of autobiographical fiction about gay culture in America. Then I chastised myself for using the word "triptych."

That wasn't even the *right* word. What had possessed me to use that word?

Everything was falling apart. This was a disaster.

Triptych? There was no recovering from this.

The conversation was polite, but I could tell he didn't think much of me. In the cab on the way home, I called my father.

"Everything okay, Sam?" he said. "I'm in Washington."

"I think it went okay, Dad, my Princeton interview, but it

wasn't great, I guess, it wasn't the hole in one I'd imagined—Jesus, what am I doing using a golf metaphor? Whatever—and it's probably going to take something more. I mean, I know that I'm smart, but I just don't think that's enough for a school like Princeton, you know? I can't compete with those other prospective Princetonians. Those fratty trust-fundsters from Exeter and Dalton who really, honestly, feel passionately about business administration and tennis and date-raping townies in Sag Harbor or whatever else they do (we both know that's not really my scene), but I mean, I feel like I held my own, like I established an identity or something, but it's not the end, is it? It's just the start. A good start? I guess. An okay start."

"Let's talk about this when I get home," he said.

My father expressed some low-level concern over how many pills I had been prescribed, but my grades were up, which suggested that Dr. Chester's cocktail of pharmaceutical drugs was working. Yet I was sickly, pallid, temperamental, and always covered in a thin film of sweat, even in the dead of winter. I never ate, except for occasional, extraordinary binges that left me ill for days; I slept perhaps once a week, for twenty-four hours straight.

For a long time after I left New York, I wondered how he could have failed to see that I was unwell. Perhaps it was because I was finally thin after years of being chubby—and my father, who prized physical fitness so highly, couldn't see anything past the thinness that he had always wanted for me. Or maybe I was just a better liar than even I realized.

He was still administering the random drug tests my mother had begun—it had been a condition of my moving to New York with him—but through some spooky sixth sense I always knew when they were coming: when he returned from a long business trip, or just off some glint in his eye if our paths crossed in the morning. I quickly learned that a liter of cranberry juice and a long stint in the sauna at the gym flushed all traces of anything illicit I'd ingested out of my system in fairly short order—and I came up positive for amphetamines and benzodiazepines usually anyway, since I was prescribed them. It was too easy to cheat.

What he couldn't test for was how I spent my nights when he was over at Jennifer's, traveling on business, or had simply gone to bed, when I would go to the apartments and hotel rooms of men I met online, over to the homes of friends to party, or out to bars and nightclubs. On the few occasions when he caught me coming home just as the sun was rising, I told him I'd woken up early. Only once, in the middle of the night, did I return to the apartment from a nocturnal tryst with Greg and Matt, a couple with a lavishly decorated Central Park West apartment, to find my father awake and working on the couch.

"Oh, hi," I said calmly. "I just went out for a cigarette."

"It's late," he said.

"I know," I said. "I've been up working on this history paper."

"Okay," he said softly. "Get some sleep, will you?"

I nodded. I went into my bedroom and shut the door.

It wasn't five minutes later that Robert sent me a text. *Robert.* He was late thirties and bearded. He lived just a block away. He always had good drugs.

"Come play," he wrote. My muscles clenched reflexively. I checked the clock. It was past one. But I had taken a Viagra that evening in anticipation of Greg and Matt's inexhaustible libidos, and I was still a little tipsy from the wine they had served me before we all went to bed together.

"Give me ten," I replied.

I shut off my bedside lamp and waited for my eyes to adjust to the darkness. The crack under the door was dark—my father had gone to sleep. *Go to bed*, I thought. *Or at the very least take a shower.* But instead I dressed and left the apartment again.

Robert opened the door wearing just his boxer briefs. His chest was lean and furry; he had a friendly, boyish charm. He kissed me hard on the mouth, and his breath tasted odd—a metallic flavor, almost antiseptic. On his desk, I spotted a little glass pipe, a skinny stem with a spherical bulb clouded and charred with flakes of crystal meth, and a propane lighter.

"I didn't know it was *that* kind of night," I said.

He smiled dreamily.

"Want a hit?" he said.

"Sure," I said. He held the pipe gently to his lips, flicking the propane lighter to incinerate the contents of the bulb, which bubbled and browned, the color of an oxidized apple. After a long breath, he pulled me in for a kiss. I parted my lips, and he blew the smoke into my mouth.

Suddenly, I felt bright and alert and shiny. It felt like someone had turned the lights on inside me—like the first rays of sunshine after a long and terrible winter.

I exhaled the secondhand smoke.

"You should be careful with this shit," I said.

"Don't be a buzzkill," he said.

I grabbed the pipe for myself and took a long pull, holding it carefully by the stem. The smoke I blew out was white and fluffy as a cloud.

"It's so good," I said, ecstatic, getting higher. Happiness was less a thought than a punctuation mark—the period on the end of the sentence that had been my life before this moment.

"Come to bed!" Robert said, delighted. I grabbed his hands, delirious. I laughed to myself over nothing at all. *Everyone is stupid and wrong about meth. This is great. Once in a while. Just once in a while.*

"I am feeling so good," I said stupidly as Robert began to unbutton my shirt. "I am feeling so good." I repeated it as he pushed me onto the bed. Soon the words became like a mantra, a prayer that I was whispering to myself in the hopes the good feeling wouldn't end.

The next day at school, Sahara stopped me outside French class.

"Babe," she said, "how did it go?"

"What?" I asked. I was bleary. My head was ringing. I hadn't slept at all. I felt like shit. *Why do you keep doing this to yourself?*

"Princeton," she said. "The interview."

"Oh!" I said. For a split second, I considered telling her the truth—admitting that I was terrified and insecure. That my whole life was a mess. That at the rate I was going, I knew that I'd be lucky if I survived senior year.

Instead, I grinned.

"I killed it," I said.

Three

Senior year sucks," I said to Daphne one afternoon. It was November now, and we were smoking cigarettes and drinking vodka-tonics on the balcony of her parents' Upper East Side penthouse after school one day. "I'm so *bored*."

Daphne took a gulp of her drink.

"And yet you're doing a fine job of keeping it interesting for yourself," she said.

"All I do is go to detention and go to school and do my homework and, like, wait for Princeton to get back to me and do, like, extracurricular activities."

Daphne guffawed. "*What* extracurricular activities?"

"I joined the school newspaper," I said defensively.

"We don't have a school newspaper," Daphne said. She reconsidered. "Do we?"

"We do *now*," I said. The paper had been defunct for nearly a decade and I'd attempted to revive it with a faculty member, knowing that they would let me call myself editor in chief, which would look good on my college applications. I retitled the paper the *Dwight Chronicle*—emphasis on "chronic." Dwight's motto, emblazoned on all promotional materials and on posters around the school, was "Use your spark of genius to build a better world," so I'd given the newspaper the tagline "Sparking genius since 2005." We still hadn't produced an issue yet due to the propensity of the editorial staff, as I was totally willing to concede, for sparking genius when we should have been writing copy.

"Right," Daphne said. "I'll keep an eye out for it."

"I also have the Young Writers' Society," I reminded her.

"That's not a real club," Daphne said. "That's just a place where you read your poetry to underclassmen and they give you compliments."

"So? I'm still the president of it," I said.

"How could Princeton say no?" Daphne said, dry as chardonnay.

I flicked my cigarette off the balcony. "Do you think I'm going to end up at a state school?"

"I don't know what that is," she said. "But no. Probably not."

I stood. "I should go," I said. "I have a date."

"Oh dear," she said. "Park Avenue wives, hide your husbands."

"This one's unmarried," I said. "Or divorced, I think. And I have a *very* good feeling about him."

"Just remember," Daphne said. "If he promises you the moon, grab it and run."

I did have a good feeling. His name was Dean and he was forty-three. He had written a personals ad online, cross posted to Manhattan and central New Jersey—Princeton, specifically. I

wondered if he was connected to the school somehow. I hoped
he would be

Back at my apartment, I dressed in tan chinos, a light wool
scarf, a blue blazer that made me look especially boyish, and my
favorite brown leather loafers. I grabbed my wallet, keys, cell phone,
and a pack of cigarettes, and put two Ritalin in my shirt pocket.

I used to say that I was a waste of a perfectly good roofie,
but then, I used to say a lot of awful things; still, I had a bad
habit of going home with any man who would buy me a double
vodka-tonic; any man in whose shoes I could see my reflection;
any man with salt-and-pepper hair and an affectionate demeanor;
any man with sad eyes and a wedding band; any man who offered
me cocaine; any man who reminded me a little bit of my father—
not so much that it felt transgressive but just enough that it felt
like love.

Dean was different. His emails back and forth to me were
quick-witted and sharp. Even his punctuation was good. He had
been an investment banker, he said; now, he was having a midlife
crisis, and that meant wanting to sleep with strangers he met on
the Internet. I liked his honesty and reciprocated. For once, I
didn't pretend to be someone I wasn't; I used my real name and
told him that I was seventeen, which was the truth. He asked me
to bring a piece of identification proving it—seventeen was the
age of consent in New York, after all—and so I did, slipping my
passport into my back pocket before I left my apartment.

I met older men online for sex frequently enough, and often it
was just for the gratification of cheap quick thrills, guys who had

better drugs than I could afford on my own—but mostly it was for the euphoria of being desired, worshipped for my youthfulness. Supine in some dude's loft, I felt powerful in a way that even the best cocaine couldn't make me feel. But there was also a part of me that wanted, desperately, to be loved by an older man in a way that was sincere and true. Even at that age I was self-aware enough to know what that was really about. "I wonder if this has something to do with my father," I'd say with a grin to Daphne the morning after, recounting certain details of how I'd spent the evening but keeping the most lurid of them secret.

I fantasized with drug-like fervor about being held by a man, about my woes and loneliness evaporating. Each time I hooked up with a stranger, some piece of me clung to a sad little flicker of hope that he would be the one to love me. It would not have occurred to me just to date like a normal person; that involved a type of deferred gratification of which I was incapable.

And so I took the 1 train from Eighty-sixth Street down to Tribeca. I met him at a little French bistro. Inside, he was there at the bar, tall and svelte, in skinny black Levi's, a white T-shirt, and a two-button black blazer. He was good-looking yet unremarkable, stubbled. He was drinking alone.

I showed the bartender my fake ID as I sat down next to him—"Whiskey sour," I said—and then, quickly under the bar, I showed Dean my real ID, my passport. He checked it, shining it under the light, and smiled. His teeth were white. He shook my hand, then squeezed my thigh. He seemed nervous.

"I'm Sam," I said.

"Dean," he said. His voice was deep and cautious. He paused. "Would it be cliché to say that I've never done this before?"

"It would," I said. "And that would be my line, anyway, I think."

"Do you do this a lot?"

"What's 'this'?" I asked.

He gestured at nothing. "You know, this. Meet guys online."

"Sometimes," I said. "It's hard to meet people when you're"— I looked up at the bartender, who was distracted rinsing a glass— "my age."

"I can imagine," he said.

"And I don't really get along with gay dudes my age," I said. "Not that there are that many."

"Are you out?" he asked. "To everyone?"

I nodded. "Since I was eleven." Off his surprised look, I shrugged. "I like to tell myself I'm too intimidating to be bullied, but maybe I'm just lucky."

He laughed. "You *are* intimidating," he said. "And smart."

"I know," I said, taking a sip of my drink. He laughed again. I could see him starting to relax.

"Have you seen the film *Igby Goes Down*?" he asked.

I nodded.

"You're like him," he said. "I'll call you Igby, I think."

"That's ironic."

"What is?"

"This is just, like, the first time ever that I've used my real name and you've already given me a new one. It's a better name than Sam, though. Uglier, but more fitting."

"And you're in high school."

"Yes," I said. "A prep school on the Upper West Side."

"What are you prepping for?"

"Adulthood, I guess."

"Adulthood."

"I just want to be old enough to meet teenagers online for sex."

"I don't think that's what adulthood is," he said. "Will you go to college?" he asked.

"God, I hope so," I said. "I applied early decision to Princeton."

"I know it well," he said. "I have a house there."

"I know you do. You said so in your ad."

"Is that why you responded to it?"

"No," I said. "I responded to it because you sounded sexy. Your writing made you sound sexy."

"You'll do well," he said. "There are a lot of smart, good-looking kids there. Like you."

"That's what worries me," I said. "How will I feel special?"

"I don't imagine it's very hard for you to feel special," he said.

"You'd be surprised."

"What do you mean?"

"I need a lot of validation," I said. "For me to feel ordinary, everyone needs to treat me like I'm extraordinary."

"What makes you feel extraordinary?"

"This does," I said. "You're smart; you're older; you're obviously successful. You're handsome. And you want me." He met my gaze. I dropped my voice an octave. "You *do* want me, right?"

"I do," he said. I put his hand on my groin; he squeezed my thigh through my pants. I licked my lips provocatively.

"So what do you want to do to me?" I asked. He was silent. I made my voice go still huskier. "What do you want to do to me?"

He had been panting; he stopped. He looked at me a little coldly. "You know," he said. "You're a charmer. And you're very seductive. But it's all sort of transparent."

I inhaled. I felt exposed.

"You can drop the boy Lolita act," he said. "You don't have to perform. You can be exactly who you are. I mean, it's obvious that you're smart but troubled, and that's probably your narrative, and you don't want to be the victim—you want to be the one in control. But I'm not trying to control you. And the whole thing is a little practiced. You'd be much sexier if you stopped trying so hard."

I went quiet for a minute. I finished my drink. It was the first time I'd been called out like that. It was thrilling.

"Let's go back to your place," I said.

He paid the check.

⸻

Outside on the street, I was a little drunk—it didn't take much—and spinning from amphetamines. The air was tap-dancing on my skin. I reached toward Dean to steady myself.

"You okay?" he said.

"Fine," I said.

Dean's apartment was a few blocks away, on West Street, in a modern high-rise building with a glass lobby that felt like a fishbowl. The doorman waved us upstairs with a brisk nod. In the elevator, Dean's boots were black and well-worn, and his chest hair looked prickly, lying perpendicular to his clavicle. The elevator doors opened.

"After you," he said.

A blood-red foyer opened up into a dining area, both with vaulted ceilings. A golden candle chandelier overhead glinted. I stopped and took it in. He turned to face me. Then, wordlessly, I slipped off my blazer, dropping it on the floor. I unbuttoned my shirt, then my trousers. Then I tugged off my underwear, pulling them off over my shoes. I stood naked for a moment, wearing only my penny loafers.

"Oh," he said. He put his hands on my chest, then my belly. He grabbed my hand and led me into the bedroom. It was maybe thirty feet long, with floor-to-ceiling windows that framed a panoramic view of the Hudson River, and bookshelves lining one long wall; the room was painted a pale peach, which in the late-afternoon light gave it an odd dreamlike haze. He pushed me onto the bed. He kissed me, his stubble scratching against my neck, and his strong, hairy chest pressing against mine, lean and smooth, and his tongue was inside my mouth, our teeth clinking as festively as a cocktail party toast.

When I woke up it was dark outside and for a brief moment I couldn't remember where I was. I was naked in his bed, lying against him with my head leaning against his chest; his arms were resting lightly on mine.

It felt good to be held—better than I had imagined. That intimacy I had been craving that felt more substantial than just sex.

"You are so beautiful," he whispered in my ear, and it seemed true, or at the very least plausible.

At first, I had pegged Dean as a typical investment banker asshole, probably a closet case—I had been with a lot of guys like that—but he was different; he defied easy categorization. He had made a lot of money working for Merrill Lynch, he said, and then decided he didn't want to be in business anymore; at that point, he was coasting, working idly on a few creative projects. He was a self-described artist, a writer and a filmmaker. He split his time between New York, Princeton, and London. He was old money, descended from a long line of American aristocratic lineage that I couldn't entirely follow. He was progressive, intellectual, bookish; he dropped names liberally but not, at least to me at that point in my life, obnoxiously—although it would have needed to be pretty egregious for me to find it obnoxious. He also seemed like a dilettante who had gotten lucky.

He was bisexual, he said, explaining that he had mostly dated women and been involved with few men. Never someone my age, he said, and I believed him. Curiously, there was nothing predatory about him—nothing desperate or furtive in the way I'd found many older men were. He seemed at once very young and very old, avuncular in a comforting, familiar way but also like a peer to me.

Naked, I picked at the books that lined the wall. There were titles on queer studies, memoirs and autobiographies, and there were pop culture titles from the '60s, which I thought predated even him. He said he inherited them from his mother and he liked to keep them ironically.

He told me that he loved Salinger; he had just finished reading *The Catcher in the Rye*, he said. I laughed. "It's so trite," I said. "All that angst."

He asked me what I wrote.

"Some poetry," I said. "Short memoir and essays. I like writing about my life." On his computer, I pulled up a piece I had been working on and read it to him. He poured me red wine.

The piece was overwrought and riddled with clichés. He loved it.

"It's so lyrical," he said. He was pretentious and affected. So was I, especially with him, dropping the flip tone I used with my friends and making my language more deliberate, more adult.

We made love again. "You give me an erection of the body and soul," he said, thrusting into me.

At the east end of the room was a daybed in a window seat,

with one large glass pane looking out over the city, and just beneath the seat, another window; when I lay there, it felt as though I were suspended in the air, floating over a glittering Manhattan evening. I smoked compulsively, like my life depended on it, making rings that drifted out the open window into the cool night, stubbing my cigarettes out into an ashtray that grew congested with little tan tombstones.

I told him about Princeton, about the way I'd felt the day I visited the campus, that world of rarefied privilege to which I wanted access so badly. He stroked my hair. "You'll get in, Igby," he said. "We could be together there."

He told me about his friends on the faculty in the English department. A knot formed in my stomach. *This was it.* He could help get me in. "I know some folks on the admission committee, actually," he said. "I could put in a call and see what I can find out."

"That would be amazing," I said.

"It's nothing," he said.

He pushed me onto the bed again.

At the time, my proclivity for sleeping with older guys felt like a matter of taste—it took many years for me to fully untangle the snarl of pathological self-loathing that drove me into the beds of middle-aged men across Manhattan—but still, in a taxi leaving Dean's apartment, some small part of me worried that I was getting in over my head. It had happened before.

The first time I was with an older man was when I was four-teen, a freshman in high school in Portland. I'd been down the previous year reeling from my first heartbreak with Jerick and spent a lot of time online, in chat rooms, looking for connections that I couldn't find in the real world. There was no one my age there, which I liked—it was so easy to find men, even if they were just words on the screen, who would make me feel valuable. Mostly, though, it stayed in the realm of fantasy. When I chatted with a man in his forties who lived in Southern California, he told me that he wanted to sleep with me. "I'm HIV positive. Is that okay?" he asked. I jumped away from the keyboard like I had been burned—the very adult reality of this stranger's sexual health colliding with my teenage need to feel desired made my stomach turn. Another time, a man in Alabama told me that he wanted to fly me out there and spend a weekend together; mostly seeing if he'd go for it, I told him that I'd do it for a thousand dollars. We got as far as booking air travel before I blocked him, too fright-ened by the possibility that it might be real to carry it any further.

In one of those chat rooms, I met a man named Jim. He was a graduate student at a local university, twenty-four. Our conversa-tions were flirtatious but felt fraternal, too; they were less about sex and more about him wanting to introduce me to an adult way of being a gay man that I hadn't accessed yet. He wanted to talk about coming out, about gay representation in the media, about what it was like to be so young and already sure of my sexual iden-tity. In his pictures, he had sparkly eyes and a five o'clock shadow. He wanted to meet in person to talk.

This felt treacherous, but I was intrigued, too. The responsible thing to do, I thought, was to discuss it with my psychologist, Judith, whom I'd begun seeing after I had come out as gay. ("Maybe it would be useful for you to have some additional mental health resources at your disposal," my mother had said delicately.) I liked Judith: she reminded me of a television therapist, all statuesque salt-and-pepper smarts. But after I confided to her that I was considering meeting an older man I'd chatted with on the Internet, she called my parents and told them. Alarmed, they had a stern talk with me about it, and I agreed to cease communication with Jim. (I also stopped seeing Judith, who I knew I couldn't trust anymore.) A few weeks later, in an act of rebellion, I decided to meet Jim in person. The fact that adults thought the situation was dangerous enough to intervene made it much more worth doing.

So I met Jim at a coffee shop. I was wearing a red-and-white–striped rugby polo that made me look like a candy cane, and he was shorter than I expected, but just as handsome. The conversation was light. We went to an adult store downtown, on my suggestion, dashing past the curtain to where the pornography was stored, gawking at the titles and the splashy covers. The thrill of sneaking into this very grown-up space with this attractive older man was exhilarating. But he still didn't seem interested in me sexually, which only made me want him more.

By a few months later, though, something had changed. One afternoon when my parents were out of town, I met him in a park. Together, we walked through the sparsely forested woods back to

my parents' house. I had borrowed one of my father's button-
down shirts to wear, something expensive and impractical, even
though I was just walking ten minutes through the woods to meet
him. He looked sallow and thinner than he had been when we
had first met.

"You look so skinny," I said dumbly.

"I've been getting in shape," he said. His eyes were lit up.
"Well, the pills help."

"What kind of pills?" I asked. At that point, I had barely
begun experimenting with drugs. This seemed exciting.

"Don't worry about it," he said.

In the kitchen, he took off his shirt and took a swig from a
bottle of vodka in the pantry where my parents kept the alcohol.
His abdomen was taut and waxy. Suddenly, I felt afraid. This was
all too real.

"Give me some of that," I said, taking the bottle and swallowing a gulp. I had never raided my parents' liquor cabinet before,
but it felt appropriate now.

Downstairs in my bedroom, he stripped down to his underwear. "You're so cute," he said. He kissed me. I realized that I
didn't want to do this, but it also felt too late to say no. He had
expectations of me. I didn't want to disappoint him.

He was aggressive. He pushed me down on my bed. It was the
first time someone had ever done that to me, and I felt desired,
and adult, but also disgusted with myself—disgusted with this
whole situation. The *no* in my head came out instead as a garbled
"Please."

"Please?" he said. He smiled a Cheshire cat smile.

I nodded, and he tugged off his boxers. I closed my eyes. I imagined myself leaving my body.

After he finished, I went quickly to get in the shower. A moment later, I heard a noise in the bathroom. I saw his form through the frosted glass. *Please don't get in here with me*, I thought. He opened the shower door and stepped inside, stretching under the running water. He pinched my side.

"You okay?" he said. I nodded. This was what I had wanted, wasn't it? But it didn't actually feel good, not in the way I'd thought it would. I liked the attention, but the act of sex was uncomfortable, awkward, embarrassing. I told myself that it would get easier.

Or maybe it wouldn't. Maybe this was just how it was supposed to feel. The rush of anticipation, then a few minutes of intermittent pain and pleasure, and a big emptiness after. I missed Jerick. I missed my mother. *Don't be a baby*, I thought. *Don't be a little bitch*. I turned my face away from Jim so he wouldn't see me cry.

I didn't see Jim again after that. But a week later, I met another guy in a chat room. He was in his early thirties and lived just a few miles away. I told him I was eighteen.

"I don't have wheels, though," I said.

"Don't worry about it," he said. "I'll pick you up."

My apartment was empty when I got home from Dean's place on Sunday night. Where was my father? Had he even realized I'd been gone? I had homework; I'd forgotten all about it. Emerging from the cocoon of Dean's loft was strange and uncomfortable. All the noises of the city made my nerves shot. My thighs and buttocks were sore and tender. I could still feel where his fingers had pressed against my wrists as he pushed my face deeper into the pillow; even the thought of it produced some prickling in my groin, a longing for the erotic charge that had held me all weekend.

I spread my textbooks out on my bed and stared at them. I called Dean. "I need you," I said.

"Come back," he said.

I tumbled back into him. We made love. I slept. He woke me up at 6:00 a.m. and I staggered into a taxi to make it to school in time for my 7:00 a.m. detention.

There, as I read in the chancellor's office, my time with Dean felt like a strange dream, and also much more real than anything else in my life.

It went on like this for several weeks. My father stayed at Jennifer's. I went to school, went home, and dutifully did my homework, snorting Ritalin and popping Provigil so I would stay focused, and then at eleven or midnight, when the work was done, I would take a cab downtown to see Dean.

We talked about modern poetry and classical art. I told him about my mother and my father. I talked about Portland, about drugs. He told me stories about his ex-wife, making it big in finance, realizing that he was wholly unfulfilled. "I had hired a fashion photographer to take head shots of me for a business website," he said. "I was wearing a suit—I looked very corporate—and he was taking all of these pictures, but they were just all wrong. I looked stiff. I wasn't myself. We were shooting on the roof of this building, with the skyscrapers all around us—it should have been so dynamic, this visual, but it was just flat. So I got started taking shots of vodka, and I took a couple of Ritalin—I was trying to create some different kind of energy, a ferocity on the set. But I couldn't. So I started taking off the suit. And the photographer was shooting as I was doing this, this anguished, ecstatic striptease for the camera. *That* was who I was. Not this corporate jackal. But something else altogether. And so I finished out the work I had contracted to me, and I haven't worked in business since."

"What happens when you run out of money?" I asked.

He shrugged. "I'll figure it out," he said. "I'll tap-dance on street corners. I'll make art. I'll get any kind of job. I just want to enjoy my life." It seemed so romantic, the impracticality of this. It also seemed like the sort of thing that only a person with family money would say, which made it all the more romantic.

I got up to take the pills I had wedged in my wallet. He asked me what they were.

"Provigil," I said. "They keep me awake."

"Like speed?"

"No," I said. "They don't work on dopamine, the way amphetamines do. They just work on your circadian rhythms.

They're using it in the military now. See, our bodies don't need as much sleep as we think they do. And when you don't sleep, you get all this lost time back—all these hours where you wouldn't be conscious that you get to use—that *I* get to use—productively."

"It sounds too good to be true," Dean said.

"It's not," I said. "I mean, I just take it when I have a lot of work to do and I'll just stay up for a few days at a time. I couldn't live without it."

"That's a little sophomoric, no?"

"What do you mean?"

"Well," he said, "if people really didn't need sleep, don't you think somebody else would have figured that out first? Do you think that you—a high school senior—are the first one to discover that a life without sleep is sustainable?"

I didn't like this. It was so condescending. "Well, it works for me," I said.

But it wasn't working for me. I fell asleep everywhere: lying on the windowsill of his apartment, a half-smoked cigarette still burning in an ashtray; in his arms as he rubbed my neck; sitting in his kitchen as we drank wine and talked about music. I would wake up to him laughing, watching me doze.

"I worry about you, Igby," he said. "You should eat something." I shook my head no. Coffee, cocktails. Dexedrine and Adderall. I stood naked in his bedroom, chain-smoking and shivering until he wrapped my overcoat around my shoulders. His hands caressed my chest; his arms hooked around my neck.

His mouth tasted like wine as he kissed me.

"I love you," I said, meaning it.

"I love you, too, Igby," he murmured.

I met Sahara at a party in a notorious town house in the East Sixties, the home of a Greek shipping heir whose parents were always away. Through panes of dark glass off the living room was an indoor swimming pool, lined in black marble. Drunk kids were skinny-dipping. Sahara sat cross-legged by the coffee table, messy hair falling in her face, pulling from her enormous designer purse a grinder and a vial of marijuana to roll a joint.

"I'm really falling for this dude," I said.

"He's forty-three, you lunatic," she said, glancing back at me. "What—do you think he's going to adopt you? Or that you're going to go off to Princeton and be with this old man?"

"Like, Sahara, I think I love him."

She rolled her eyes. "Dude. You're young and pretty and so you make *him* feel young and pretty, even though he's old and crusty. He just wants to live forever, and so he's, you know, drinking from the fountain of youth."

"Gross," I said.

"Sorry, but it's true. He's using you as his plaything." She wagged a finger, the Cartier bracelets on her wrists clanging. "If you're going to do that, at least find, like, a sheikh or something. What do you even have to show for this relationship?"

"So why am I in it?" I said.

She turned to me. "Sam," she said, "how oblivious are you? You're the poster child for daddy issues."

"Not *everything* is about my relationship with my father," I said. "I think this is about a lot more than that."

"Well, of course *you* do." She sighed. "Why can't you just find a nice, early-twenties gay to date? Maybe one of those corn-fed midwestern types, all bright-eyed and bushy-tailed, freshly out of the closet—somebody whose life isn't all dysfunction and drama. NYU is *crawling* with guys like that." She cocked her head. "Or so I've heard."

"That sounds boring," I said. She tapped the contents of her grinder out onto a rolling paper.

"Whatever," she said. "Then keep fucking him until you hear back from Princeton so at least he can pull some strings for you—if he's such hot shit there. Just don't delude yourself into thinking it's more than that."

"But that's the thing that's completely infuriating," I said. "If I didn't love him, that's exactly what I'd do. It's *because* I love him that I feel bad using him."

"Then you'll always be known as the boy who didn't go to Princeton," she said.

"I'm so exhausted," I moaned.

"When was the last time you actually got a full night's sleep?"

"Sunday," I said.

"Sam," she said, agitated, "it's *Friday*. Why are you out? Go home. Don't go to Dean's. Just, like, get takeout from Mr. Chow, take an Ambien, and get some sleep. Like a normal person. You're going to die."

I told her I would, fully intending to keep that commitment, but by the time I got home, I was too tired to sleep—a feeling I had often. I envied the clarity with which Sahara saw the situation. I knew there was a part of me that was manipulating Dean, just as he was manipulating me, but it was thornier than that: I had grown to care about him too much to be so opportunistic, and I had no poker face. And if my youth was what he coveted, why did he talk to me like I was a peer?

After tossing and turning between the sheets for a few minutes, I texted Dean. He told me to come over, and so I did, jumping into a cab and speeding down the West Side Highway.

We lay in the window bed, facing each other. He massaged my legs.

"I hate school and I hate my life," I whined. "I just want to be with you."

"How do you want to be with me?" he asked.

I shook my head. "Maybe forever," I said. "But that's a long time." I paused. "How do you want to be with me?"

"Let me think about it," he said.

Later, he sent me a note. "I want to be with you in many more discombobulated and recombobulated states . . . to see that smile of yours which is half-visible . . . to touch the most vulnerable pieces of you, circulating energy that I wish I could call by a more nuanced name than love . . . to feel your body modulate, in my experience of it, from very manly to boyish . . . to know things after being with you that form a new pattern, things not having to do with you directly but that fit together as a result of some cohesion and opposition—some alternating current—between us . . . to feel our power: yours, mine and ours."

"That's, like, the very definition of sweet nothings," I wrote back. "Or maybe sweet everythings."

Later, I read his note to Sahara over the phone.

"Dude," she said.

"Isn't it romantic?"

"No, it's *weird*," she said. I could hear her sucking on a cigarette. "Maybe you two deserve each other."

"I could do worse, though," I said. I hacked a low, guttural cough. I'd had it for a few weeks and it just wasn't going away.

"It's funny," she said. "He's so old, but he's probably going to outlive you."

It was mid-December when I got a letter in the mail from Princeton. I could see clearly that it wasn't big enough to be an admissions packet. My heart stopped. I tore it open, scanning it for the rejection that I knew was coming.

It wasn't a rejection, at least. It was a deferral to the regular admissions cycle.

I called my father and told him. "That's disappointing," he said brightly. "But what a great opportunity for you to strengthen your application by January—to give them a really strong case for accepting you in the regular round. Maybe get involved with some more extracurriculars." *Fucking extracurriculars.* I hated extracurriculars.

I didn't see it that way. I called Dean. Surely he would know how to cheer me up. "Oh, Igby." He sighed. His husky baritone gave me chills. I could smell his neck.

"I feel thwarted," I said. "Not defeated but thwarted. I lost the battle, I guess."

"Without thwart, there can be no character," he whispered. He often did this: murmuring poetically in a way that made all my rhythms go haywire, like he knew exactly what I needed. "Without character, the colors of your soul would dull. You're supposed to be a prophet of the last generation, a more vivid prophet than the easy experience of successful early admission to Princeton would allow."

A more vivid prophet? I had no idea what that meant, which made it seem all the more profound. "No," I said. "It was supposed to be easy."

"Buck up, Igby," he whispered.

I went out with friends that night and drank too much, falling down in the street. I couldn't be inside my head anymore. I had failed.

Who was I if I wasn't the person who belonged at Princeton? What would my future hold? The fantasy life I'd been leading had been so beautifully rendered in my imagination. I couldn't conceive of a future worth living anywhere else.

I hatched a plan. Dean could be my savior, I thought; he could help me at Princeton where I couldn't help myself. He was powerful and well connected. Surely he would do that for me—surely he loved me enough to pull a few strings.

I brought it up one night, on the patio of a dimly lit restaurant in Tribeca, the kind of place where we could make out in the back without anyone noticing. "Maybe you could put me in touch with Ed," I said, as casually as I could.

"Right," he said, sidestepping the question. "I bet he'd like you, even if you were angling for a good word with the admissions committee." He reached for a drag of my cigarette. "But I think he's on leave in London or somewhere like that for a few months. I saw him a few weeks ago at Yolanda's house for a little dinner with Steve Martin, who was in town."

"*Steve Martin*–Steve Martin?"

He smiled. "Shameless name-dropping is part of the courting ritual of a May-September relationship, isn't it? You keep flaunting your youth and I just keep flaunting my cocktail-swirling panache with the big-timers."

"Do you know when he's coming back?" I asked.

He shrugged. I gulped my cabernet.

"Too bad," I said.

There was a moment's long hesitation.

"Well, if you talk to him," I said, "tell him his pubescent doppelgänger wants to buy him a drink."

"Will do," he said, smiling at me, but it felt strained.

"What other of my literary idols can you hook me up with?" I said, trying to break the tension. "Hermann Hesse. Can you make that happen?"

He grinned. "Oh, I wish I'd known you'd be so impressed with Hermann," he said. "I reconnected with him the other night, actually. Nietzsche was such a scandal, drunkenly trying to pants Schopenhauer—and then he got really irritated and spilled his drink all over Hannah Arendt. Oh, what a marvelous party."

He could see me trying to manipulate him, but he wasn't taking the bait. And I could feel myself beginning to pull away from him, just the slightest bit. It wasn't that I loved him any less for what I perceived as his unwillingness to help me—it was a fissure within myself. I could envision the life where I clawed my way into Princeton and we stayed together there, a love that grew deeper and more profound with time. But what if I didn't? Would I go to some other college and take the train to New Jersey on the weekend to see my middle-aged boyfriend? Wouldn't I want to be young and unencumbered?

There were too many variables—too many moving parts. I was going back to Portland for Christmas, and I thought it would be good to be there for a little while—away from the city, and away from him.

I spent my last night in New York with Dean, not knowing if it was exactly where I wanted to be. We had sex, although I didn't want to. The thought spun around in my mind like water circling a drain: *If I don't sleep with him, what happens to Princeton?*

I didn't wake him up in the morning when I left for the airport, but I left a note on the kitchen counter telling him that I loved him.

I still meant it.

I was almost sure.

Four

*O*utside baggage claim at the airport in Portland, I could see my mother idling in her black SUV, the passenger-side window rolled down. She had cut her hair since I'd seen her in the summer; now it was styled in a fashionable bob that showed off her angular jawline and high cheekbones. I walked toward her car, tugging my suitcase behind me. She scanned the throng, and I could see her looking right past me. I raised a hand in greeting.

"Mom," I called. She looked directly at me without recognition, then did a double take. She stepped out of the car and walked toward me.

"Oh, Sam," she said. She wrapped me in a hug. "You're so thin, honey." She looked alarmed. I took it as a compliment.

"I know," I said.

She touched my hair. "And you need a haircut," she said.

"I know."

"I'm glad you're home," she said.

"This isn't home anymore," I said sharply.

If this hurt her, she didn't show it; she had gotten better at deflecting my anger, or depersonalizing it. I knew she had been going to a support group for families of addicts, but she said it was about her father, who had been an alcoholic—I wouldn't learn until much later that it was for me.

I was always angry at my mother, usually unfairly: for her emotional irregularity, which I privately believed had pushed my father away and resulted in the collapse of their marriage; for not fighting harder to keep me from going to New York with my father when, I thought, she should have wanted me to stay in Portland, my home; and for the way she interacted with me, which usually involved efforts to police my behavior that resulted only in conflict.

None of this was actually her fault. My father had been passive or absent, leaving her to overcompensate for his unavailability with explosive outbursts and dramatic gestures. I'd been set on going to New York anyway, and besides, there had been so much tension between us in the preceding years, she would have been power-less to parent me; my resentment toward her was transparent and ugly. Most of all, though, what I couldn't see then was that she was floundering, too. In short succession, my brother, Ben, had left for college, her husband had left her, and I had moved thousands of miles away. In the space of two quick months, she lost the two identities that had given her purpose for decades: wife and mother.

She tried to set limits, but I quietly flouted them: if she told me not to go out, I simply waited until she went to bed and went out anyway; if she told me she was concerned about my weight or how many pills I took, I threw back in her face my academic suc-cesses and college prospects, which were certainly brighter than they'd been in Portland. "Oh, like *you* did such a good job being the parent," I'd say, and I could see her face fall, but it was better than the alternative—having to change. She had stopped fighting back. In personal essays I wrote for school and in the stories I told my friends and therapist, I made her out to be the villain in my family's narrative, embellishing details of our arguments and taking things she had said out of context to give her the shape of an emotionally volatile, glamorously self-involved narcissist. (I might have been projecting.)

Often we got along well, but her attempts to parent me were, I thought, too little, too late. I much preferred my father's hands-off approach. My mother often seemed to be trying to save me from real or perceived harm, and this annoyed me. I knew what I was doing. I couldn't see then that we were both unraveling, each of us angry about the other's instability.

We drove through the night in silence, making switchbacks up the hills toward the house, her occasionally asking a question and me responding as briefly as possible.

"I'm sorry about Princeton," she said.

"Me, too," I said.

"Maybe you'll get in regular decision."

"Yeah, that's what Dad said, too, but I don't know how good my odds are," I said.

"You have to finish your other applications, right?"

"Yale's the other reach," I said. "Vassar and Swarthmore are probably doable. NYU and Sarah Lawrence are my safety schools."

"That's a good list," she offered.

"I guess."

"You must be excited to spend time with your friends back home." She corrected herself. "In Portland."

"Yeah," I said. "It'll be nice to see Kat."

A pause. "Are you seeing anyone in New York?" she asked.

"Couple guys," I said.

"Anyone serious?"

I thought about Dean. I considered the option of telling her the truth: that I'd gotten in way over my head with a man more than twice my age; that I had no idea what I was doing anymore; that I was trying to sleep my way into Princeton.

"No," I said.

"Anyone not serious?"

"Mom, I'm not going to talk to you about my sex life," I said. She raised her hands defensively.

"Honey, I ask your brother about who he's dating," she said. "I've known you were gay since you were a toddler."

"Right, because I'm so fucking mincing," I said.

"Why are you being so hostile?" she said. "You don't have to be secretive about your life." She sighed. "It's not like your father's giving me updates."

"If I'm being honest," I said, preparing to lie, "I've been too busy in the city to date anyone."

"Is that healthy?"

"I'm not your patient," I said.

She sighed heavily.

A long pause. I felt guilty. "I really missed you," I said. "I'm sorry. I'm just tired."

She smiled. Her eyes looked watery. "I missed you, too, sweetheart," she said.

———————

I loved and hated my parents' house in Portland in equal measures. The year that I was ten years old, as I was finishing the fifth grade, my parents had sold my childhood home and moved across town, up into the wooded area on the other side of the river.

The first time I saw it, my parents drove my brother and me to a part of town I didn't recognize, along Burnside—the gritty thoroughfare that bisected Portland into north and south halves. Turning from Burnside, we curved up a series of long, winding roads, and although it was daylight it seemed to get darker as the elevation rose, as the broad oak and chestnut trees grew thicker and cast shadows over the streets. We took a sharp turn onto a dead-end street, boxed in on both sides by trees. There, at the end of the road, was the property they had bought. The house was big from the front, painted a pale forest green that made it blur into the landscape if you squinted, with a large garden contained by thick stone walls and a pergola that led down to the front door.

Inside, it was expansive and sterile. A foreboding black chandelier hung in the foyer. Upstairs, there was a screening room with a large projection screen; the previous owner was leaving it behind, my parents said, for us to use. A formal dining room was painted a rich cherry red, which made the space feel gracious but oddly womb-like. The lower level was unfinished; it would be the wing where my brother and I would live, separated from my parents by two floors. I didn't grieve the loss of my old home—the new one was a nice, shiny distraction.

That was the fall I began attending an arts charter school across town, which I had chosen with my parents' encouragement. I was expected to get myself there on public transportation. The new house was a short walk from a light-rail station that dropped me in downtown Portland, from which I took a public bus to school.

I resented that my mother wouldn't drive me and pick me up, like most of my friends' mothers did, and as I rode the bus through the grimier corners of downtown, where crackheads ambled through the streets and a cluster of homeless shelters and methadone clinics created packs of panhandlers at the bus stop, I was angry at her for what I experienced as abandonment, or neglect. But on another level, I felt empowered by my independence. My father was often away and my mother was distracted furnishing our new home and starting her new career—she had launched a small practice as a financial planner after working as a therapist for years—which made it possible for me to spend the hours after school how I pleased, with little oversight.

Moreover, I liked my new school, where everyone was at least a little bit strange: artistic introverts, kids who already worked professionally as dancers in the local ballet, musical theater geeks. The grades were mixed, meaning that I, young for my grade at ten years old, was in classes with kids who were several years older.

It was there, in a theater class, at age eleven, that I met Cassie; at fourteen, she seemed impressively worldly. She wore men's T-shirts and had buzzed her hair; she was the first person I ever heard say that "gender is a spectrum."

In my beginners' dance class, I was introduced to a boy named Jerick. He was already popular and well liked; the older girls fawned over him, and I envied both him for being so adored and the girls who were close to him. He was taller than I was, and slimmer. He had shaggy hair that he colored with Sun-In or lemon juice. In class, he stood at the front while I preferred to hide in the back of the room, but as I stared at his back, I wanted to run a finger down his spine, to make him shiver. I felt a desire to be close to him that I couldn't quite explain, some tingling when he passed in the hallway that felt strange and intimate.

I told Cassie that I liked Jerick. "You should," she said. "He's adorable." She studied me. "Do you have a crush on him?" she asked. There was no judgment there, just curiosity.

"Maybe," I said.

"That means you're gay," Cassie said, with a brusque authority.

And so, after some deliberation, I wrote my parents a letter—explaining that I was gay, or at the very least was attracted to boys, and I knew so because I was in love with a boy in my grade and also because Cassie had told me so. I left it in their bedroom for them to read.

A few hours later, the three of us—my mother, my father, and me—met in my mother's office to discuss the contents of my letter. My mother told me that she understood and loved me unconditionally, and my father said it didn't change anything at all. It was a nonevent. I told my friends at school that I was gay and they seemed unimpressed.

Jerick's feelings for me didn't seem to change one way or another after I came out, but we grew closer as time passed. I had large groups of friends over to my parents' house, ostensibly to watch movies on the big screen in the theater room but mostly just to have an excuse to spend time with him. While friends packed onto the couch and spread out onto the floor, lips smacking on popcorn and jelly beans, I watched him watch campy movies—the way he tilted his head back when he laughed, the way Cassie rested her head on his shoulder affectionately. He was effete in a way that I didn't know how to be. I'd had no sexuality crisis, no struggle with my own self-identification, and so being gay changed nothing more than who I was attracted to—but Jerick seemed drawn to a type of cultural gayness that I didn't understand. He experimented with makeup, went to midnight showings of *The Rocky Horror Picture Show* dressed up in costume, talked abstractly about "camp" in a way that was precocious.

I still got along better with a coterie of boys from my old neighborhood who were straight but often stayed the night at my house on weekends. Quickly, we discovered Internet pornography—grainy, low-quality clips of women thrusting and moaning, their enormous breasts slapping wildly against their chests—which we watched together with a low-decibel mix of lust and curiosity.

Then, for my benefit, we queued up gay porn, all waxy chests and spectacular ejaculations, evaluating its erotic quality together. Later, we retreated into separate corners of that big house to masturbate in privacy, armed with tissues and the instant replay of those sequences, then came back to compare notes.

But as I lay on the floor of my bedroom trying to will myself into a state of sustained arousal, those worked-out porn stars did nothing for me. Instead, I thought of boys twirling in endless ethereal ballet, leotards taut against flexing limbs. Same with the mornings when I awakened early and allowed my hands to explore my body, the tensing in my groin, the pressure and release—I thought mostly of Jerick. Afterward, sticky and full of self-loathing, when the weight of my budding sexuality was too much to bear and I couldn't believe what a mess I'd made, I didn't wish for him to be near me. I felt dirty and disconnected, shame descending all over me like a scratchy wool blanket, like the sheets I used to sweat and piss in as a child, hot and terrified, dreaming of Brooks. Masturbation made me want to molt. It made me feel like my body was a tomb, and I was desperate to get out.

No, sex was always better in theory.

Dean called me every day that I was in Portland. Instead of picking up, I wrote him emails.

"Sorry, handsome," I said. "I have no cell service at my mom's house." (This was true—reception was spotty—but mostly, I didn't want to talk to him.)

A few days before Christmas, I bought ten hits of Ecstasy—twenty dollars a tab—from a friend who sold it as a side hustle. I hadn't taken it before but had always wanted to.

I took the first tab alone, walking downtown, which was often how I liked to experience drugs—to test the waters to see how I would respond to them, to know what to expect so when I did them with others, I could talk about it with an air of worldly confidence. I took the train up into Washington Park while the sun was going down and walked home through the forest. My heart was thudding in my chest, and I could feel the trees moving inside me, their branches crackling and snapping underneath my rib cage, and euphoria thundered up and down my spine. The sky was a field of grass and the stars were beneath my feet. I was in love with everything.

I texted a guy I occasionally slept with when I was in Portland. I had met him online when I was fourteen, right after I had first slept with Jim; he would drive up to the woods and park his pickup truck and we would fuck in the front seat or outside, on the grass, our clothes wet from the dew. He was older and swarthy, maybe Latino; his belly was a little round and smooth.

I pulled him from the driver's seat, dancing in the moonlight.

"Steve," I said.

"That's not my name," he said, tugging me back toward his truck. I got in and pulled my pants down.

"I'm rolling so hard right now," I said.

"Shit," he said. "Got any more?"

I shook my head no. He unbuckled his belt.

"I've heard that once you fuck on Ecstasy," I said, "it ruins regular sex for you forever."

"Am I worth it?" he said.

"You better be," I said, bending him over.

Walking home from where I'd met the man I called Steve, I thought about the times I had walked through those same woods with Jerick. By age thirteen, I remembered, he had become a rangy teenager, the oval circumference of his face indented with haughty cheekbones and a keen jawline. I was chubby, and I envied his growth spurt, his ability to become more in tune with his body. He had taken to dyeing his hair any variety of Manic Panic colors, bright neon shades that made him look like an alien, all translucent skin and otherworldly hue. Even if I hated this, thinking it deeply uncool, it didn't matter: he was my best friend and my partner in crime. There were so many times I had stood with him in the foyer of that house, looking up at the black chandelier that hung from the ceiling and imagining it, as I always did, impaling us. I would touch his hair, the smalt of a fresh bruise or buttercup yellow. "You look like shit," I'd say, mostly joking.

"You're an asshole," he'd say.

And I would kiss his forehead. "You know I'm just kidding," I'd say. "Don't leave. Take me with you."

I told Judith that I thought I was in love. I could see it as a Venn diagram. I could almost draw it. Jerick and I were the only two boys in the eighth grade who had already come out—even though there were plenty of others who would soon, I was sure of it—and we were both precocious and hypersexual, prone to theatrics. We both liked it when things were "dramastic," which was Jerick's portmanteau of "dramatic" and "drastic," which we found very droll at the time.

But we were different, too. Jerick had that pretty-boy bone structure, and I didn't have that, but I knew all the answers to exam questions, even when I hadn't studied. He ebbed and prowled in his body, like he was nothing but appendages, so relaxed in his skin. I envied him that. Checking my reflection was like looking into a house of mirrors. I would discover some distended ugliness I had somehow missed the day before, the bloat of how awful I'd been in eating so much; or, if I had been starving myself, my figure looked severe and attenuated. Jerick didn't hate himself the way that I did.

If we could meld into one person, I thought, we would be unstoppable. Supergay, or something.

We shared a locker and five out of six classes. He was a middle school celebrity: pulling at his polo to expose the gooseflesh between his pelvis and navel, batting his eyes to the click-click-click of imaginary paparazzi. In ballet class, he always found a way to take center stage, waving to a multitude of adoring fans. We had a recital that year and he and I were choreographed to be the last two dancers onstage in our number; we wore purple leotards and black tights and, per the dance teacher's instruction, made triangles on our bellies with our hands. We laughed about it for hours after, how very *gay* it was, us alone onstage, bathed in yellow-white light, dressed like that.

But they were cheering for him, not me; he was the star; he didn't usually share the spotlight. So when he pushed me up hard against the brick wall behind school one September afternoon, so hard I could feel my hot breath stinging at my tonsils, and he clasped my wrists in his spindly hands, the air was thick with significance. I looked up at the security camera, which swiveled in a robotic waltz above us. *Finally, equal billing.* Jerick opened his mouth, and I was distracted by the tooth that he'd chipped on a bottle of wine when he was twelve.

And when he kissed me, even though it was my first real kiss, I wasn't there in the moment. I was thinking about how it was different from the tentative pecks in clandestine games of spin the bottle, from the touch of that blond boy from Texas the previous summer whose timidity made me afraid I might break him. Jerick's kiss was strange and soft and wet, so I kept my eyes open and tilted my face to stare at his ear.

He intertwined his fingers with mine, a gesture that felt disconcerting. We didn't usually hold hands. On the bus, once, locked beneath my backpack. Another time in the dim retreat of a movie theater, Jerick's palm clammy from holding the cup of soda. My hesitation wasn't a fear of homophobia—we were probably too young to get hate-crimed, anyway, although I worried sometimes for Jerick, who was so girlish. Sometimes when his limply gesticulating hands flicked I would think he was too ineffectual to love, even as I did love him.

But Jerick touching me still made me uncomfortable. Moments into each embrace, my skin began to crawl. I wasn't old or mature enough to face my cognitive dissonance. *He loves me; I am unlovable. He finds me attractive; I am disgusting.* If I concentrated hard, I could try to spin the paradox into something more digestible. *I am broken; he wants to fix me.*

My face was still wet with his kisses when, on the walk to the bus stop, a homeless man asked if we could spare a little change.

"True change comes from within," I sneered with the same derision as always, thinking myself very clever. I looked at Jerick for approval. But he fingered his worn jeans, then fished out a fistful of dimes and nickels. I always noticed the ways we were different: the reduced-fare lunch card courtesy of the school office; the strips of cardboard Jerick's mom had glued to the inside of his shoes so his socks wouldn't get dirty; the constant allusions to the long-delayed check from the car accident that left his mother's coupe all busted up, one shattered headlight like a black eye. The money was coming soon, Jerick would say.

We sat together in the back of English class, scribbling notes to each other in the margins of young-adult paperbacks.

"My parents are going to Washington next week," I wrote.

"Love is like bumper cars," Jerick wrote. "No, it's like swimming. It's better if you aren't afraid to get wet."

After school let out, we rode the train to my house. In the cool, still air of the underground station, Jerick touched his fingers to my lips and paused, listening for the clarion whistle of the train through the tunnel. The one long, high note.

At the front door, I looked at Jerick.

"You know, my parents are gone," I said. I let that hang for a moment.

"Let's go inside," Jerick said.

As he went down on me, I thought of Brooks, and it didn't feel like it had before—velvety damp, that wriggling sensation like I was going to wet myself, the emptiness of a phrase as stupidly sincere as "bad touch." No, with Jerick, it felt warm and intimate. I just wanted to be close to him, and for once, I really was.

It felt like I couldn't belong to my family anymore. I loathed the sparkle of clean silverware, the hum of C-SPAN left drawling in the living room, my mother's idle conversation. I lived for the weekdays, which hurtled forward madly. Jerick and I spent most of our time in the second-floor boys' bathroom. Time never knocked on the bathroom door; it passed by in a haze as we stood for hours, glued to the wall of a toilet stall. I traced the ellipse of Jerick's mouth with one hand and shaped it with the other, listening for the groans of pleasure, Jerick's fist slamming lightly against the spackled wall.

"We're so lucky to have found each other," Jerick said. It was a stupid thing to say, I thought, and it sounded familiar—like I had heard it in a movie somewhere. I didn't say anything back.

On the afternoons when someone interrupted us by entering to wash his hands or urinate, Jerick's eyes darted mischievously, firecracker glances going off on the Fourth of July.

Where will I fall, I wondered, *that place, when the sparks are all gone?*

I criticized him endlessly—for the way that he dressed, for how effeminate he was. I slapped his hand away when he reached out for mine in public. I wasn't sophisticated enough to know that these things would push him away: I wanted to mold him in my image, make him clean-cut and presentable, but I also wanted him to stay exactly as he was. I wrote him love letters and poetry in the dim light of my computer screen, in my bedroom late at night; then at school I was chilly to him until it was time to pull him into the bathroom to make out. My mother didn't like him; she objected when he stayed the night, probably because she knew that we were sleeping together, but I convinced myself that it was because his family was poor and he had dyed hair and strange clothes; it made it easier to be angry with my mother.

Then, after some fairly mundane quarrel with Jerick, a friend from school called me and told me that Jerick had spent the night with two other boys from school, and *things* had happened. *Sex things.*

"I don't believe you," I said.

"He told me himself," she said. "I'll call him again and you can listen in." And so we did, and I sat there numbly on the other line as Jerick told my friend, in more detail this time, about what had happened.

After several hours of planning my speech, I called Jerick to announce theatrically that I knew—I knew about everything, and it was over. And it was.

In the months after that, I spent a lot of time in bed, my face suffocated deep in a mass of pillows, and I listened to emo music and smoked clove cigarettes, and I watched bad television and cried a lot, from the sting of rejection, from the perverse satisfaction of having pushed someone I cared about away, from getting to be *right* about the fact that I was unlovable. My mother knew that I was in pain; occasionally, I would awaken to the sound of her precise voice, reading poetry out loud to me. Khalil Gibran, or Rumi. I pretended to keep sleeping, but sometimes I would sit up, wrap my arms around her middle, and sob.

It was my first heartbreak: I didn't know that it could hurt so deeply.

One spring afternoon, I sat outside after school, on the playground where my sneakers had dragged in the beaten sawdust, by the field where I had tripped like a coward during a game of capture the flag, choosing to lie motionless, inhaling the smells of grass and rain rather than playing along, across from the basketball court with the ragged hoop where Jerick had first kissed me in streaks of summer light. I hated that place, hated all my memories.

Monkey bars squatted behind the portables, adjacent to the chipped clay tennis courts that had been abandoned decades earlier. I cornered Jerick there, shielded from sight by a wall of ivied fence. The physical proximity to him made me hard, and also angry.

"I miss you," I said. My thumb grazed his waist, tiptoeing across the band of exposed skin.

"You know, Sam, I guess there are times when, I mean, I miss you, too, but now I'm sorry," he said in clipped breaths. "I just don't love you anymore."

I pulled closer, wanting to kiss him, wanting to punish him, to grab his full lower lip and sever it from his face with my teeth. He pushed me away.

"No," he said. He sprinted off, across the blacktop to the field. His movements were elegant, like he was in slow motion, his long strides forceful and deliberate. I heard a distant thumping as a basketball was dribbled across the cement, rhythmic as a drumbeat.

My mother and I had Christmas dinner at a steakhouse downtown, all twinkling candlelight and the smell of cedar in the air.

"What will you do for New Year's?" my mother asked.

I shrugged. "Probably go to Marquee," I said. "I dunno. Everyone's away."

"What's your dad doing?" she asked, in a way that was so casual it felt practiced.

"He and Jennifer are going to the Caribbean," I said.

"When?" she said.

I shrugged again.

"Surely he'll be home by the time you get back," she said.

"No," I said. "He's gone until the second week of January, I think."

She looked incredulous. "So he just . . . leaves you alone there?" she said.

I nodded. I knew that I was fanning the flames, but I didn't care.

"Oh, honey," she said, as if to say: *That explains everything.*

"I'm dreaming of a white Christmas," I said to Kat later that night, emptying another baggie of cocaine out onto the mirror on her center console. She laughed, even though it wasn't funny. Quickly, I chopped up lines and we snorted them. Some of the coke blew onto the thigh of my jeans and I wiped it off with a finger, then smeared it on my gums. We were getting sloppy.

She locked the door and we headed down Ash Street. It was cold outside in downtown Portland, and I was moving fast, walking quickly, sucking down a cigarette and then tossing it onto the asphalt, and out of the corner of my eye I saw the sparks spray like a firework, and I paid the guy at the door and we went inside. It was a terrible club, just like all the clubs in Portland, but I was high and it didn't matter because everything felt good when I was this high, except when it didn't.

I don't like it here, I thought, my teeth chattering involuntarily, my nose running. I wiped away a gossamer film of pink snot. The dance floor smelled like sex and apple juice, and the hardwood beneath my feet was chintzy, scarred with age. Men stood on the periphery, and they looked like clowns with leering smiles and hungry eyes. A boy in a cage, his body provocatively bent, snapped the elastic on his jockstrap. His skin was waxy with sweat. His face was frozen in some pose of grief, I thought, although I was probably projecting. I wondered if this was the seedy underbelly of the city. I wondered if people who found themselves in the seedy underbelly of something were ever able to identify it as such, or if that delineation could only come later—but if this city had a seedy underbelly at all, I thought, it had to be there, in the black-walled amphitheater of that nightclub where the strobe light was elongating each second like a flip-book, where everyone was blanketed in darkness.

In the bathroom, I did another few lines, and that familiar metallic clarity coursed through me, and I felt a surge of power, of numbness and virility, but I was already thinking about the next lines that would necessarily follow, and I wanted to freeze the instant, distill the high into something that I could take home with me and keep, but I could already feel the intangibility of that palpitating rapture slipping through my fingers—never graspable, almost like sand but not as gritty, the moment's texture was wispier and more powdery. Like the texture of cocaine.

On the dance floor, a man with red hair whose name I didn't know put his hands in my back pockets, the bulge of his erection suddenly pressing into me. I jerked like a marionette.

"Baby," he whispered, and I felt his tongue caressing my earlobe, slimy. "Baby, let's go to my car."

I'd lost Kat. Where had she gone? Whatever. It had gotten crowded. All these gays home for the holidays, their miserable interactions with the families whom they hated, sneaking out for an escape, a fumble in a nightclub with a stranger before they went home to their childhood bedrooms. How sad, how awful. The man pulled me toward the door and I didn't feel good about him, whatever darkness inside him was trying to take me away, or maybe it was the other way around. My heart was hammering in my chest in a way that felt alarming, even to me, and I turned back around to catch one last glimpse of the club. I wanted to etch the image into my mind, to remember what it had felt like to be there. I looked for someone I knew and thought with the same halfhearted resignation as always that if we got too coked out and he threw me down a flight of stairs or cut me up and left me in a dumpster, I wanted a witness, but Kat had gone and I didn't know anyone there. I didn't know anyone, and that was so much more frightening than the threat of whatever might happen, because if nobody saw us leaving together, what would people think if they never saw me again? Would they think that I had run away to start a new life in some godforsaken flyover state? Would my friends in New York talk about me over cocktails, thinking of the bright young spirit I had once been? Would they even remember me? This fear was so primal, the fear of being forgotten, the fear that I might be forgettable.

Would Dean even remember me?

And then, with a bubble of hope catching in my chest, I recognized someone through the crowd, silhouetted against the deep-red crushed-velvet curtains up onstage. It was Jerick. He was in drag, wearing full makeup, ivory concealer crusted under his eyes, his cheeks a violent fuchsia rouge, his lips drawn into a smile.

Cocaine stung in my throat.

I pulled away from the man with the red hair and threw myself into the mass of writhing bodies, swimming toward the stage to get a closer look. Jerick was skinnier than he had ever been before, his clavicle jutting out above his torso and his bow-legged stems miles long beneath a pink tutu. I waited for him at the base of the stage as he howled an off-key Shirley Bassey rendition.

Hey, big spender . . . spend a little time with me . . .

After his set, he tottered down the stairs and stood before me. I reached out and caressed the indications of his androgyny: his mouth outlined in garish pink lipstick, the fine hairs along his neck, the protrusion of his Adam's apple. I hadn't remembered that, I realized. His smell flooded my nostrils, clenching my knuckles and locking my jaw in place.

"You look like shit," I said.

Jerick looked down at his battered high heels, then back at me with wounded eyes. "Some things never change," he said.

For Christmas, my grandmother sent me a hundred-dollar bill with a note that said, "Please don't use this to buy alcohol or cigarettes." I laughed when I read it but still felt a twinge of sadness; it wasn't who I wanted to be.

I finished my college applications on New Year's Eve, the night they had to be postmarked, frantically printing out final drafts. I couldn't ask my mother to take me to mail them—she would know how irresponsible I had been and judge me for it—so I called Kat.

"You're always doing shit like this," Kat grumbled as she maneuvered her car toward downtown, the hood of her sweatshirt pulled up over her messy blond hair. I took a swig of vodka from a bottle in a paper bag.

"I know," I said. "What's wrong with me?"

"You've got to be the only kid in the world mailing your Ivy League applications, drunk, the night they're due," she said. Then she looked over at me, more compassionately.

"It's not my fault," I said.

"I know it's hard to come back here, dude," Kat said. "There's way too much history. I don't blame you for needing to be, like, numb."

I was silent.

"At least you got to leave," she said. She sighed. "Sometimes I worry about you out there. Remember when we first met? You were such a sweet kid. The city is changing you."

"It's not like I was doing well here, Kat," I said.

"No, I know," she said. "It's just scary to think of you. All alone in New York."

As I dropped those manila envelopes in a navy-blue mailbox, a shudder rippled through me. One more milestone I could cross off my list. Would I get in at any of them? Or all of them? I deserved to celebrate.

Back at my mother's house, I railed lines of Adderall in my bedroom off an oversize square of mirror before a group of friends came to pick me up: two stoner girls I was friendly with and their friend Seth, with whom I'd had English class sophomore year. Then, he'd had bad acne, pink and red against his fair skin, and his blond hair was shaggy. He was quiet and withdrawn and a little off-kilter. That summer, his mother had sent him to a wilderness therapy program in southern Oregon, and he came back clean-cut and almost militant. Now, he stood up straight, and his creamy complexion was marred only by a dusting of freckles. He still smoked pot and experimented with other drugs, but it all seemed pretty harmless—psychedelic mushrooms and painkillers.

I distributed to the group the remaining tabs of Ecstasy that I had bought, and we took them in the basement of Seth's house, then drove to an apartment complex downtown where there was a pool. Laughing, swathed in moonlight, we jumped the fence and stripped off our clothes, the undulating waves, rolling on euphoria. I had wanted everything to go away, the hazy shame of Jerick and that club, but now, high and blissful, I wanted to stay forever in the glory of the instant.

In the pool, I bobbed up to the surface and stood in front of Seth, both of us waist-deep in the water. We gazed into each other's eyes and I saw him for the first time. His chest was thin but strong, freckled, his shoulders a little sunburned, his eyes glacier blue. He was wearing briefs in the water, a V of pelvic bone jutting from the calyx of his groin. I could see the outline of his bulge, could feel his heart beating from three feet away. The moon tattooed its fingerprint between his nose and lips; the water glistened in the indentation there. His torso looked like sculpture. His cheeks were winded-breath mauve. I reached out and touched his groin. He gasped.

And then, abruptly, we were back at home, in my bed. He had a girlfriend, but this registered somewhere deep and unreachable. Our bodies stretched out, infinite. His musk was different from Dean's—no cologne. Instead, pine needles and dirt. I felt the hair on his muscular calves. His hands were cold, but my body was warm. I felt as bonded to him as if we had emerged from the same womb.

As the sun came up, we smoked sticky green marijuana out of a bright red apple. The colors were too bright in the light, too vital.

"What does this mean?" he whispered.

"I don't know," I said.

Neither of us had expected it; he was straight, I thought, and I was strange and damaged and in love with someone else. I was always convincing myself that I had fallen in love with guys while I was on drugs, fusing with some relative stranger, yet there was something different about this.

We passed out on the floor. I curled up against him. All the pain I'd ever felt was unimaginably far away. I didn't know if any of it was real or if it was just the drugs, but it didn't matter.

"I think there's a you-shaped hole inside me that I didn't realize I was missing until just now," I said.

"Don't go back to New York," he said. "Don't leave. Take me with you." I couldn't place where I had heard it before, but it felt like an echo, ringing out in the trees.

Five

*I*t was January, and Dean's friend was having people over to some loft, so I agreed to tag along, although I was loath to leave Manhattan. The streets of Brooklyn were glossy black, bleeding into the winter sky. We slid along side streets into Greenpoint in Dean's car, then squealed to a stop before an unassuming industrial building.

I checked my reflection in the mirror: my eyes glassy-pinned, bones jutting from my chest.

I hadn't known Dean very long, but I felt like I had known him a lifetime. And suddenly, there were so many things that I hated about him. I hated that he was divorced. I hated that his purported bisexuality seemed to be the last vestige of a hip youth instead of an actual preference. I hated that he was old money, just like everyone else I knew. I hated that he managed to do nothing, all the time, lucratively. I hated that he was always unshaven. I hated that all of his friends were artists and writers of considerable repute, none of whom I'd ever heard of and all of whom I claimed to be fans. I hated that he wasn't Seth.

In the morning, waking up in his place to the smell of coffee in the kitchen, I didn't want to be myself. I didn't want to be with

him, but I didn't know how to stop. I was too much of an adult
to feel properly victimized by the relationship—the power differ-
ential in the decades between us—but I was too much of a kid to
know how to extricate myself from it gracefully. But most of all,
I had grown bored with him, in the same way I grew bored with
everyone. Not that I could have admitted this at the time.

Upstairs in the loft, a limitless sprawl of hardwood floors.
Red wine in a paper cup. Twee pop tinkling in the next room. A
miasma of smoke and the damp, earthy fragrance of marijuana. I
made small talk with a dull woman named Cecilia. She was thin,
rouged, severe like a ballet teacher. She had an asymmetrical bob
and a shrill laugh.

"This is my protégé," Dean said, referring to me. I hated this,
too; he never called me his lover. "He'll be at Princeton next year."

"Hopefully," I said, lighting a cigarette. "If all goes according
to plan."

"We're not all that worried about that," Dean said. He winked
at me. Hope made me catch my breath. *Was that still a possibility?*
I wondered.

Later that night, after he had sex with me, I counted the wrin-
kles on his face, hating myself for doing so. I went to the bathroom, turned on the water, and left it running. I knelt over the
toilet and stuck my fingers down my throat. There was nothing to
throw up. I choked, gagged, retched.

Eventually, I gave up and flushed anyway.

I took the elevator downstairs and went out onto the street.
I called Seth.

"What are you still doing up?" he asked.

"Stupid question," I said. I hesitated. "How's your girlfriend?"

"Sam," he said.

"Come to New York," I whispered. The winter chill was cold on my arms. My nose was running. "Remember when I did too much Oxy over New Year's and you just stayed there in bed with me until it stopped? Remember how you promised not to leave? Didn't that feel good? Don't you want to do that again with me?"

"Yeah," he said.

"I don't know how many times I'm going to wake up in the morning with my skin irritated from an older man's stubble on my face before I realize how much it's hurting me," I said.

I'd been rehearsing that line for a while; I thought it sounded poetic. Saying it to Seth, though, made it feel real.

"I'll see you over spring break," he said.

I stayed on the phone with Seth for hours, walking through Riverside Park and chain-smoking, high on Adderall, using the same lines on him about love that Dean had used on me. I didn't feel guilty for this act of plagiarism. The love that Dean had given to me I could now give to someone else. Someone, I thought, much more deserving.

"What happened with Princeton guy?" Daphne asked me one afternoon, smoking cigarettes down the block from school.

"I dunno," I said. "I'm over it."

She shook her head. "Last month you were telling me you were in love with him."

It was odd: I could vividly remember being certain that I loved Dean, but I couldn't even project myself back the few weeks to the point when I had felt it. "I got swept up, I guess," I said.

"What about Princeton?"

I shrugged. It seemed less important now than it had before. "I mean, I got deferred. How good are my odds, really? Is there really anything he can do for me at this point? Like, I'm still hopeful, but what can I do?"

Daphne shook her head. "You're infuriating."

"What?"

"I can't keep up with you," she said. "One minute it's Princeton, then it's some closet case you met in Oregon. You're always looking for the next thing that you think will tell you who you're supposed to be."

She was right, although I hated to admit it. "I'm on a journey of self-discovery," I said.

She rolled her eyes. "Well, can you discover some self-respect, please?"

"I think we both know *that* ship has sailed," I said.

Seth and I stopped for gas only an hour south of Portland, in a one-pump town where the wind sang in the fields and the sunlight was obscured by clouds. While the station attendant filled up Seth's old sedan ("Oregon," I remarked, "the only state where

they let you kill yourself, but not pump your own gas"—I had
heard someone say this once, a commentary on the controver-
sial legalization of physician-assisted suicide in the state, and I'd
found it pithy; Seth laughed dutifully), I spotted what looked like
a high school track off in the distance. I pointed toward it, and
Seth followed the direction of my finger. "Let's go there," I said,
"and get high."

The air streaming from the open car window felt good on my
bare arms.

By the time we got there, the sun had moved in the sky so it
beat hot on our heads. We parked at the top of the bleachers and
took a seat in a row halfway down. Seth lit a joint and passed it to
me. The Adderall I had taken had me feeling sparkly, lean. I put
my arm around his shoulders. We were alone.

"I'm happy," I said. "I love you."

"I love you, too, man," he said.

It was March now and we were driving from Portland to Los
Angeles, to visit friends along the way (my friends, mostly) and, I
thought, to be young and free.

Things were going to be different.

We'd left Portland early in the morning, stopping for brunch
with his mother at a café; she had given Seth extra cash for gas,
looking at him worriedly, reminding us to be safe, to be good. We
headed south on I-5; I played bad pop music that Seth hated but
tolerated for my benefit. Three other friends had been supposed

to join us, but they had pulled out of the trip at the last minute, and the journey as we had originally conceptualized it—the five of us taking a long drive down the coast, taking as many drugs as we could and crashing wherever we landed along the way—had been eroded, so suddenly it was just me and Seth. I had never learned to drive, which meant he was stuck behind the wheel the whole way. Whatever tension there was between us over what had happened that winter went unarticulated. I knew that we loved each other, and in my head it made a funny sort of sense. Seth and I had slept together that first time when we were both on Ecstasy, and subsequently on other combinations of drugs, but those moments when our bodies seemed to collide felt more like the natural expression of a powerful friendship than any genuine romantic sentiment. I only dated older men, and Seth was straight, ostensibly, and his off-again, on-again girlfriend, Marissa (a bulimic cheerleader with a gritty complexion and a rigid smile; once I'd seen her vomit into her handbag while driving on the freeway as I sat frozen in the backseat, paralyzed by fear), was always sort of in the shadows. It didn't matter who I was sleeping with in New York, or that he wasn't interested in men in the first place. We wrote each other long, emotional letters trying to decode the nature of our friendship, this bond between us that I was so certain was immutable.

When it came time to make plans for spring break, the rest of my class at Dwight was going to the Bahamas, and I wanted to go but more desperately than that I wanted to see Seth, to feel the rush and calm of his presence, to get high and be happy.

It wasn't about sex, but it was about something sexual, some tether to a sense of my own youth. Sex with Seth was different. I loved sex with older men: their confidence, their experience, their mouths that always tasted like Listerine, musk, and stubble, orgasm noises in a rich baritone, the delight of seeing strange apartments, Hell's Kitchen walk-ups and Park Avenue duplexes, the unromantic decadence of entering these lives for a matter of moments, these men who were lawyers, doctors, executives, husbands, fathers, bachelors, their bookshelves and family photos, and getting each other off—eyes rolling back, toes curling, semen and spit—and then I would leave and they would remember me or they wouldn't, and I loved that, this intimacy shared that faded away, the rapture that ended as quickly as it began. There was shame after, of course, an urgency to leave, to stumble into a taxi and get home and take a shower and forget that it all had happened. As right as it felt in the moment of consummation was exactly how wrong it felt as soon as it was over.

But with Seth, it wasn't like that. That sex seemed pure, somehow. He didn't know what he was doing, and there was a symmetry to our bodies, the feel of his ribs against mine, the tautness of his skin. I had forgotten what it felt like to be with someone my own age, but more importantly, I had forgotten myself that I was young. With the older men I slept with, from message boards or shitty gay bars, we were two men coming together to do something quick and dirty; with Seth, I was suddenly aware of my own boyishness, my youth, the feeling of our lives stretching before us, time yawing forward like an ocean of untapped possibility. Whatever happened between us was sacred.

Or maybe it was just the drugs—it was always the drugs.

People who loved to take drugs as often and with as much variety as I did were hard to come by, but Seth—ultimately a scratchy kid from Oregon who had a certain outdoorsy, freewheeling, psychonautically curious streak—loved the numbness and the electricity, the escape of chemicals, with the same zeal that I did. Half the goal of the trip was to get as fucked up as possible as often as possible, so I had brought a litany of pills from New York—Adderall and Ritalin, Xanax and Klonopin, Ambien and Vicodin and Percocet—and he'd been on the ground in Portland stockpiling a solid ounce of weed, some muscle relaxants that Marissa had given him, hallucinogenic mushrooms baked into chocolates, and we'd buy more in California. I'd asked him whether he could get any ketamine, which was my favorite drug but was so hard to find, but when he'd called the dealer, his voice mail message had said, "I'm in fuckin' jail!" which made us break into peals of laughter.

I still took more pills than he did, of course. I knew that he knew that I was in danger, but I also knew that he couldn't say anything, too complicit in it to offer any kind of judgment or warning. After going through wilderness rehab, he had the vocabulary of recovery even if he didn't really use it. It was easier to just get high and run away from it all, to be at once less and more present in our bodies and in the moment, to be happy and voluble and full of only the good feelings, to chase away the monsters until the drugs wore off and the next ones kicked in.

And that was the mood as we drove south through the brush of central Oregon, the pastures and scenery, as I packed bowls from the little wooden pipe that he had brought, nothing but the open road and the Xanax hitting my system, serenity flooding through my body. I looked over at him as the sun illuminated his face, handsome and spangled with freckles, his tawny hair going white in the light, his laughter and delight at how happy I was, at making me happy. I thought that was the happiest I'd ever been, that I could ever be.

Our first destination was Ashland, Oregon, a resort town near the California border where my father's sister lived with her husband. They had bought the property a few years earlier, moving up from Orange County to escape suburbia for something more remote. My father had told my aunt that Seth and I were driving to Southern California and she had offered the small guesthouse on their property as a stop-off.

By the time we arrived, just as the sun was setting, after about six hours on the road, the Xanax had worn off and I was feeling tense, but I didn't want to take any more downers. I hadn't eaten; Seth was hungry. I wasn't in the mood to see family.

"Sam, you're so thin," my aunt said to me. I loved when people said that. "Have you boys eaten?"

"Yes," I said quickly. Seth shot me a look.

We dropped off our things and drove a few miles into the town. I had fond memories of Ashland; when my parents were still married, it had been an annual vacation destination for our family; we would stay at a bed-and-breakfast and go see shows at the Shakespeare Festival. It never felt particularly natural—things in my family never did—but it had been the site of some of our happier memories, and being back there (the smell of the air and the grass, the small-town charm) made me a little sad.

The water in Ashland was unusually high in naturally occurring lithium. "There are no bipolar people in Ashland," my mother had said once, laughing. "Maybe if we all moved here we'd level out a bit."

We went to a brewpub, brick-walled and rustic, and I sat nursing a Diet Coke while Seth wolfed down a burger. He knew better than to ask me whether I wanted to eat anything.

That night, we smoked a joint in his car down the road before we went up to bed. It was colder than I'd expected, and—sharing a bed—I curled up next to him for warmth. I inhaled the smell at the nape of his neck and wrapped my arms around his thin chest.

It felt like he was a million miles away from me.

Somewhere outside of Bakersfield, we stopped for the night and took mushrooms, rolling around on the threadbare carpet and looking at the coffeemaker with slack-jawed wonder; then, on the comedown, we began to argue about something, a fight that continued for hours. I was so frayed from all the Adderall it felt like my brain was made of putty, and Seth wanted some, too, so I shared it with him. Then I realized that I was going to run out if

I didn't pace myself, so I started hoarding them and taking them in secret.

On the third day I got a terrible head cold (probably from taking so many pills) and my nose wouldn't stop bleeding. We drove through the desert in the darkness, past the fields of wind turbines, like ghostly figures waving their arms. We crashed in Palm Springs, where Kat's mother had a home; I tried to convince Kat to steal some of her mom's Ambien for me.

She looked at me strangely; I knew she wanted to ask me to leave but couldn't.

The next day, as we drove toward Los Angeles, the rain started. At first it was just a drizzle, and then out of nowhere, the downpour was torrential. The windshield wipers on his old Corolla swished back and forth swiftly, but it was hard to see, and he was squinting, hunched over the steering wheel, the way my grandmother drove. I could tell he was scared.

"Go toward Claremont," I said. "Just get on the 10." I fished around in my bag for an Adderall, but the prescription bottle made a sinister rattle—it was nearly empty. *Shit*, I thought.

My phone was ringing; it was my father. I didn't want to talk to him, but I picked up anyway.

"The mail came," he said. I stopped breathing. "There's something from Princeton. Do you want me to open it?"

I made an indistinct moaning noise.

"Is that a yes?"

"Yes," I said. "Is it big or small?"

"It's medium-size," he said.

"What the fuck does that mean?"

"I don't know."

I turned to Seth. "Pull over."

He hit his turn signal, preparing to get off at the next exit.

"Dad?" I said into the phone. "Yeah, open it."

I heard the rustling of papers, pictured him sitting at the kitchen table with the mail, tearing at the envelope. I could almost feel it in my own hands. Seth pulled into a fast-food restaurant.

"You didn't get in, kiddo," my dad said.

"Okay," I said. "I'll talk to you later." I hung up the phone. I felt numb. I turned to Seth. "I didn't get in," I said.

"Sorry," he said. "That sucks, man."

I exhaled. There was a buzzing in the back of my head. It was getting louder.

"You still got into all those other schools, right?" he said. "I mean, that's good. I wish I was going somewhere besides U of O."

"Kiss me," I said, and he begrudgingly complied.

"What do you want to do now?" he said. We were still at least a half hour from my friend Hanna's house in Claremont, where we would be staying the night.

"I want champagne and foie gras," I said. "I want to get some coke. I don't want to feel this way." I half realized I was shouting. "I don't want to feel anything."

"You never want to feel anything," he said.

I looked out the window. It hadn't even registered with me that the rain had stopped.

Once we got to Claremont, the mood improved a bit. My friend Hanna took us to a dealer who sold Himalayan opium, and we spent all our money on an ounce, then drove around in her car, filling it with fragrant white vapor and giggling. In a parking lot, we fell asleep; when we woke up, the gauzy white smoke was so thick we could hardly see. It took a mile for all of it to clear out of the car, streaming in big white clouds with all the windows open. We spent a week in California, and we did not go to the beach once.

Seth dropped me at the airport in Long Beach to catch my flight back to New York.

I knew he was growing tired of me, that his patience had dwindled to the point of no return, that I'd run him into the ground, and the ways in which I made my life appear fast-paced and thrilling and glamorous while his was rather average and staid, this sweet stoner boy from Oregon whom I'd suckered into getting caught up in the madness of my universe, the slick shellac of all that glitzy adolescent posturing—it had all just turned him cold. He'd been tricked by how dazzling I could be and then gotten close enough to see the bracing emptiness of it, how ugly it was when exposed to the light. I knew he wouldn't want to get high and make out with me anymore, which was all I'd really wanted anyway—that, and to feel good all the time.

We smoked the last of the opium from a pipe in his car. I was out of money and out of drugs. The sky was a grim shade of gray.

"I still love you," I said. "You know that, right?"

"I love you, too, man," he said, but I could tell it was only out of obligation.

He was just another person I'd worn out.

———————

Back in New York, Dean called me and wrote me, but I didn't reply—I felt strange and empty. I hadn't gotten in to Princeton. What was the point? I'd failed in my pursuit of becoming the person I'd hoped I might become. I started taking even more pills than I ever had before, going home from school early to lie in bed in the dark, dreaming strange benzodiazepine half-dreams.

Although I'd been rejected by Princeton, I had been accepted to several other schools to which I'd applied. It seemed likely that I would go to Vassar, though that was based solely on its ranking. It was hard to imagine myself going off to college—hard to imagine where I would end up, who I would turn into.

I began spending more time with Ronan, a boy from school who lived a few blocks away from me in a town house in the West Nineties. He was Irish, with shoulder-length, oily brown hair that he raked his fingers through anxiously as we waited for the dealer to come. We smoked pot or drank bottles of cough syrup and sat on his balcony, tripping and looking at the light in the trees.

I had a fling with a television producer who lived in the West Village; I took his Ambien and sprawled in his body heat.

I went on several dates with Evan, an NYU student whom I'd met on Fire Island the previous summer. He was blond and good-looking and, for once, not so outrageously old that I couldn't introduce him to my father. We took Ecstasy and wandered around the East Village, making out on the street. Some nights he crashed at my place; my father brought us coffee in the morning, which felt refreshingly normal. He was the closest thing I'd had to a real boyfriend in years.

But I was listless and lost. At school, they called it senioritis, but my case felt somehow more urgent than that. It was spring now, after a long, cold winter, and the flowers blooming should have felt like the start of something good. But I felt empty.

I took more pills, and the more pills I took, the emptier I seemed to feel.

"You're looking thin," Dr. Chester said. I hadn't seen him in two weeks. Why did everyone keep saying that to me? Did I really look that much thinner than I had two weeks earlier? Was that possible?

I thought of all the things I could say in response: "Thanks. You always give me the best compliments." "Thanks. My target weight is 'sickly.'" "Thanks. I haven't eaten since the '90s."

But I didn't say any of those things. I just laughed. I could feel my jaw working, some telltale twitch betraying me.

"I know, and, like, people *keep* telling me that, you know?" I laughed again. "But, like, I remember you telling me this, back when we *started* with the Ritalin, right, that it's, like, a side effect of stimulant-based medication that it often *causes* weight loss but it's not necessarily a *problem* because maybe your body is just restoring itself to the weight where it was *supposed* to be because maybe you were eating for *other* reasons, like stress or emotional problems and so you were eating *more* than your body needed, like, nutritionally or whatever, but now you don't *have* to anymore, so isn't it probably, like, a *good* sign that I'm thin?" I laughed a third time.

"Yes," he said.

"Right," I said. "Yeah, so."

"This is the last time I'll see you before you head home for the summer," he said.

I nodded. "I think this is going to be a really great summer," I said. "I'm excited to, like, work on repairing my relationship with my mom or whatever."

"And Vassar in the fall."

"Yeah, Vassar," I repeated.

I didn't tell Dr. Chester that Vassar felt very far away. I didn't tell him that the very idea that I would ever get there was laughable.

"I'm writing you some prescriptions," he said, pulling out his pad. "For the summer. Ninety days' worth."

"Okay," I said. My mouth, which had been sticky-dry a few minutes earlier, was suddenly filling up with spit. I wanted to grab the prescription pad from his hand and run for the door.

What a stupid little man, I thought, suddenly filling up with contempt, an odd and distant rage that I couldn't entirely name. I knew I hated him, but I didn't know why. I didn't know if I hated him because I believed he had turned me into a monster or because he couldn't fix a monstrosity in me that was innate.

"This is for—" He laid them down on the coffee table one by one, scribbling on them with a silver pen. He had a jaunty mode of expression that often made him seem younger than he was, but his hands were dotted with liver spots, and I suddenly felt food I hadn't eaten coming up in my throat. I choked, disguising it as a cough.

"Ninety Adderall XRs," he said. "One hundred and eighty short-acting Adderall."

"Fives or tens?" I said, my heart pounding.

"Tens," he said, smiling at me. "And then—ninety Lexapro. And ninety Ambien. I'm going to stick with the original formulation since you didn't tolerate the CRs. And ninety Xanax."

"Two milligrams?" I said.

"One milligram," he countered.

"Okay," I said. "That's probably good. I don't want to take too much."

"I'm glad you've been able to maintain a moderate relationship with these drugs," he said.

"Me, too." I looked down at the prescriptions. They were levitating.

I took a cab back to my apartment and went straight into the Duane Reade on the corner to drop off the prescriptions. The lights inside were suspiciously bright. I felt dizzy.

"It'll be about thirty minutes," the pharmacist said.

"I'll wait," I said.

I walked up and down the aisles, studying competing brands of toothpaste. I picked up a tabloid and flipped through it. Everyone was too fat or too thin. I took a pack of candy off the shelf and began to eat it mindlessly without paying for it. I stood by the pharmacy counter and checked my phone.

Then, a tap on my shoulder. I turned around. It was my father.

"Hey, Sam," he said.

"Dad," I said.

"What are you doing?"

"Picking up some prescriptions," I said. "Just came from seeing Chester."

"Oh, good," he said. He took out his wallet and handed me his credit card. "Use this."

I woke up two days later in a hospital bed. Everything hurt.

A nurse, her scrubs sea-foam green, her expression grim, was seated across from me. She had a clipboard in her hand. She was asking me questions. I knew that I had been answering them for a while, but I also knew that I hadn't been conscious while that was happening. Consciousness, like everything else, was so ephemeral.

"Were you trying to harm yourself?" she was asking me.

"No," I spat. "Of course not."

"Then why did you take so much?"

"I don't know," I said. "It was an accident."

Then everything went dark again.

The next flash of memory was getting out of a taxi with my father in front of our apartment building. He held my arm as he walked me up the stairs into the lobby.

Later, I pieced together accounts from various friends about how I had met them in Central Park, where I had been handing out pills from my freshly filled prescriptions, taking too many myself. We'd gotten drunk there, but they said I didn't seem normal. Eventually, I stumbled off toward Fifth Avenue.

Nobody saw me after that until Jesse found me lying under a bench, in the middle of the night, my face cut up and bleeding. He figured I must have been hit by a car, he said, and I needed to go to the hospital; this wasn't something I could just sleep off. He called my father and dragged me into a cab.

My father came downstairs at four o'clock in the morning and I fell out of the cab, my figure wraithlike, my skin luminescent in the lamplight. He took me to the hospital and waited for me to wake up.

"You were comatose," my father said, his voice threatening to break. "I was so scared."

The doctors said I'd taken probably twenty Xanax over the course of the evening. It was only my high level of drug tolerance that had kept me alive. It was funny, almost—the tolerance that had been such an annoyance to me as I'd had to take more and more pills to achieve the same effect had turned out to be my life raft.

The day after I went home from the hospital, I went to see Dr. Chester to talk to him about what had happened. I had bandages on my face.

"Maybe we should try putting you on Neurontin," he said.

If I wasn't scared straight, at the very least I was rattled—deeply. I decided to stop drinking, at least for a little while, although I wasn't sure I was ready to give up the pills.

Daphne's father had been sober for over two decades. I met him at his office in midtown and told him, in brief, what had happened. He shook his head. He didn't seem shocked or surprised to hear my war stories, but he offered to take me to a twelve-step meeting.

And so I went with him, down to a converted brownstone in the West Village that now served as a clubhouse. It was a funny mix of people: glitterati in heels, grizzled old men who looked (and smelled) homeless, white-collar commuters, and a drag queen named Brownie who pushed my face into her décolletage.

"Welcome home, baby," she said.

It didn't feel like home: it felt like an anthropological experiment. I was too young to be doing this, I thought—too young to be *seriously* getting sober. I was supposed to go to college. There were far too many things that I had yet to do.

I went a few times, but after the meeting one night, I took the train up to Ronan's house. He was sitting on the fire escape, smoking a joint. I took a hit and exhaled.

"Yo—I don't know if, like, going to meetings is for me," I said. "Part of me thinks that maybe this was all just a big over-reaction—so I went too hard and ended up in the hospital. It happens, right?"

The truth was, I *missed* drinking. I'd thought that I could get by on just pills, but there was nothing that produced quite the same marvelous effect in me that alcohol did: that fizzy, loose liberty.

"Maybe you *aren't* an alcoholic, Sam," he said. "Maybe you're just kind of messed up."

"You really think so?" I said, trying not to sound too eager.

"Yeah, man," he said. "Like, you're fine. So you took a few too many pills and fucked up your face. That doesn't mean you have to stop drinking for the rest of your life."

He was right, I thought. I had gone way overboard.

"Give me a beer," I said. He opened the minifridge in his bedroom and handed one to me. I cracked it open. I didn't even like beer, but nothing had ever tasted quite so sweet.

Senior prom was a week after the overdose. I almost skipped it—it felt like an odd way to punctuate the end of my high school experience—but decided at the last minute to go.

The night was balmy, the streets crashing with taxis. Pedestrians muttered on sidewalks. All the lights were on in midtown, blinking jumbotrons with video screens flashing logos, graphics, cleavage.

The event was at an upscale restaurant downtown. On the glassy dance floor, I stared at the swirling rainbow of couture dresses and dark suits. I drank champagne in the bathroom, waking up once it was in my body, vitalized again.

"I can't believe this is the end," I said to Daphne. "I can't believe it's over."

At eleven thirty, we left the dance and took a cab up to the Waldorf, where the seniors had split the cost of a penthouse suite. I smoked a joint on one of the many-tiered terraces. Gangster rap, spitting gutturally, lurched from the speakers inside. In the master bathroom, I could hear laughter; a trio of girls had filled the tub with bubbles and jumped inside, their bodies glistening.

I was sitting on a floral-printed chaise, talking with Daphne, when I heard a scream—alarming and constant and wrenching, ululating as a tribal song. It pulled me into its eye.

In the hallway, there were three boys, tanned and muscled, their fists flailing. There was a boy beneath them—he was a little odd; I wasn't friends with him—and he was writhing, delirious with pain. They were hitting him, and blood was everywhere, dripping from him, puddling below his nose and into his ears. They beat him mercilessly as he screamed and wailed. The noise was piercing, like the screeching of feedback over a loudspeaker. The scream spurted blood all over the white carpet. They were winning, fueled by cocaine and adrenaline and bravado, I figured, but there wasn't really any fight to win. The kid was choking, his tongue lolling uselessly in his mouth, his eyes slitted into wrinkled indentions. He opened them to see everyone watching. Then the scream turned into a kind of muted gagging.

"I need a drink," I said. I turned away. Later, I heard they had accused him of stealing their drugs, though it wasn't clear whether he actually had, not that it would have made a difference.

I called Kat that night. "Maybe it's good that I'm coming back to Portland for the summer," I said.

"Why?" she asked. "What's wrong?"

"I don't know," I said. "Too many beautiful people doing too many ugly things."

I could practically hear Kat rolling her eyes through the phone.

"That sounds like something you would say," she said.

The graduation ceremony was a few days later, in a ballroom at the Metropolitan Museum of Art. I was wearing a trim black suit under my robe. All the other graduates looked so happy with their families—so normal. It made the day feel slightly sinister, weighty with portent.

My mother flew out for the occasion. It was the first time she had met any of my New York friends.

"Your life here is so different," she said.

"You don't know the half of it," I said.

Six

They appeared in the night, as in a dream. Two men shadowed in beams of charcoal half-light. They stood in the doorway of my bedroom, dark-skinned and hulking, impassive as sculpture. They didn't speak, but their presence was as rattling as a shot of adrenaline. I jolted awake in a snarl of knotted linens. Perspiration stung on my brow. I licked my lips. My tongue felt useless, like it didn't belong in my mouth.

As my eyes began to adjust, I looked stupidly at the men, and they looked back at me.

It seemed like only minutes before that I'd stumbled out of a packed nightclub in a coruscating blur of neon lights, cigarette smoke unfurling in the air, the taxicab sprawl, my doorman leering, the slickened walnut panels of the elevator spinning around me, a clumsy face-first collapse into bed. I could still taste the evening's vodka-tonics, feel the sticky hubris of lip gloss tingling on my cheekbone. That telltale clenching in my jaw from the two tabs of Ecstasy that I'd taken shortly before midnight with Sahara. She was just a few blocks away, across the park.

I should call her, I thought idly. *I wonder if she's tripping out, too.*

One of the men snapped his fingers, jerking me into alertness. I had dozed off.

I looked at them, trying to will them into nothingness. Then I glanced at the clock. It was half past four. I moaned. The men were still standing there. I was awake, suddenly. Acutely awake.

"You should pack a bag," one of the men finally said. His face was inscrutable. Was I being kidnapped? A frisson of anticipation scaled my spine. *Kidnapped.* It was so glamorous.

"Where are you taking me?" I asked. "Who are you? Where's my father?"

My father.

I sat up in bed and I could see his silhouette in the hallway. He was quaking, his face buried in his hands.

"Daddy?" I said. He disappeared into the dusky light of the corridor and I focused back on the two men.

"Where are you taking me?" I repeated.

"Rehab," the other man said.

"Rehab?" I said. My voice cracked. "Oh no. This is a mistake."

"It's not," he said.

"Where?"

"Aspen," one of them said.

"Aspen," I said. "Oh. Great."

I let my imagination project me into a ski lodge. I would be nestled in an overstuffed armchair before a fire, its flame crackling. I would be sipping from a mug of peppermint cocoa, wearing a chunky-knit argyle turtleneck and suede snow boots. I'd talk about my feelings and then maybe hit the slopes in a fur-trimmed parka and oversize sunglasses. Aspen would be okay.

"Get your things," one of them said, brandishing a tan canvas duffel at me. It had come from my father's closet, I knew. The realization that he'd planned this suddenly dawned upon me. I lurched to my feet and tossed a few essentials into the bag: my laptop, a diaphanous cashmere sweater, facial moisturizer, a fistful of jewelry. The drugs left shimmering trails on my bare feet as I shuffled into a pair of leather bedroom slippers.

I heard a gust of laughter. I looked up at one of the men.

"What are you packing?" he said.

I eyed him warily.

"You're going to the wilderness," he said.

What?

"You said I was going to Aspen," I countered, arms akimbo. I studied the contents of my unzipped bag. I had been so pragmatic.

"Aspen," he said. "Aspen is the name of the program. Wilderness rehab. In Utah."

Panic prickled in my scalp, then corkscrewed down through my fingertips. My father materialized in the doorway.

"Sam," he said, "go with them."

"Shit," I said. "Shit." Then, with gusto: "Shit shit shit."

I began to cry, momentarily deafened by a ringing in my ears. Feebly, I punched a pillow.

Could I escape? As I straightened my back to my full height, tears gushing down my face, I realized that the men dwarfed me:

I was six feet small. A ripple of muscle poked from the sleeve of one of them; he tensed. A getaway attempt was futile.

"You better not try and run," he said, working some eerie telepathy.

"I won't," I said. I meant it. He motioned me out of my room and I limped forward into the kitchen.

At the front door, my father put a hand on my shoulder, then pulled me into a hug. I allowed my arms to dangle limply at my sides for a moment; then I pulled away.

He would pay for this later.

"Don't fucking touch me," I spat. His beard was wet with tears.

Through the hallway, in the elevator, down through the lobby. The night doorman raised a hand in greeting and opened the doors to the front vestibule for my unlikely entourage. He was the one who had always looked at me funny when I stumbled in half drunk at midnight on a school night, again when I left at one thirty to go pick up drugs, stranger still when I returned reeking of smoke at four, and most strangely when I left for school at six in the morning, no trace of slumber clouding my eyes.

On the street, the sun was rising over the brownstones on Eighty-eighth Street, and I raised my hand to my eyes, blinded by the starkness of the morning. Croissants cooked in the patisserie beneath my building. A taxi purred past in a yellow blur. I tried to suck in as much of that smoky morning air as possible.

More than anything, I did not want to leave New York.

I could not leave New York.

I called Seth on the way to the airport. I was hysterical.

"They're taking me to wilderness," I cried. "Some program called Aspen."

I heard a heavy sigh on the other end of the phone. "Okay," he said. "You're gonna be fine. It'll be tough, but you can get through it. And you will."

"I don't think I can do it," I said.

"This is the best advice I can give you," he said. "Keep your head up, but keep your head down."

At the airport, I sat dumbly at the gate, flanked on either side by the two men. There was a bluebird hopping along the floor of the terminal, dodging the wheels of rolling suitcases slapped across the tile by fat tourists.

You don't belong here any more than I do, I thought.

I slept on the plane to Salt Lake City, awakening to one of the men nudging me to life. I couldn't remember where I was—and then it came rushing back to me. A swirl of terminals and shuttle buses.

In the bathroom at the airport, I sneaked the emergency Adderall that was tucked into my wallet. They rented another car and we drove on the freeway. I felt peppier. *Everything is going to be okay.*

At a convenience store, I bought a tabloid and a bottle of water. I smoked a cigarette while one of them stood beside me. His name was Tim, he had said.

"That's going to be your last one," he said.

"I'll enjoy it, then," I said.

I took in the sights and sounds of this unfamiliar terrain—the low scrub of the suburban landscape. Where *was* I? Surely they wouldn't actually take away my cigarettes—that would be inhumane. Dean used to say that I didn't seem like I could be me without smoking. "You'd be much less profound if you didn't smoke," he'd say, reaching for a drag. "You're always enwrapped in a cloud of smoke. Literally, or metaphorically."

"You hungry?" one of them asked.

"No," I lied.

After about an hour on the road, we turned onto a cul-de-sac spotted with small, ranch-style tract homes. A white van was parked in front of one; Tim pulled up behind it.

"Out," he said.

They led me inside. A cluster of teenage boys, all of whom looked as haggard as I did, sat on a faded sectional, watching a movie. One of them raised a hand in greeting, while the others looked forward at the television. I turned to Tim.

"This isn't what I was picturing," I said.

"This is the safe house," Tim said. "Your program isn't ready to admit you yet, so you'll be here a few days."

He took my duffel bag. "Tell us if you need a change of clothes," he said.

"I don't," I said. "But I need my pills. Do you have my pills? I haven't taken my Lexapro today." Privately, I was more concerned about the Xanax—that would certainly take the edge off this experience.

"You're not going to get any pills until you get to Aspen and see a doctor," he said. "We can't dispense them."

I sputtered. They might as well have told me that I'd be going the next two days without air.

"That's unacceptable," I said firmly.

"Kid," he said. "We're not giving you any drugs."

"I'm not asking you for *black tar heroin*," I said. "I'm asking you for my *psychiatrically necessitated medication*. You don't have to go cop for me. I brought my pills. Give them to me. Now."

"I'm sorry," he said. "I can't help you." He turned to leave, but I grabbed his arm.

"Let me explain something to you," I said. "I take benzos for anxiety. I've been taking them for months. Now, you probably don't know this because you're, like, an *inbred fuck*, but there are only two types of withdrawal that can kill you: alcohol withdrawal and benzodiazepine withdrawal. If you don't get me my fucking Xanax, I will have a fucking seizure and die right here and my dad will fucking sue you for everything you are worth. Do you understand me? You are putting me in immediate medical danger."

He shook my hand off and laughed, like he had heard this pitch before. *You brat*, his face said.

"Eat something," he said. "You'll feel better. Maybe if you sit down and behave, we'll get you Taco Bell later."

"I don't want Taco Bell," I barked. "I want my fucking Xanax."

He left the room. On-screen, a high-speed car chase terminated with a massive explosion. The boys didn't react. Not knowing what else to do, I crumpled onto the couch next to one of them.

"'Sup," he said.

I was livid. I needed a cigarette. I was starving, but I couldn't possibly eat.

I hoped the withdrawal would cause a grand mal seizure. It would serve them right—all of them, but especially my father.

I imagined myself convulsing on the floor, white foamy spittle on my lips, their helpless faces as they scrambled for a phone. It would be too late. I'd already be dead.

Was there any chance that I could run? I had no money, no phone, no contacts, and certainly no life skills—even I wasn't naive enough to think I could make it as a runaway. I looked to the windows.

I had been so distracted that I hadn't even realized that they were covered in bars.

I was given clean sheets for a lumpy twin bed; on the top bunk was a dark-haired boy with a sparse mustache that belied his age. Fourteen, fifteen, maybe. In the night I heard him weeping, which gave me an erection for reasons I couldn't explain.

Dizzy from hunger, I ate macaroni and cheese for breakfast. I poured myself a tumbler of milk and mixed a few tablespoons of Nesquik chocolate into the glass with a long spoon. The taste was chalky and saccharine. After, in the privacy of the bedroom, I nursed my protuberant stomach with one hand.

And then, in the bathroom, one of the escorts sat on the toilet and watched me as I lathered my face with shaving cream and ran a razor across my chin. Hand quivering, I swiped my neck. A stinging, the metallic smell of blood, a crimson glistening. He grabbed my hand.

"You're finished," he said. It had been an accident. Even at my worst, I had never been a self-mutilator.

Later that day, they gave me a letter from my father. It was reasoned, cautious, and positive. He told me that he wanted to see me move into a life without dependence on drugs; that he knew this approach was not in my comfort zone, and he hoped that I would embrace the program as a new and exotic experience (those were his words, "new and exotic"—the absurdity of this was laughable); and that he apologized for not involving me in the decision-making. "I know this will be a great few weeks for you," he concluded.

I gave the letter a cursory read, then tossed it aside.

"Don't you want to keep that?" Tim asked.

"No," I said.

Tim picked it up and tucked it away. I hated my father for doing this to me, hated him for his optimism and concern. I had already started going to twelve-step meetings, even if I hadn't been staying sober. I would have been willing to go to a real rehab. Why was this necessary? Pulling me out of bed in the middle of the night, sending me to some godforsaken shithole in the desert? Making me *hike*?

It wasn't, I concluded. The whole thing was bullshit. I would play along for as long as I had to, but my father was dead to me.

On the third day, a van arrived. The fat woman in the driver's seat was all teeth. Tim pulled my bag from a locked closet and passed it to her; I watched this exchange with hawkish intensity. My *pills* were in there, and my *phone*.

There was another boy in there already, sitting in the back-seat of the van. He was shorter than I was, and muscular, broad-featured. He introduced himself as Eric. I shook his hand.

We talked about what had brought us to Aspen. Eric was from the Jersey Shore, a stoner and a football player who had ingested what he had thought were psychedelic mushrooms—they turned out to be poisonous. He'd nearly died and landed in the hospital for two weeks, and his parents, fed up, told him that the only way they'd release him was if it was to a wilderness program.

The landscape grew sparser as we drove south past Provo. Hours on the freeway. We stopped at a fast-food restaurant off the highway and I studied the menu as if it were written in a foreign language. Hadn't it been just a few days earlier that I had been drowning my soft-shell crab in a tangerine cosmopolitan? *What had happened?*

Eric devoured a bacon cheeseburger while I effeminately nursed a Diet Coke. I told him stories from the city, about how hard I partied, about seeing celebrities in nightclubs.

"Dude," he said. "Sick."

Finally, we pulled up to a brick building in a small town called Loa. A wooden sign posted in the yard read: ASPEN ACHIEVEMENT ACADEMY, FIELD OFFICE. Inside, we were weighed and measured. I stood in a dimly lit room until a man entered. He put on plastic gloves with a resounding snap.

"Strip," he said.

"Seriously?"

"Cavity search."

I pulled off my T-shirt, then my pants.

"Everything," he said. Shamefully, I tugged my underwear down to my ankles. I felt hideously exposed.

"Bend over," he said. I complied. He probed me, checking under my testicles and in my anal cavity.

"Buy a girl a drink first," I snarled. "What exactly do you think I'm hiding in there?"

Satisfied, he pulled off the gloves.

"You're good."

"It's not the first time a guy has told me that after putting his fingers in my ass," I said. He ignored me.

I dressed and followed him to a long, narrow closet where shelves were lined with stacks of folded clothes—Spartan, military issue. Methodically, he pulled my size in each garment. Two plain blue cotton T-shirts. Two heather-gray crewneck thermals. One pair of cargo shorts. One pair of cargo pants. Two pairs of boxer briefs. A pair of Converse All Star sneakers. A pair of hiking boots. Two pairs of thick gray socks. A black fleece sweater that zipped up. An olive green rain poncho.

"You'll want to change," he said, handing me a blue T-shirt, a pair of underwear, and the cargo shorts. I slipped out of the jeans and gray cashmere hoodie I'd been wearing for the last few days and put on my new uniform. (In fairness, my old uniform had developed a stale, locker-room odor.) He piled the rest of the clothes in his arms, and I trailed him out into a large, open warehouse. On the floor was a rectangular silver tarp, about ten feet by eight feet, on top of which was a snakelike coil of something black and ribbed—seat belt webbing—and a few other odds and ends: a length of bungee cord, some rope, a tan canvas knapsack, a small black bag, a sleeping bag, and my eyeglasses, absurd in their lilac Christian Dior case.

"What is all this?" I asked.

"This will be your pack," he said. "They'll teach you how to make it later, so I'll make it for you now." He deposited the contents of his arms into the center of the tarp, knelt, and began to fold it, making tight creases in the silver material. He folded it into thirds, like a burrito, then folded the top and bottom thirds over the center. Nimbly, he wrapped the bungee cord around the pack, several times in short succession, then tied it longitudinally, too, as though he were tying a ribbon bow onto a wrapped gift. Then, expertly, he threaded two pieces of black seat belt webbing between the bungee cord and the tarp. It only took him about twenty seconds to turn this mass of stuff into something that resembled a backpack—albeit a squishy, bulbous one.

It was impressive, but it looked more like a cocktail party trick than anything I could ever be expected to do, and I told him so.

"You'll get the hang of it," he said, holding up the backpack so I could slip it onto my shoulders. To fasten it to me, he tied the seat belt webbing tight around my belly in an awkward knot. It was heavy on my back, heavier than the agility with which he'd picked it up had suggested. I waddled behind him as he headed back out to the front of the building.

"You need to use the bathroom?" he asked.

"No," I said.

"Think carefully," he said. "It's the last time you'll be able to shit indoors for a while."

"I'm fine," I said.

He shrugged. "Your call."

I stepped out the front door, where Eric was waiting by the van, also changed and with a pack of his own. It didn't fully resonate for me then that it was the last time I'd be indoors for two months.

We drove another hour out of town, through a hardscrabble landscape that was magnificent in its desolation. A sign on the highway read: WELCOME TO DIXIE NATIONAL FOREST. Eric and I were silent in the backseat.

Past the perimeter of the park, we wound up a winding, bumpy road that was littered with boulders that jostled us; a few times, it felt as though we might topple over. (That, I thought, would be a blessing.) Finally, we stopped at a plateau where a man and woman with backpacks (*real* backpacks) stood, unsmiling, against a backdrop of crystalline sky. We stepped out of the van and surveyed the scene. The scope of it was daunting, incomprehensible. An endless panorama of sagebrush and juniper trees, the soil ruddy and thick with clay, interrupted by only the rare riparian area where a dejected creek sputtered across the landscape and the dust sprang forth with a flash of life, then hills to the horizon. More dust, more hills. It was alien and indifferent.

The sun was going to set soon. The counselors—Rob and

Liz—told us that the first step of the program was to not speak for twenty-four hours, so we sat in opposite corners of the camp in silence. I wrote in a stenographer's pad I'd found in my knapsack, doodling about New York and the friends I missed. Rob built a fire as the summer sun faded away into a night of unprecedented potency. It was getting cold. I ate a bag of peanuts and raisins from my knapsack.

That night, nestled into a sleeping bag under the dispassionate desert sky, I prayed for the first time I could remember. I begged a God I did not believe in for a hurricane, a coyote attack, a wildfire, a nuclear holocaust—anything that might swallow the state of Utah and everything in it.

———

The program combined elements of survivalist training, cognitive behavioral therapy, a boarding school, and a type of New Age spirituality inspired by Native American mythology, which I found odious. Students moved through different phases, starting as a Mouse, then continuing up to Coyote, Buffalo, and finally Eagle. Certain tasks and checkpoints were required to progress to the next level of the program, some as straightforward as successfully building a fire, others as subjective as "accepting responsibility for behavior."

I learned later that the typical experience at Aspen was entirely unlike mine: Most students joined groups that were already fully functional as the veteran students graduated and left Aspen. But the program had experienced a recent influx of students—perhaps at the onset of summer, or due to rising popularity (a reality show had been shot at Aspen and broadcast the previous year)—and so they'd had to create new groups and hire more wilderness counselors. Eric and I were the first two students in our group. It would have been easier had we joined an existing group, with students at all phases of the program demonstrating what was required of them, but instead we were starting from scratch, with no one to model how a successful group ran; accordingly, there was more telling than showing.

The only objective for the Mouse level was to be quiet for twenty-four hours and resolve my anger about my placement at Aspen; this seemed fairly straightforward. I was given a workbook that asked me leading questions about my past behavior and, dutifully, I answered them dishonestly, writing that my father had sent me to Aspen because I was out of control—although privately I felt that it wasn't my fault that he didn't see my drug use as the only way I was able to *maintain* my control over the chaos of my life.

The structure of the program seemed suited for kids who had behavioral problems, not active drug addictions, but I reasoned that there was nothing that I could do about it.

I read the answers to the workbook over the campfire, and Rob and Liz nodded thoughtfully as I read.

"This is how you become a Coyote," Rob said. He led us to a rocky cliff a few hundred yards from the campsite, which jutted out over a spectacular vista, and began to howl—high and eerie.

"You, too," he said. So Eric and I howled at the moon. It felt stupid, but the ritual still gave me chills, not that I would have admitted that to Rob and Liz.

That second night, they showed us how to build a shelter using the same silver tarp that served as a pack: Find two trees spaced not much more than ten feet apart and tie a bungee cord a few feet off the ground, then drape the tarp on the cord to make an upside-down V. Place rocks on each of the four corners to secure the tarp in place, providing a makeshift tent.

At Aspen, there was a lot of talk of "busting," which had an ejaculatory connotation that I disliked; it was such a vulgar word, I thought. To bust an "I feel" meant to pause the conversation to make an emotional statement, since most patients had a hard time articulating their feelings. (This had never been a struggle for me.) To bust a fifty was to step away from the group to urinate, at a distance of fifty feet; to bust a hundred was to leave to defecate, one hundred feet away from the group. When we were out of sight from the counselors, we had to call our names every few seconds loudly enough that we could still be heard, which meant it was difficult to go far enough to be comfortable, and made actually executing the act near impossible; peeing was easy enough, but I learned quickly it was very difficult to focus on getting relaxed enough to go while shouting at the top of your lungs in the woods.

To bust a fire was to create flame with a bow drill, the pieces of which I received on the second day. I had assumed that it was possible to create a fire by rubbing two sticks together, as the old cliché went, but at Aspen, the preferred mode of fire lighting was

with a bow drill—an ancient kit comprised of two pieces of wood,
a bearing block, and a bow formed from a curved branch and
some springy cord. I watched as Liz knelt on her right knee, with
her left foot holding down the baseboard—a piece of flammable
wood, like cedar. Then she wrapped her spindle—a narrow cylin-
der of wood with one edge rounded and the other one cut into a
point, like a pencil—into the bow by twisting the cord around it
once, which kept it taut. Placing the point of the spindle into an
indentation in the baseboard, she pressed down with her left hand,
in which she held a stone, to exert pressure onto the rounded top
of the spindle. Then, quickly, she worked the bow back and forth,
rotating the spindle in the baseboard; this created friction, which
eventually would produce an ember that could be blown into a
flame. She made it look effortless, but when I tried it, I found that
it was difficult.

"You have to learn," Liz said. "This is a skill that you need to
survive."

"Yeah," I said. "*Here.* Give me something I can use in the real
world." I fantasized about my vintage Dupont lighter. It was sitting in my duffel bag at base camp.

On the third day, we began to hike, breaking for a makeshift
lunch of foodstuffs from the black nylon bags in our packs—tor-
tillas with lukewarm cheese and leftover rice and beans, dry packets of ramen noodles (when you ate them uncooked, they tasted
like crackers), peanut butter on apples. It seemed that we would
descend from forested areas, hike downhill through long expanses
of high, scrubby desert, then hike back up to greener spots, where

we would set up camp in little clearings in the woods not far from water sources. We built our shelters, made a fire, and completed a series of chores—filling up tin cans that we carried tied to our packs with water from a nearby pond, digging a latrine, gathering wood for the fire—and completed the day's curriculum, which included some light academic components (mostly studying about the flora and fauna of the region; I wasn't particularly interested in the ecology of Utah) but focused more on a type of structured group therapy.

It moved slowly.

We cooked over the fire—often beans and rice, which I ate out of a tin cup—then continued the discussion after the sun went down. We wrote in our journals for an hour each day or so. I mostly wrote about things that had happened in the past, although years later I wished I had better documented what was actually happening, to have left a record sturdier than memory. At night, we set our pants and shoes outside our shelters, and the counselors collected them—to keep us from having the temptation to run, they said. Out in the desert, our only supply of water was from cow ponds, brackish little holes in the ground. We filled up thick Nalgene bottles with that water; then a counselor administered a few drops of iodine into each bottle to render it potable.

But it wasn't potable—not really. The water was viscous, gray-green, and coagulated, with clumps of algae floating in it, and even after the iodine it had a bitter chemical taste that reminded me of cocaine. We had to drink four quarts a day to stay hydrated. One afternoon, swallowing a gulp of gritty water, I felt something wriggling in my throat. I choked and reached into my mouth, pulling a brine shrimp through my front teeth.

After a few days, Rob and Liz were cycled out and replaced with two new counselors, Medeina and JT, who would be with us for the next week. I liked both of them more than I wanted to. Medeina was tough, with long curly hair and a militant affect, but her no-bullshit front masked a motherly kindness. JT spoke with a flat, stretched timbre and his patience was boundless; he looked like a young Mel Gibson, too, which I didn't mind.

With them came a week's worth of food and clean laundry— the decadence of a fresh pair of underwear felt glorious—as well as a psychologist named Kathianne, who sat with each of us for a half hour to talk in more detail about our issues. She was stout and spackled with rosacea, and unlike our counselors, she didn't seem totally at ease being out in the wilderness; I wondered if she'd been unable to make a living in private practice. I told her about my drug use, my affairs with older men. My fraught relationships with my parents. I tried to make myself sound glamorous and wild, the casualty of a rarefied world that had taken me down.

"The narcissism and manipulation that have served you in your life so far aren't going to work here," Kathianne said. "So you better start getting honest."

I fumed over this later as I knelt on the desert floor with my bow drill, rotating it until my hands were chapped and raw, making little jets of steam rise from my baseboard and then drift away.

She doesn't know me. How dare she?

But no matter how intensely I worked the drill, I couldn't seem to get an ember going, just some charred black dust and a lot of smoke. Frustrated, I threw the bow across the camp.

"If you can't bust a fire," Medeina said, "you can't have hot food."

"I don't want hot food," I said. "I don't want any of this food."

"Good," she said. "Because you're not getting any."

"What if I just don't eat?" I said. "What if I go on a hunger strike?"

She laughed. "I can't force you to eat," she said. "But you can do that, if that's what you want. We'll just send you back to base camp, hook you up to a feeding tube, and then send you back out to start the program over again once you're healthy."

"What happens if I break a leg?" I said.

"We'll get you medical attention," she said, "and then put you back in the field."

This was always the response to any hypothetical catastrophe: the consequence would simply be that the program would take even longer to complete. There was no way out.

That night, they cooked beans and rice over a fire while I sat on the sidelines, waiting for them to finish. After the food had gone cold, it was served to me in a tin cup. There were no utensils; I picked a twig off the forest floor and used it as a makeshift fork. Most of us did this, figuring that it had to be more hygienic than our fingers, since we had no way of washing our hands.

At our local water hole, we found a cow standing dumbly at the surface of the water, defecating directly into it—fat green-brown pellets thudding into the murky pond.

"This is the only water for miles," Medeina said, more than a little gleefully. "Drink up."

With Kathianne that week came documents from our parents: "impact letters," which described how their lives had been affected by our behavior. We were given them over the campfire and were asked to read them out loud for the first time. I didn't stumble over my mother's, which was clear and thoughtful, but my father's made me blind with rage. He described his concern for me, his mounting fears, his anger over feeling manipulated and used.

After I finished reading, we sat quietly for a moment. "How did that make you feel, Sam?" Kathianne asked softly. "Do you want to bust an 'I feel' statement?"

"Sure, I'll bust," I said, my voice low and quivering. "I feel angry. I was a fifteen-year-old with a drug habit—that he *knew* about—and he left me alone in New York City with his credit card for two years. He paid for me to fill my prescriptions. He was too busy to give a shit about me. Where does he get off being so self-righteous?"

"This isn't about what *he* did, Sam," Kathianne said. "This is about *your* behavior."

"So I'm just at fault for everything?" I said bitterly.

"You wouldn't have ended up here if your parents hadn't already done *everything they could* to try to help you," Kathianne said.

"I don't know if you have my case file handy, but he didn't do shit," I said. "In fact, he only noticed that I was in trouble once I was already in a fucking coma."

"You have to learn to take responsibility for your own behavior," Kathianne said. "He got you here. Isn't that enough of a sign that he cares?"

"Yes," I lied.

"Is there some part of you that sees that he is right?"

"Yes," I lied again. I was flushed hot with self-righteous anger. Hadn't it been my father's job to make sure that I was safe? Hadn't my father been the one who had failed?

That week, around midday, as we were hiking across a meadow, Medeina stopped us suddenly.

"What?" I said. She held a finger up to her lips, then pointed out toward the horizon. There, a few hundred feet away, was something lumbering toward us. As it got closer, I could make out what it was: a brown bear, smaller than I had expected and predictably cuddly, bounding through the tall grass. After it had passed the group, all of us standing silently and shaking, I cleared my throat to speak. But Medeina shook her head.

"That was just a little guy," she said.

"So?" I said.

"That means Mama Bear isn't far behind."

And indeed, a few moments later, a second bear easily twice the size of the first came blundering through the field—but unlike the baby, which had been crawling on all fours, the mother was walking two-legged like a human. She was fearsome, dark-eyed.

The thought struck me like a bolt: *What if I run toward her?* She would maul me. She might kill me. But surely they wouldn't make me come back out to the wilderness if I was mauled by a bear. It was too ridiculous. I tensed my body. I was ready to run, to see what might happen. Would she run in the opposite direction? Would she see me as prey, smell my flesh, rip into my belly with her jaw? Adrenaline coursed through me, making the hair on my body stand up. I tensed my legs, then—

I felt Medeina's hand on my shoulder. She had seen my posture shifting, read my body language—or maybe she was just psychic.

"Don't," she whispered.

A strange energy passed between us. I obeyed, and the impulse left me.

After the bears passed, we hiked to the far edge of the field and began pushing up the side of a mountain; it was greener there than it had been in the desert we had just walked through. In the deafening quiet of the woods, I heard an unfamiliar noise—a quiet whooshing that turned into a burble as we approached it.

"Running water," Eric said. His eyes were electric.

We reached a brook that sliced through the terrain, water slapping euphoniously over slick gray stones, pushing downstream with satisfying velocity. It looked so perfect—it was a movie creek, a prop. I emptied the contents of my water bottles onto the ground, then dipped into the stream. The water was fresh, clear, ice-cold—otherworldly blue. I drank from it gluttonously, like I hadn't had water in years, until my stomach was swollen. The trees created a canopy of cool shade overhead. We sat quietly for a moment before we got up, tied our packs to our bodies once more, and began to climb another mountain.

⸺⸺⸺

After seven days, I still couldn't bust fire. Each night, I worked the bow and the spindle, twisting it into the branch of supple, flaky cedar as it blackened and smoldered. But the top point of the spindle skipped along my top rock, which was a piece of gray stone with a slight indentation in the middle; the more I put pressure on the top rock, leaning into it to maximize the friction generated by the spindle, the more the spindle would slip off the rock, unfurling from my bow with a vengeful *snap* and sailing across the campsite. It wasn't working to spite me.

Eric wasn't having any of this trouble; his top rock had a more pronounced indentation that made it better suited for fire starting. Quickly he was spinning away at his bow, bent down on one knee like a marriage proposal, creating fat orange embers that he blew gently into a nest of dry grass, then built into a satisfying blaze that roared as he whooped and hollered, dancing through camp. But better still was JT, who used for his top rock an anklebone he said once had belonged to an elk; he called it a talus.

"Is this, like, a Native American thing?" I asked. "You have to use all of the parts of the animal's body after you kill it?"

JT laughed. "Nope. I'm a white dude from Salt Lake City. It just makes for the best fire starting, that's all."

I held the bone in my hand. It looked like a hinge: slightly smaller than a fist, smooth and curved, with four bulbous quadrants. It almost resembled a miniature loaf of challah bread. In the center of those four bulbs was a natural depression that fit the point of a spindle perfectly, and when I held it in my hand, my middle finger and thumb wrapped nicely between the grooves, creating a firm grip.

While collecting wood for the fire—another one I hadn't built—I searched the forest floor for rocks that might work better in my bow drill. I turned them over one by one, running my fingers across each smooth surface in pursuit of the perfect stone. But I knew what to look for, and the rock they had given me was still better than anything I found. I hurled them to the ground, loading my arms with fallen tree branches to take back to the camp. I sat apart from the group, eating the food that had gone cold after they had finished. I felt sorry for myself. I imagined my father having dinner at a chic downtown eatery with Jennifer, then enjoying a leisurely walk home.

I bit my lip so hard it started to bleed.

The next day, we walked along a path that cut through a large open field. The yellowed grains, tall and sharp, slapped against my arms. It was hot, brutally hot, so hot that my glasses steamed up as I walked, a cloudless sky split only by the white-hot sun. The seat belt webbing that kept my pack tied tight to my body was digging into my side, chafing painfully. As we turned a corner, I caught a whiff of some fetid smell, rank and skunk-like.

Eric smelled it, too. "What *is* that?" he asked.

As we approached a whitish form that lay motionless on

the side of the trail, the stink grew stronger. Eric and I groused and groaned while JT and Medeina laughed at our disgust. It was a dead cow, collapsed on its side, and it had been dead for a while by the look of it: its stomach had rotted or been torn out, revealing the tines of a rib cage curving like long, macabre fingers. That warm carrion stench filled my mouth, and I gagged reflexively.

"Circle of life," Medeina said.

As we started to move past it, I stopped suddenly. "JT," I said, "would the anklebone from this cow work as well as your elk bone does?"

"Probably," he said.

"Will you help me?" I asked.

He studied me skeptically. "Are you serious?" he said.

"Yes," I said, sucking in a big gasp of breath before I closed my mouth tightly and walked closer to the cow. Flies buzzed and snapped in the air, crawling along her Dalmatian hide, perched on the line of mauve-brown decaying flesh. I grabbed her rear right leg and tugged at it, half expecting it to just snap right off, but it didn't give. I looked to JT for support.

"Please?" I asked. He approached the cow, stepping hard onto the joint where her leg attached to her decomposing belly. Bones snapped. He put pressure on it while I pulled, and the leg bent a little, but it wouldn't budge.

"Move," I said, circling the cow. Bending at my knees like a gymnast, I jumped onto her body, stomping my feet down as hard as I could. More bones crunched. The flies hissed around me. With my hands, I leaned down and detached the leg, wrestling away the sinuous threads of rotted tissue, maggots squirming away from the activity. I cried out, triumphant, as it tore away from her belly.

"I want one, too," Eric said. He raced over to the carcass and began working on one of her other legs.

With the right leg successfully detached, I began wrestling out the bone in her ankle, beating it against a boulder until a fissure formed just above the foot; I broke it at that point with a sonorous crack. Once it was split open, I could see the bone that connected the leg to the hoof—and then, just below, the white curve of a talus. I peeled away the hide and pressed hard on the underside of the leg with my fingers and out it popped—the talus, still sticky with gray-pink flesh, my holy grail.

I looked over at the rest of the group, paused in the path, watching this scene take place. I was caked in dirt and sweat, and the stench of the cow's festering carcass was all over me, on my hands, in my mouth. But I lifted that bone over my head, victorious, and laughed out loud, the hardest I had laughed since I got to the wilderness. It was *mine*.

That evening at camp, under a silvery Utah moon, I made a fire so big and blue that I thought it would burn for a thousand years.

Seven

I was beginning to give myself over to the program, piece by piece. Kathianne asked me pointed questions about my childhood and, without much difficulty, she teased out of me the story of my first sexual experience with Brooks. I understood cognitively that what had happened was wrong and that I was not at fault, but I surprised myself by how emotional I became when recounting it—or maybe I was just trying to earn her sympathy. She seemed satisfied by my tears, which were sincere, but I also suspected that I'd given her a nice, straightforward causality to why I was the way that I was—something she could write in her notes that made me simpler to crack.

"Do your parents know?" she asked.

I shook my head no.

"It's probably time you tell them," she said, "that you were sexually abused."

Was it even something that was appropriate to categorize as abuse? He wasn't much older than me, and I'd participated willingly in some of it; it wasn't as if I'd been molested by a priest. Still, it felt like that was what she wanted, and so I wrote each of my parents long, emotional letters, explaining that I had been secretly suffering for years as a result of childhood sexual abuse. It felt reductive, but it was what Kathianne wanted me to say, and it was certainly much tidier than trying to parse out any other reason.

Still, as I lay under my shelter at night, waiting for sleep to take me, I did wonder how things had gotten so out of control. Surely there was something profoundly wrong with me, even if I couldn't name it, exactly. That big emptiness inside that clawed at my throat when I awakened in the morning until I went to sleep at night—the emptiness that I was always trying to fill.

There was no way to fill it at Aspen, so I tried to cherish the little things. A hot meal. A stunning vista. The camaraderie of the group. The moments when I woke up as the sun was rising, before the morning's chores, and let myself flash back to how things had been. The sound of Jerick's laugh. The splendor of Dean's loft. The smell of Seth's skin. The people I had loved, if I was even capable of that. Maybe they were just people I had tricked into loving me.

We hiked nine miles through a hailstorm, little shards of ice beating down in stinging tides, volleying into my skin like needles. We huddled under a tree for warmth, shivering, freezing from the odd anomaly of a summer ice storm; a nurse was helicoptered in to check our vitals, then promptly left upon establishing that none of us were going into hypothermic shock. My body was covered in mosquito bites and grime. I was blistered and strained; my head pounded constantly; my feet were calloused and bloody.

Yet I was pleasant and compliant. What had started off as sheer manipulation—pretending to be taking it seriously in order to expedite things—had transformed, through no effort on my part, into something much more sincere. Eagerly, I fetched wood for the fire and helped to organize breakfast in the morning. The program had its own logic, rhythm, and parameters; before I realized it, I had internalized them.

Two new boys, Justin and John, joined the group. Justin was from Indiana, and young—fourteen, maybe—and he had a bad temper; after punching a hole through a wall, he had been given the choice between Aspen and juvenile detention. He liked what I considered boy things—dirt bikes and hiking—and so he had decided to try wilderness.

John was my age, from Marin County, and had a laid-back, surfer-stoner demeanor; I got the sense that he was a pretty normal kid, just with conservative parents. All three of the other boys had at least a passing interest in the outdoors, and I felt that my father had been particularly spiteful in sending me to that program, given my manicured affect and propensity for quoting Fran Lebowitz: "To me the outdoors is what you must pass through in order to get from your apartment into a taxicab."

I said this to Medeina once. She just rolled her eyes.

Justin and John looked at Eric and me as if we were experienced veterans, which—having been there for a few weeks—we were. I taught them the ropes, patiently teaching them how to make their packs and even how to bust fire. They were almost as pissy as I had been during my first week, and I understood their frustration, but the program was straightforward: The more upbeat and acquiescent you were, the sooner you got to go home. Refusing to go along with it only protracted the stay unnecessarily.

Once a week, for hygiene, we filled the billies—old tin cans about a gallon large—with pond water; a counselor would squeeze a dollop of soap into the water, and we would set off to the edge of camp, with a shield of trees providing some semblance of privacy, shouting our names all the way. I stripped, trying to wash myself with the soapy water—but I was standing in the dirt, with nothing to dry myself other than the dirty clothes I'd already been wearing for days, crusted with mud. It felt like a fruitless exercise, and so eventually, I just gave up trying.

I looked tan, but it wasn't just the sun: I was covered in a thin layer of dust and grime that sweat made adhere to my skin—we called it permadirt. A can of cold water and soap were no match.

One morning, I awakened in my sleeping bag with an unfamiliar stickiness at my groin. I'd had a wet dream—my first ever. Sex had been far from my mind for weeks—it was almost impossible to be aroused in those conditions. But I felt strangely enlivened by this: I'd always assumed that I had never had a nocturnal emission because I'd been sexual at such a young age. It felt like my body was restoring a boyishness that I had assumed was lost forever, like the first normal teenage thing I had done in a long time. I wiped myself clean with a dirty T-shirt, hoping that a laundry drop would come before I'd have to wear it again. There were no tissues, no towels, only the single bottle of hand sanitizer that was dispensed to us when we returned from busting a hundred.

A few days later, I noticed a sharp, painful stinging when I urinated. It wasn't going away. I panicked. *Which sexually transmitted disease was it?* I wondered. I didn't know what to do.

I told Medeina, unsure whether she would believe me— would she think this was just a ploy to get me out of the field?

"We'll call a nurse," she said. "But you're not going anywhere."

And indeed, later that day, a field nurse arrived. (They must have driven staff to within walking distance of our campsites and had them hike in; I never saw a car; people just seemed to materialize out of nowhere.) In a circle of trees, she knelt before me, examining my genitals with plastic gloves.

"Is it gonorrhea?" I asked. "Or chlamydia?" I shook my head. *Fucking tweakers.* I wondered who had given it to me.

"No," she said. "It's a urinary tract infection. Happens sometimes." I hiked my pants up. "We'll get you on some antibiotics."

The field staff seemed accustomed to the sickness that accompanied living in nature, and this was unfathomable to me. JT had been terribly sick with giardia from the drinking water years earlier; now, he said, the bacteria were dormant in his gut, which meant he didn't need iodine. At one particularly rank cow pond, he bent his head down to the surface of the water and gleefully lapped it up, chunks and all, as we recoiled in disgust.

Justin fared worse still. Much later, I heard from him that a few days after he finally left Aspen, he was hospitalized with horrible stomach pains, shitting blood with a violence that terrified the emergency room doctors. He had E. coli from the water.

But there were good times, too, as I beat back my cravings and grew more facile with the survival elements of the program. We sang as we hiked through the mountains, songs that had been ubiquitous on the radio or old animated movies we had all watched as kids.

Justin, who was pretty handy, borrowed a penknife from Medeina and carved us all spoons from branches he picked up along the way; as we sat eating our beans and rice with actual utensils for the first time in weeks, we all felt like kings. We talked about home, what we would eat when we got out—Eric wanted Little Debbie Nutty Bars; I craved tuna tartare—and the television shows we missed watching the most. And we studied the stars, which gleamed like jewels in the sky.

Suddenly, three weeks had passed. I still wanted out, but staying wasn't impossible.

One afternoon, we hiked down to a field that looked more developed than our typical terrain. In the distance, I could even see something that resembled a road.

"It's gonna be a big day," Medeina said, rubbing her hands together. Her face shifted: she knew something that we didn't.

We approached a fence. Behind it was a large wooden contraption. It looked like a big wheelbarrow—a deep bed with two enormous wheels taller than the wagon itself, built of sturdy wooden spokes. In the front was a rectangular wooden crossbar that created a space big enough for two people to fit into.

"This," Medeina said, resting her hand on one wheel, "this right here is a Mormon handcart. We'll be traveling on these for now."

"For how long?" Justin asked.

"No future questions," Medeina said.

"So does this mean no more hiking?" I asked. "We're just going to push this thing?"

JT nodded. "You load your packs into the bed," he said. "One or two of you will take the front, and the rest of you will push from the back." This sounded straightforward enough.

"And we'll be on roads," I said. "This whole time?"

"Yup," Medeina said.

"Awesome," Eric said. We high-fived. Medeina smiled, tucking her hair behind her ear.

We untied our packs from our torsos and tossed them into the back of the cart. Eric took the lead, slipping between the bed of the cart and the crossbar, while Justin, John, and I took the rear.

Medeina pointed. "Over to that road."

"On the count of three," Eric said. "One, two—"

We started to push. The cart creaked and groaned, and so did we. It wasn't just heavy—with six packs inside, it weighed as much as a car.

"Push!" Eric yelled. The three of us shoved with all our force and the cart edged forward about a foot. We pushed again, and it moved another foot. I turned to Medeina.

Thompson-Nicola Regional District Library System

"This is a joke, right?" I said.

With an extraordinary amount of force, we managed to push the cart over to the road. It wasn't paved with concrete, just worn down and jagged with rocks, small enough that an automobile would have rolled right over them but big enough to disrupt the movement of the cart. Along a smooth surface, it would have been easy, but the wheels weren't designed to pass over any irregularities.

We continued pushing, Medeina and JT trailing behind us, watching the struggle. Each time a wheel got stuck on a rock, we had to stop and wrestle it into rotation again, pushing from the underside to move it along. It bumped and skidded, stopping every minute or two. The sun beat hot and heavy overhead; my glasses steamed up. But still we pushed on, up an incline and down the other side, pausing to catch our breath. Eventually, the road flattened out and it got easier; then more bumps would emerge and it would get difficult again. Another hill, and then on the other side another.

It went on like this for hours. My fingers were crushed between the wheel and the axle as I pushed; Eric complained of having welts on his hands from the crossbar; all of our shoulders and arms ached from pushing. By the time we reached camp, the sun was already beginning to set.

"Carts sure are frustrating, huh?" Medeina said as we unloaded our packs, panting and bruised.

"They're awful," I said. All my goodwill had been sapped out of me.

Thompson-Nicola Regional District Library System

"Does it remind you of anything?" she asked. "Having to work together as a team—learning to support each other when things get hard—being patient with the limitations of others?"

I was silent.

"It sounds like a family to me," she said.

"All of these metaphors are a little ham-fisted, don't you think?" I said.

Medeina laughed. "Oh, kiddo," she said. "If you don't like metaphors, you're *not* going to do well here."

The third day on carts, passing through a red-rock desert, we reached a flat, straight road that led all the way down to the horizon, where the path stretched upward at a sharp incline. I looked over at Eric. Sweat poured down his face, ruddy and filthy with grime. He looked back at me and shook his head.

"Fuck this," Justin muttered.

We edged closer to the hill, which loomed before us. I stared at it, not knowing how we would make it. Surely it couldn't be done. The cart itself weighed five hundred pounds; with our packs, it felt like it was close to a ton.

At lunch, we conspired. "We have to break the cart," Eric whispered. "We can't go on like this."

"But then what happens?" I said. "You think they're just gonna let us hike?"

"Yes, dude," he said. "They'll have no choice. If the cart doesn't work, we can just leave it and keep going. We have to sabotage it."

"No talking out of earshot!" Medeina called. We returned to our dry noodles and chunky water.

Closer and closer, we pushed toward the hill. As the incline got steeper, our progress got slower. We grunted and squawked, nudging the wheels over boulders and kicking up clouds of dust that made my eyes fill with tears. I spat a ball of dirt and phlegm. My hands were bloody.

"It's Hell Hill, dude," Eric said.

"Can't we take out our packs, hike up, and then come back down for the cart?" I asked. Medeina shook her head no.

As we approached the apex, the slope was getting dangerously steep. We pushed one foot forward, thrusting with all of our collective force, and if any of us stopped pushing for even a moment, we rolled back two or three feet. The road curved into the hillside, creating switchbacks lined with rocks. Painstakingly, slowly, we pushed over each rock. Justin was weeping.

"I can't go anymore," he cried. "I'm so tired."

"Come on, Justin!" JT shouted. "Almost there!"

Every part of me was soaked in sweat. I had put my glasses in my pack because they kept steaming up, though I couldn't see three feet in front of me without them. Blindly, I pushed, crying out in frustration and pain.

And then, suddenly, we were at the top. There was nothing more to push against. We had reached a plateau with panoramic views of the valley, one lone acacia tree providing a little shade. I collapsed onto the ground, heaving.

"All right," Medeina said. "Five minutes. But we've gotta keep going if we're going to make it to camp by nightfall." I looked at her with what I knew was unmasked loathing and she smiled at me.

We unloaded our packs and sat for a minute, hydrating. I looked up at the sun inching its way across the Utah sky; that was the only way that I could tell time. The cart was perched on the edge of Hell Hill. I looked over at Eric, who looked back at me. I nodded and he stood up.

"I think I left my hat in the cart," he said, walking over to it. I saw him looking in the bed, busying himself with its contents.

"Hey, JT," I said. JT and Medeina, in conversation a few yards away, looked up at me. "Can I have a bandage? My hand is bleeding."

Then, while they were distracted, a creak and a rapid-fire thudding noise. The cart was sailing down Hell Hill. We sprinted over to the edge, where Eric was standing, feigning horror. The cart skidded and bounced down the incline until—he couldn't have *planned* it better—it collided with a boulder set off from the path. One wheel popped off and went spinning down through the dust, landing a few yards away.

"Oh no!" I yelled. "The cart!" It felt good to get back to my roots—melodrama and lies.

Medeina studied Eric for a moment, then Justin and John, who looked aghast. Then she turned to me. I was waiting for her to blow a fuse, to yell or shout, but instead, she smiled and pulled out her walkie-talkie.

"This is Medeina with group eight. We have a broken cart up

here. Where's the nearest cart parked?" She waited as a lo-fi mur-
mur on the other end spoke. "Ten-four," she said.

"There's another cart a mile south of here," she said. "So we're
going to carry this broken cart to the drop so it can be repaired.
And then we're going to load up a new cart. And then we're going
to keep going."

Eric and I blinked wordlessly, mouths agape.

"So—so we're going *back* down the hill?" Justin said, incredulous.

"Yup," Medeina said.

"Oh," I said.

"And in case it wasn't clear," Medeina said, flashing a nasty
smile, "we're going right back up it."

The wilderness staff had made several opaque mentions to "solos"
over the course of my stay at Aspen, but didn't expand on what
that meant when asked. But I had heard of it from Seth, who had
gone out on solo at the wilderness program in Oregon he'd completed three years earlier. We had been on carts for about a week
when we arrived at one of the prettier sites we had visited—at
high elevation, the grass yellow-green with plenty of shady trees.
There we were told we would be on solo for two days, or maybe
three: in complete isolation in the woods. This didn't intimidate
me. After so many weeks of traveling in a group with no privacy,
the idea of a little solitude was appealing.

I was camped on a grassy hillside, with a fallen white aspen tree that served as a perfect bench for sitting. They had given me a copy of *Alcoholics Anonymous* and a workbook; plus, I had two blank stenographer's pads to fill up.

I wrote.

I read the AA book from cover to cover, then read it again. I built a fire. I sang songs to myself, strange wordless lullabies to snatches of melodies. I walked to the top of the hill and surveyed the landscape. I could see gray smoke rising in the distance where someone else had taken shelter.

I wrote letters to my father and my mother, who each had sent me several more pieces of correspondence.

My father's, again, had infuriated me; he had described my recollections of sexual abuse as "very troubling," and then, one sentence later, began discussing the marathon that he and Jennifer were preparing for. He had vacated the apartment where we'd lived for the past two years, he wrote, and was now living full-time with her.

How could he gloss over my pain? I wrote in reply that I was excited to hear about his marathon, and that I was glad he'd been able to move out of the apartment on Eighty-eighth Street, and that I hoped Jennifer was well.

All lies.

It seemed strange to imagine my father going about his life just as he had before: bicycling through the park, picking up takeout, waiting for the subway. I wondered how much they told him about how I was doing, and what the progress reports from Kathianne revealed. I thought of how I'd looked on the day of my graduation, the day he sent me away—shiny black shoes, crisp black suit. Now, in my well-worn fatigues, covered in dirt, I was an urchin.

The two days passed, and I returned to camp with the rest of the group, unfazed. Eric seemed swoony.

"I didn't think I could do it," he said. "But I did. It really makes you think about, y'know, the choices you've made and where things went wrong."

Justin, too, seemed altered. "Man, I thought I was going to go crazy toward the end of the first day," he said. "Just pacing back and forth, stuck in my head. I had no idea how hard it would be." I tried to read both of their faces, to see whether they were performing it for the counselors' benefit, but they both looked sincere.

"How was it out there, Sam?" Medeina asked. "All alone, with nothing but your thoughts?"

"It was fine," I said. "All good."

Medeina and JT exchanged a look.

"That's it?" JT said.

I shrugged. I wasn't trying to be deliberately blasé, but I didn't want to fake it, either. I didn't know why whatever effect solos were supposed to have hadn't worked with me.

One night later, at the campfire, we were just finishing dinner when JT tapped me on my shoulder. On carts, we could carry more food with us, which meant better meals: the previous drop had included a pound of bacon. We cooked it in a skillet over the fire, then made macaroni and cheese. Normally, that was beyond our ken since we had no milk or butter; here, we poured the bacon fat into the macaroni and cheese with a half cup of powdered milk. It was delicious, the noodles greasy and smoky and decadent.

"Follow me," JT whispered in my ear. "Bring a thermal." I dropped my blue spackled tin cup by the side of the fire, returned to my shelter to grab a warm layer, and met him back at the center of camp. The other boys looked confused. I raised my hands—I was as bewildered as they were.

I followed him up into the forest, the bobbing beam of his flashlight marking a tenuous path through the trees. I stumbled over the gnarled roots of aspen trees, with their distinctive oviform markings like eyes. In the shadows of the night, the exposed roots looked like ghostly tentacles. After what felt like hours, we stopped in a clearing. There was only darkness around us, and eerie silence. He dropped his flashlight onto the ground, then knelt. I heard the whistling of his bow drill and then, quickly, the neon glow of embers.

"Blow this into a fire," he said, "and keep it burning all night. If it goes out, you fail the test."

And then, in a ballet of hushed footsteps, he was gone, and I was left in the night with only the flickering flame and nothing but darkness around me.

"Oh God," I said out loud. "Oh God."

I was alone, and it was dark, and I couldn't have found my way back to camp if I tried. There was truly no way out, not even the security that I'd felt on solo, of knowing approximately where the other boys were, of being able to crawl into my shelter after the sun went down. I was *alone*. The aloneness spread through me until it felt like it was possessing my body. I gazed into the inky beyond. A gust of air galloped through the clearing, and the hairs on my arm stood up on end, saluting the night. The fleece of my thermal stiffened against my sunken chest. I could feel the drumming of my quickening pulse. Dread prickled at the nape of my neck.

I got onto my hands and knees and blew into the fire, a bud of orange-blue flame now waning in a wispy nest of dried grass. Mercifully, it grew. Twigs and bark fueled its strength, but there weren't enough pieces within arms' reach. I stood and hurtled forward into the darkness, tripping over my clumsy limbs, groping madly for kindling. I snapped a branch off a tree and tossed it into the fire, spraying embers to and fro. Pain needled in my eyes. The wind scattered embers and ash all over the clearing.

Good, I thought. Some rage turned white-hot within me. I wanted to burn down the forest, burn down every lying teenage dream that I'd been stupid enough to have.

Then, as the fire waned, I began to cry. I sobbed and blew ashes everywhere, and the world crumpled around me—there was nothing but my breath. How many minutes had it been? How long would I be out there, alone in the darkness?

"I can't do this!" I shouted into the empty night. "I can't do this."

I could hear my hysteria escalating, feel my heartbeat rising, but it didn't matter—there was no one around.

"How the fuck did I end up here?" I shouted. "What am I doing here?"

And then, instantaneously, my tears stopped. The night was still.

"God," I murmured. "Please help me. Please see me through this." I hadn't prayed since the first night in the wilderness, and even that prayer had been half ironic, a plea for catastrophe to befall me. But this prayer was sincere. And as I prayed, I felt a calm settling—not the presence of God, in whom I didn't really believe, but the presence of some notional feeling that I wasn't entirely alone out there after all.

I counted the minutes until morning, blowing into the fire to keep it alive.

Then, at daybreak, there was a rustling behind me. I turned slowly and stared into the watery umber eyes of a fawn. Her ears perked up as she studied me. I inhaled and exhaled slowly and deliberately. She looked at me for a long time until I realized that I'd forgotten the fire. I turned back to blow in it to keep it going, and when I turned back around, the fawn was gone.

When JT came back for me, the sun now shining brightly over the forest, I was dumbfounded and motionless, the fire still shuddering a sooty pile at my feet.

"You did it," he said, with something like pride.

I looked up at him. I felt a new vitality coursing through me. I was *different*.

He led me back down to camp, where the boys were gathered around the fire pit, eating breakfast. Eric looked at me funny.

I could feel it in my movements—I was standing up straighter. Things were graver.

I knew myself, knew what I was capable of.

"You aren't a Coyote anymore," Medeina said. "You're a Buffalo."

In my previous life, this would have been laughable, but Medeina was serious. She touched my arm. The moment felt sacred.

"Yes," I said. "I am a Buffalo."

Things changed after that, some division between me and the rest of the group. We weren't in it together anymore; I was separate from them. Even Eric, with whom I'd grown so close, felt like a stranger to me, like I had waded in over my head. I could still see my friends on the shore, but they were too distant to touch.

By this point, more boys had joined the group—first as Mouse, sitting silently, gnawing on their peanuts and raisins, then howling triumphantly at the moon. I didn't get close to any of them—I didn't know quite how to relate. Their brusque resistance and occasional good cheer, both of which had been my primary modes just days before, felt altogether foreign.

When we were at camp, I stayed in my shelter, journaling. I cried several times a day. I prayed feverishly, begging anything that might resemble God to take my pain away. Over and over again in my notepad I wrote: "There is only clean, there is no in between," a paraphrase of a line from an Elliott Smith song I had always loved but never really understood.

So, I decided, if part of the purpose of Aspen was to strip away the ego and defenses, that piece had worked. I felt vulnerable, cut open: a mass of exposed nerve and tissue, all tender to the touch. All the ways I'd medicated—from the drugs all the way down to sarcasm—had been taken from me, but nothing had been resolved. I was just as sick as I'd ever been, but I had no medicine; everything hurt all the time.

I didn't know what I was going to do about it, or how I could possibly be fixed.

Neither did Kathianne.

When she came for her weekly visit after I had been in the field for about six weeks, she told me that my parents were working on formulating an aftercare plan—determining where, exactly, I would go once I left.

"I think your work here is almost done," she said softly. "You're ready to move on to the next thing."

"But where?" I asked.

"We'll see," she said. "First, you'll go to the graduation week. Your family will be there."

I grimaced. We were so fractured.

"I'm not ready for that," I said. "I mean, I'm ready to go, but I'm not ready to see them. They're going to be disappointed by where I'm at."

"Why do you say that?" she asked.

"I just— I know them," I said. "I know my dad. He expected me to come out of this fixed. That's what it was supposed to be—a fix, somewhere he could send me off to and they'd return me all better. And I'm not. I feel so ugly. So messed up. Who wants to see that in their kid?"

"I know you don't feel ready, but I think it's time," she said.

A few days later, in our morning meeting by the camp-fire, Medeina abruptly announced: "Sam, this is your good-bye group." I looked up at her, startled. "They'll be coming to take you to grad week in about an hour."

Slowly, methodically, each member of the group said a few words; the mood was elegiac. It was as though I were attending my own funeral.

"Dude," Eric said, "it's been you and me from the beginning." His voice cracked. "I hope you can get out of all of these rehabs."

I didn't cry until Medeina began to speak. "You and I both know what my greatest concern for you is," she said. "Be mindful of the signs."

She gripped my hand and I wept openly. I didn't want to leave, didn't want to face my parents, didn't want to know where I would ultimately land, and I was puzzled by that feeling, so counterin-tuitive. On some level, I must have known that the person I had become at Aspen—serious and independent and unguarded—couldn't possibly translate into the real world. The quiet rhythms of my daily routine, the certainty of the sun rising and setting—it was so soothing in the narrowness of its scope. Real life was com-plicated, messy, unpredictable. Paradoxically, it was the natural world that felt artificial. I wanted to take a hot shower, wear real clothes, smoke a cigarette, call my friends, but more than any of that, I wanted to stay in a place where the variables were all known.

But I couldn't. I cried again as I left the campsite, fiercely hugging the other boys good-bye, though I couldn't even remember their names today. And I sat silently in the passenger seat as a man with a beard drove me away from camp in a pickup truck, through the white aspen trees and the hot red-rock desert, not knowing where I was going.

As it turned out, grad week wasn't so different from the weeks that had preceded it—the main difference being that this was a new crop of kids, the graduates from all of the other groups. There were girls, too, a development that the other boys found exciting.

On a dusty new terrain several miles from where I'd spent the past seven weeks at Aspen, we hiked for a few days, the focus of therapy now shifting onto our families. I felt detached from this upcoming rite of passage; there was a low-level, distant concern for where I would go and what I would do, but there wasn't much more to it than that. Other kids had already been told that they were being placed into therapeutic boarding schools, but that wasn't an option for me: I had already completed high school, and I was nearly eighteen—too old for an adolescent program. But I also knew that it was likely that I needed more treatment, both because Kathianne had told me so and because I felt it—like a broken bone that had yet to completely heal.

I knew this would disappoint my father, even as I still bubbled with hot rage for how he'd sent me away in the first place.

There could be no way to explain to him the holy moment I'd had with a deer at sunrise in the middle of the woods, the triumph of building a fire with my own two hands—and yet I couldn't take any of that with me, not really. All those accomplishments, but his disapproval could override any sense of having made progress.

I immediately picked out a girl named Laurel as the other most interesting person in our group. She rattled off her addictive behaviors in a long list, her affect flat and humorless—"Alcohol, cocaine, crystal meth, bulimia, truancy, prostitution," she said. She was from Staten Island, and although that was a world apart from the city I knew, there was a toughness to her that I associated with New Yorkers. Her stringy brown hair was pulled back, so matted with sweat and dirt it looked marbled; the girls, too, wore sack-like tan khakis; her skin was caramel-hued and crusted with the same permadirt.

Laurel had almond eyes and freckles and a guileless smile (albeit with yellowing teeth), and even at seventeen, she bore the physical trappings of having endured some profound trauma. (I could almost imagine my mother sizing her up and saying, "She looks like she's had a hard life," in that theatrical way that I loved.) Somehow, Laurel seemed fundamentally broken: even the way she walked was like a marionette with twisted strings, every step a shudder.

Perhaps I liked her because I could see that she was even more damaged than I was, or perhaps we had more in common than I could even see at the time. We were pushing up a hill together on the third day, the sweat unremitting on our faces, and I could see that she was close to breaking. I touched her arm. Her eyes were dark and empty.

"We're not doing it for them," I said. "We're doing it for all the men who have hurt us."

She looked at me with awe. "How did you know?" she whispered. I wondered if it was the first time anyone had seen her as a victim rather than as the instigator of chaos and conflict.

Over the fire, we talked quietly about her past. She told me that she had been a crack whore—literally, she said, she had rented her body for crack cocaine. I'd hustled older guys for drugs or money, too, but something about the starkness of her admission made me want to rescue her. Because of its colloquial popularity, the term "crack whore" had assumed a larger-than-life lexicographical mythology, and so it was almost hard for me to swallow the reality that there were *real* crack whores, let alone seventeen-year-old ones who might cross my path. Before she had come to Aspen, she said, her pimp had kicked her in the face with a steel-toed boot and shattered her jaw. Desperate, Laurel's parents sent her to Utah.

"Just stay close to me," I said. "We'll get through it together."

A therapist led us through a psychodrama workshop where we re-created our family dynamics, acting out the parts of our parents; I rolled my eyes through it. A conversation about relapse prevention focused on peer pressure felt impressively far removed from anything I knew would be my reality.

"I'm not worried about my friends pressuring me to get high,"

I said under my breath to Laurel. "What am I supposed to do when I'm bored and alone and empty and some guy I used to bang texts me that he just bought an eight ball?"

She shrugged. She didn't know any better than I did. It was so clear: our triumphs in the wilderness existed only for the wilderness.

On the fourth day, we were led into the field and blindfolded. After several minutes, where I could make out rustling and some quiet conversation, I heard the blast of a bullhorn. We removed our blindfolds and turned around.

Our parents were waiting there, a few hundred yards away.

"Run!" someone yelped.

The other kids began sprinting toward the crowd—they were doing it to embarrass me, surely. I resented their eagerness, their willingness to forgive, and envied them, too—all I felt toward my parents was a dull apathy.

I walked slowly and deliberately. I could see my mother and father standing together, scanning the crowd of runners for me— then they spotted me, the lone straggler. I twisted my face into a grim smile.

I hugged my mother first, then my father.

"Oh, sweetheart," my mother said.

"Why weren't you running?" my father asked.

I shrugged. "I don't know," I said. I looked around at the other families—they were crying, jubilant, so happy to be reunited.

What is wrong with us? I wondered. *What is* still *wrong with me?*

We met with Kathianne, who, it seemed, had been expecting a level of catharsis that wasn't in play. The main question on my mind was still where I would go from Aspen—what the aftercare program was. A week earlier, Kathianne had said that another thirty days in a program specifically designed to treat drug addiction, as opposed to behavioral issues, would be appropriate, and while that didn't sound attractive to me, I didn't have any better ideas. She had promised that the plan would be revealed when my parents came, and I was ready.

"So have you figured out where I'm going?" I asked.

"Well," my mother said carefully, eyeing Kathianne, "we're not exactly sure yet."

"What?" I was flabbergasted. "I've been out here for two months. You haven't come up with anything?"

"Honey," my mother said. She had her mental health professional voice on, calm and clear. "It doesn't look like any of the adolescent treatment programs are what you need right now. Your issues are too . . . too advanced, too specific. We can send you to a boarding school to do a postgrad year—"

"I'm not doing that," I said. "I'm supposed to go to college."

"I've called every adult rehab in the country," my mother said. "None of them will take you. You're underage. It's a liability for them. Basically, you're too old for the programs for teenagers and not old enough for the programs for adults."

"That wasn't my responsibility," I said. I could hear the old anger creeping back in. For the first time in weeks, I sounded like myself again. Bitter, spiteful, bratty. I heard those notes in my voice, but I didn't know how to control it. "My responsibility was to come out here, hike ten miles a day, talk about my feelings, and shit in the woods. Your responsibility was to fulfill the *relatively minor task* of finding somewhere to go from here that might actually help me *get better*."

"We really tried, sweetheart," my mother said.

"Jesus," I said. "Give me a working phone and *I'll* do it."

I kept waiting for Kathianne to interject, but she just sat back, watching the spectacle.

"And you," I said, turning to my father. "Have you made any progress on this front?"

He shook his head.

"Busy with Jennifer? Having a nice summer?"

He looked pained. "I have thought of you every day since you've been gone," he said.

"Too little, too late," I said. "Maybe if you had paid an *iota* of attention to me while I was actually *living with you*, I wouldn't have ended up here."

I had been wanting to say this for months, dying to say it, and it felt so gratifying to purge it from my body. I could see that I was hurting him, and I didn't care. Never mind that he had been trying to reach me in his own way—that I had been the one deliberately diverting his attention away from my downward spiral. I couldn't feel anything bigger than this flashing, irrational rage. In it, I felt powerful once more.

"I don't know if there's any parent who could have given you what you needed," my father said.

"You're probably right, Dad," I said. "But would it have *killed* you to try?"

His face fell. Horror filled me, at how ugly all this was, at how little I'd actually changed, and how good it felt.

The program hadn't worked.

Late that night, I was awakened by one of the counselors shaking me. "Get up," he whispered.

I crawled out of my shelter and pulled on my pants, quickly tying my laces and rising to my feet. Through the campground, past makeshift tents and spindly trees, I followed his flashlight.

This gimmick worked better the first time, I thought.

In a wide clearing, there were two clusters of people: in the first were my parents, with two other sets of adults; then Laurel and another boy stood perhaps a dozen yards away. I joined them, raising a hand in greeting to my parents.

"This is your Eagle ceremony," a counselor said. His voice boomed. "You are being inducted into the next level of achievement because of your hard work and dedication to the principles of this program."

I reached for Laurel's hand.

Then, as if by magic, a circle of flames ignited around us, roaring and crackling. I could smell gasoline. It lit up the clearing, casting shadows across my parents' faces; I could see them through the fire.

"Congratulations on your accomplishments," the counselor said. Laurel gripped my hand tightly. I looked across at my mother and father. I didn't want them here, observing this ritual; I wanted it to feel as sacred as it had felt when I was alone in the woods. Their presence cheapened it, reminding me of the world outside—the world that had hardly existed for months, the world to which I would soon return. And the person I would become once I had to go back to it.

I wanted to cry, but I blinked back the tears. I held my face up to the sky, letting the heat of the flame warm me. I tried to look strong and proud. I stared at the fire until my vision went blurry.

—

Eventually, we decided—or, rather, my father decided—that I should travel to Portland with my mother for a few days while they figured out where I would go next. I was booked on the same departing flight as she was. On the final day, we were shuttled back to base camp, where there was a celebratory barbecue with both patients and parents.

I asked my mother whether she could take me back to the hotel in Loa where she was staying instead, and she agreed. It was strange to see buildings, a town—even such a small one, which suddenly felt like the apex of all civilization. Paved roads. People in real clothes. Automobiles.

In the hotel room, I opened my duffel bag, the contents of which I hadn't seen for two months. There was the cashmere sweater I had packed foolishly, the David Yurman chain I had received as a graduation gift from Jennifer. I had no sensible clothes, nothing to wear except the filthy uniform I had been living in.

I stripped naked and studied myself in the mirror. My facial hair had grown in patchy and irregular. I was sunburned and lean. My skin was a strange color from the dirt that I hadn't been able to wash off. Burnt sienna.

Who was I?

I ran the shower and stood in it for the better part of an hour. The water that spiraled down the drain was black as ink. I waited until it ran clear, turning the heat up, scrubbing until my skin was raw.

"There is only clean," I whispered. "There is no in between."

Eight

*E*verything was heightened: the smell of exhaust fumes at a gas station were noxious, going straight to my head; the yogurt pretzels I grabbed from a convenience store were so sweet they made my mouth fill up with spit; a first cup of coffee had me feeling warm and bright in a way caffeine hadn't in ages.

Stopped for a bathroom break somewhere outside Provo, I booted up my laptop, combing through two months of emails. Here was a message from Dean, asking how I had been: "Igby. I dreamed of you last night."

A note from Evan, whom my father had called to explain where I'd gone: "When the big house lets you run free and clear," he wrote, "give me a call—because memory, it can only thrive for so long before I start craving the real deal."

And a message from Kat: "I'm just going to keep emailing you in hopes that one day when you're home I'll see your name in my inbox."

I closed my computer. It was too overwhelming. I felt seasick. In my pocket was my top rock. I ran my fingers over its indentations, the round dark hole in its center that my spindle had worn into it.

It left my fingers covered with a fine soot, powdery as cocaine.

Back in Portland, my mother continued her efforts to find a program that would take me. I heard her in her office as I walked past, pleading on the phone to intake officers, explaining that I would be eighteen in just a few short months, I was a high school graduate, I wasn't a good fit for adolescent programs. "Please," I heard her in snippets, "please. My son . . . nowhere to go . . . poly-drug and sexual acting out." She didn't sound desperate, just resigned.

I found a pack of cigarettes I had stashed in my bedroom and sat on the steps that led down from my brother's room to the garden and smoked. It didn't occur to me that I should stay quit—from that, at least.

Kat picked me up the afternoon after I got back, hugging me warmly. "You look *so* weird," she said.

"How?"

"I dunno," she said. "Like, *normal.*"

Being on drugs all the time had given me a sickly pallor—now, lean and toned from months out in the woods and sunshine, I looked healthy for the first time in years. I hardly recognized myself.

Downtown, we parked at a coffee shop. It was July now, and all my friends would be celebrating their last weeks before heading off to college, while I was on a brief hiatus between stints in rehab. I envied them their freedom. That jealousy burned bitter in my throat.

What did sober people do? I wondered. It seemed peculiar, the idea that I would go about each day with total clarity—and, the more I thought about it, unattractive. I was still so young. Too young to be quitting everything. And back in Portland, where it all had begun, there were so many trigger points. As I walked up the busy street toward a department store, there was the bench where I had sat with Jim for the first time. I had been so young, so stupid. The memory made my palms sweat.

But moreover, I reasoned, there was no point in staying sober now if I was just going back to rehab in a few days. If I were back in Utah, sure, I could stay sober, but that environment had been artificial. The real world was fraught with temptation, and I had no defense—but I knew I would *find* one.

Just not quite yet.

"Do you have any Adderall?" I asked Kat. She looked startled.

"At home," she said. "But aren't you— Wasn't the whole point of this to stop, like, doing that?"

"I have to go somewhere else, like, tomorrow," I said. "I might as well enjoy myself while I'm out."

"But haven't you been clean for two months? Do you really want to give that up?"

"The success rate for wilderness programs is abysmal," I said. (I had looked it up after I'd gotten home, to use in situations just like this.)

"Why?"

"Because it doesn't fucking work, Kat," I said, surprised at my own sudden anger at her. "Okay? It doesn't fucking work."

"I'm sorry," she said softly.

We chopped up lines of Adderall in her bedroom and snorted it. As that familiar euphoria flooded my body, I felt no twinge of guilt.

"I deserve this," I said to Kat, feeling powerful again. "I deserve to be happy."

"Whatever you say," she said, but I could see the disappointment in her eyes. Yet another person I had let down.

—————

Finally, after several days of placing phone calls, my mother got a hit on an adult rehab in Tennessee. It was called, clumsily, the Bridge to Progress.

"It's the low-budget Betty Ford of Appalachia," she said enthusiastically. I looked at pictures online: the bridge, it seemed, wasn't just a metaphor but also an *actual* bridge that was visible in their promotional photos, wooden slats leading over a creek that cut through the campus.

"It looks nice," I said flatly.

"They specialize in treating cross-addiction," my mother said. "Sort of a holistic approach." She looked at me. Her voice carried the measured clinical detachment that she had spent years practicing, but her eyes looked so helpless. "That's what you need, right? Something that treats not only the chemical dependency issues but also the sexual dysfunction, PTSD, inappropriate attachments . . ." She trailed off.

"I don't think I have any chance of staying sober unless I deal with the root issues," I said. This was true.

"They can take you on Thursday," she said, clicking open the calendar on her computer. "If you'll go."

"I'll go," I said.

———

The program was outside of Chattanooga, on several acres of sprawling grassland, rolling hills, and forested land that didn't look unlike Oregon. After two months in the wilderness, even the thin institutional sheets on my twin bed felt luxurious, and I was just happy to be eating the morning's rations of biscuits and gravy with a side of cheese grits with a utensil that wasn't a stick.

We held morning meetings in a lodge built out of thick wooden logs. The clinical director of the program was a self-help guru named Debbie Dixon; she had a cartoonishly sculpted bouffant and the steely but kind bearing of someone who had spent her entire career talking crazy people off a ledge. She'd written a book called *Pain No More* about how the roots of addiction were in codependence, its title scrawled in cursive on the sickly pea-green cover. We each received a copy, as reliable as a Gideon Bible. I unpacked my clothes in a shabby white dresser in the bedroom, but everything I owned felt baggy on my frame, which had grown lean and muscular in Utah, those months I'd spent hiking all day.

Too bad, I thought, that there was no one in Tennessee to appreciate it.

My roommate was a career alcoholic from Knoxville named Frank Bacardi who had careened into a family of four on the freeway, driving drunk. He'd been spared jail time if he agreed to inpatient rehab. From a distance he was an Adonis, but at night, after he had stripped away the foundation he wore, I saw that his handsome face was mottled with acne scars. He was effeminate in a way I found threatening, and though he treated me with a cool dispassion, I could sense his curiosity about me.

Our days were spent in sessions that felt more like a corporate seminar than actual group therapy, slideshows and lectures that included liberal excerpts from *Pain No More*.

"Any substance or process which distracts you from your highest self," Debbie explained, presiding over the assembled group with a sage, grandmotherly authority, "—that's alcohol, drugs, spending, sex, compulsive overeating, obsessing over romantic relations—is unsober."

I resented this, even as I helped myself to a third serving of chicken-fried steak in the cafeteria, trying to fill up an emptiness that continued to gnaw at me while I idly worried that I'd lose the muscle tone I'd developed in Utah. I wondered whether the type of sobriety that Debbie described was even attainable. It didn't feel very realistic.

The campus was nicotine-free, but I smelled cigarettes on Frank's breath one afternoon; it made me clench my fists.

"Have you been smoking?" I asked him. He pulled me in for a conspiratorial whisper.

"I'll give you one if you don't tell," he said. On our next break,

I followed him down a dirt path to a covered spot underneath the bridge, obscured from view. I lit one of his Marlboro Lights and inhaled rapturously. There was something symbolic about us breaking the rules to smoke cigarettes *under* the literal bridge to progress.

Each afternoon, we loaded up into a white van—the druggy buggy, Frank called it, with a roll of his eyes—and were driven to twelve-step meetings in the town of Chattanooga. The other attendees were grizzled, older—straight white dudes crowded into church basements that smelled like stale cigarettes. Frank pointed to the only other young person in the room, a lean blond boy.

"See that little twink?" he whispered. "I blew him in the bathroom last week." He looked at me, expecting a reaction. I shrugged.

"Not my type," I said.

"Oh?"

"Find me an old drunk with family money," I whispered. "Then let's talk."

He laughed loudly. Heads turned in our direction.

Lying in bed that night, I saw a blue light glowing from the other side of the room, where Frank slept. I stood and crept around the corner to look closer. He had a laptop computer open. I cleared my throat and he looked up.

"We aren't allowed to have those," I said.

"You gonna narc on me?" he said playfully. He tilted the screen so I could see; he was watching porn. His hand worked under the sheets.

"No," I said.

"Come here," he said. I stood paralyzed for a moment, feeling a heat inside me rise. "Come here." He lifted the sheet, exposing himself to me. My pulse quickened. I hadn't slept with anyone during the few days I was back in Portland; I hadn't been with anyone since before I'd left for wilderness, which felt like an eternity. I'd half resigned myself to celibacy.

"Um," I said.

I saw him grinning in the darkness. "You want to?" he asked.

Oh well, I thought as I crawled into his bed. *Old habits die hard.*

Frank had already left for breakfast when I woke up in the morning. I showered and headed to the main lodge. He was sitting with two other patients, picking at corn bread; he stared at me as I walked in, and I could feel his discomfort radiating from across the room.

I cornered him before we headed into group. "You don't have to make this awkward," I said. "I'm not trying to date you. We were just having fun."

"It's fine," he said, bypassing me.

Later, in group, I sat fidgeting with my notebook as Debbie droned on about forms of acting out. If I'd been at a more conventional rehab that just dealt with drugs, that would have been one thing, but I'd gone to treatment specifically to deal with *all* of the issues, including—as my mother had come to call it—"sexual acting out."

What kind of progress could I possibly expect to make if I was sleeping with my roommate while in treatment? If my time in the wilderness had taught me nothing else, it was at least to be honest, even when it was uncomfortable; there could be no growth if I wasn't transparent. I *did* want to develop self-restraint, the ability to say no. I resolved to tell the staff what had happened; surely, I thought, they would let me switch rooms to eliminate the temptation.

And so, later that day, I met with Debbie in her office and told her that something inappropriate had happened between me and Frank. "Maybe you could move me to a single room," I said helpfully.

She made a low humming noise that sounded like thoughtful deliberation and cocked her head, her hair tipping perilously.

"I'm just not sure, Sam," she said.

"Not sure about what?"

"Well," she said, "this is more of a secondary program that we provide here—we're not equipped to handle *acute* issues."

"There's really nothing acute about it," I said. "I just— I fucked up, I guess."

She made the humming noise again. "If you had come here with a drug problem, and then you had *used* drugs while on campus, we would send you off-site, to a detox facility. Do you see what I mean?"

"Sort of," I said.

"I'm just not sure that we can provide you with the level of care that you *need*," she said.

"I think I've been doing great otherwise," I said. "I just think maybe it would be best if I, you know. Moved to another room."

She wasn't getting it.

"I know of a *great* program that can help with sexual issues," she said. "In New Orleans."

"New Orleans," I repeated.

"New Orleans!" she said cheerfully. "Have you been?"

"No."

"You'll love it," she said, reaching for her phone. "I can make a call and see if we can get you in for treatment there."

"So, wait," I said, processing. "I have to leave to go to some program in New Orleans? Does Frank have to leave, too?"

"Frank has been here for thirty-five days," she said patiently. "You've been here for—four days, I think? Or five? He's been making wonderful progress, without incident. And you get here, and, well . . ." She motioned at nothing. "*This* happens."

I pulled at the hair on my arm anxiously. "What if I want to stay?" I said. "Are you just kicking me out?"

"No!" Debbie said. "Not at all." She looked at me kindly. "I'm just asking you to leave."

———

The program they were referring me to was the sexual trauma and compulsions unit at a psychiatric hospital called River Oaks; it looked considerably more drab than the style of the Bridge. Debbie had called my parents and told them what had happened—I didn't want to know how she had managed to sell them on a unit in a psych ward.

I had a sneaking feeling that the cost of my stay had been prepaid and was nonrefundable, but I couldn't think about that—there were more pressing issues.

I walked along the road that led away from campus, tears stinging in my eyes, but I would not cry. I lit a cigarette I had stolen from Frank's dresser and called my father.

"I'm going to come down south and pick you up," he said with a sort of practiced even keel, though I could hear anger simmering just below. "It'll be nice. We'll drive from Tennessee to Nola. A little road trip."

"Okay," I said in a small voice.

"There's a famous ribs place in Tuscaloosa," he said. "I've wanted to try it my whole life." I could hear him softening a bit. "I had hoped that we would be able to spend some time together this summer. I was going to get a rental in the Hamptons. But maybe this is the perfect opportunity."

"That's nice," I said miserably. "You probably didn't think the conditions would be driving me to a new rehab after I got kicked out of the last one."

"No," he said crisply. "I did not."

Once it had been decided that I was leaving, the staff at the Bridge were in a hurry to usher me out. The next day's activities involved a day trip to Nashville; they dropped me off there, at a busy shopping street downtown. I stood on the side of the road with my duffel bag and waved good-bye to the new friends I had made as the van sped away.

Six days, I thought. *I only made it six days.*

I wandered into a department store and listlessly bought a sweater.

When my father pulled up an hour later, I was standing on the street with shopping bags. I could see his disappointment in my impulsiveness.

My frivolousness.

My inability to stick with anything.

"Let's go, kiddo," he said.

We took the freeway as far as Birmingham, then turned onto a winding country road. The summer was lush and humid, the road expansive and sun-dappled, and I thought back to previous adventures: the drive to Princeton nearly a year earlier. My future had felt so full of promise, hadn't it? Driving through southern Oregon with Seth—that had been only four months ago—high and happy, warm and loved.

I didn't know why things had taken such a sharp turn. It wasn't part of the plan.

We stopped for those ribs in Tuscaloosa, at a squat red building with posters on the wall and big Budweiser signs. I craved a beer, though I didn't even like it. We stayed at a roadside motel, and I sat on the curb while my father slept, chain-smoking, dreaming of New York nights, the heady rush and spin of nightclubs, sex with strangers, the freedom of being desired.

"How long will they make me stay?" I asked my father. He kept his eyes on the road.

"I don't know," he said. "Maybe a few weeks."

"College starts soon, though," I said. I was still planning on going to Vassar, though I hadn't even bothered to visit the campus before applying. It was just the most prestigious school that had accepted me.

He shot me a look. "You still want to go?"

I shrugged. It had been too difficult to think about it as a real possibility when I had been in the wilderness; I had been focused on the immediate future, getting through each day. But I was out—even if I was just en route from one rehab to the next—and it was close enough now that I could consider it as an option.

"I want to go eventually," I said.

"Of course," he said smoothly. "But I think you should defer a year. Or a semester, at the very least. That would give you some time to get everything in order. Save up some money."

"Why would I have to save up money?" I said.

He looked over at me again. I saw something in his body language: he was nervous.

"That's part of why I wanted to come down here," he said. "We need to talk about that. College."

"What is there to talk about?"

He hesitated. "Jennifer and I have discussed it, and—given

the shape of this summer and how unpredictable your behavior has been—well, I can't stop you from going to Vassar if that's what you really want, and if you think you're ready for it. But"—he hesitated again—"I'm not going to pay for it."

My stomach dropped out. "What?"

"If you want to finance it yourself," he said, "that's fine by me. But the money I had set aside for you to go to school—I spent that on Aspen."

"I didn't even want to *go* to Aspen," I said.

"I know that," he said. "But I was acting in your best interest."

"It was a waste of money," I said. "It didn't do anything. How much did it cost—thirty-five thousand dollars? And for what? All it did was get me ready for *more* rehab."

"Well, I didn't realize that was going to be the outcome," he said.

I was furious. "And you spring this on me when I'm *so* vulnerable."

"Sam," he said, "after this program, the one in New Orleans—that's it. I'm done helping you."

"No," I said. "I get it. I know I've been an expensive project." I crossed my arms. He didn't say anything. I could feel his tension and uncertainty. Maybe if I said the right thing I could convince him.

"You know, Dad," I said, "I have a *lot* of friends with problems. I have a *lot* of friends who have been to rehab and back again. Most of them ended up there because their parents don't give a shit about them. But at least they have the decency to keep paying for the mess they made."

"I love you," he said. "You know that."

"I know you do," I said. "I'm not arguing that point." I struggled for words. I wanted to get this right. "Things would have gone differently if you had *been* there. For me. Maybe all of this wouldn't be happening."

"Your problems are not my fault," he said. "You have to take responsibility."

"I'm not saying they are," I said. "I *am* saying that you were completely fucking negligent, and I ended up ruining my life. The least you could do is foot the bill."

"I'm paying for your treatment," he said helplessly. "I'm not going to spend tens of thousands of dollars on an education that I can't be sure you'll even show up for."

"Can't we just see how the first semester goes?" I said.

He sighed and rubbed his temples. The sun was blinding. "Let's talk about it once you're out of this program," he said. "You may end up seeing this differently." He brightened. "This could be a really great opportunity for you to take more ownership for your future. It could be empowering!"

I resented this attempt at spinning it into a positive most of all. I leaned my head against the window. I wanted to get away from him, to get away from everyone.

Maybe a stint in a psych ward was just what I needed.

Angela looked a little bit like Teri Hatcher, her face gaunt and tight against her keen cheekbones, and she was engaging in one of her addictive behaviors. She sat crisscross-applesauce on the bedraggled sofa in the common room, the sleeves of her cardigan rolled up messily to reveal the mutilated skin along her forearms. She was scratching her arms with gnawed fingernails, and the scratching was loud against the heavy silence.

She's not supposed to be doing that, I thought.

"There's something wrong with Angela," I said to Joni. Joni nodded. Her left eye twitched.

"That's one of her addictive behaviors," Joni said.

"We have to stop her," I said.

The therapeutic staff kept on saying that I was lucky to be there, since River Oaks didn't admit patients under eighteen and I wouldn't be eighteen until the following month.

Eighteen.

I repeated the number over and over again as I lay in my bed. I would be an adult. I would be free. No, I would never be free.

But River Oaks had the best program for sexual trauma and compulsion in the country. Lucky.

Joni stood up awkwardly and rested her weight on the metal frame of her walker. She was forty-seven, she said, and she was a hunchbacked Sisyphus, pushing her walker in laborious strides as though defeated by its staggering weight. She looked splintered. She had been raped in a parking garage, she told us during process group, and then she got hooked on Oxy-Contin and turned tricks for a while, and at a certain point she didn't walk right anymore. Maybe she'd said why. Was there an accident? I couldn't remember. They put me on Trazodone after my intake exam, for sleep and depression, but it had made things so fuzzy.

"We should get the nurse," I said.

In group, we described our feelings by transmuting them into a tangible object. We gave them shape, color, and definition.

"My self-loathing is a black cube," I said.

The clinician, Melissa, smiled warmly. "Tell us more about it," she said. I closed my eyes.

"Shiny black like what you see under your eyelids when you're trying to fall asleep but you can't," I said. "It sits in the pit of my stomach, and its edges are cutting me from the inside."

I belong here, I thought. *I'm really good at this. Maybe better at this than I've ever been at anything before.*

That thought troubled me.

"I wanna get high," I said. "I wanna get fucked up."

"Why?" she asked.

"Because I have too many feelings and they're all too much for me all the time and drugs take them away so I don't have to feel anything," I said. "Why do I have to feel so many things?"

And then the med nurse gave me an Ativan and I couldn't remember anything after that.

Joni pressed her palm against the top of Angela's head. Joni was a shaman and her hand was noiselessly vacuuming up the pain,

through the top of Angela's skull and upward, away. Angela rocked
back and forth. She moaned.

"Angela," I said. "Name your addictive behaviors."

Angela stopped scratching. Her arms were slung in repose.
A vermilion lattice of blood was sketched on her arms, shining.
"Um. Prescription drug abuse. Unmanaged dissociation. Self-
mutilation. Euphoric recall. Suicidal ideation. I can't remember
any more."

Joni looked at me. "What do we do?"

I shrugged and wiggled my toes in my slip-ons. I had bought
those in Nashville, too. My father had dropped me off at the
nurse's station with my suitcase and sped off into the bayou, just
disappeared like a ghost. They took all the shoes that had laces.
They took my mouthwash, my cologne. A sweatshirt with the
elastic cord in my hood. Risperdal, administered orally, dissolved
into a grainy mash of periwinkle sleep under my tongue.

—————

Later, we were out on the terrace smoking. Joni and Angela
and me. A clinician stood by the door with a cigarette lighter;
we weren't allowed to have those, either. I was smoking menthols because everyone there smoked menthols. It was all women
at that hospital. I was the only man in the program, which
wasn't unusual for sexual trauma and compulsion units, they
told me.

Women get raped and go to psych hospitals; men rape and go
to jail. That was the best-case scenario, anyway.

It was late summer, and New Orleans was so muggy I could choke.

"Why are you here, Angela?" I asked.

"Courts said I had to come 'cause of the dissociative identity disorder, but it ain't me who needs the help," Angela said. "It's one of my alters. She's the one who fucked Kenny up in the first place." She took a long pull of her cigarette. The clock ticked overhead.

I closed my eyes and tried to become someone else.

I closed my eyes and tried to become normal.

Inside, on the television in the common room, several women sat on the floor, gazing up at the screen. Sandra Bullock was crying. Her pain was her streaked mascara. I couldn't see my pain.

My pain is a set of marbles that I keep on rotating in the palm of my hand.

"What about you?" Angela said. "Fuck are you doing here?"

I shook my head.

"I don't know anymore," I said. "I'm not supposed to be here."

She looked at me funny.

"This really, really, *really* wasn't supposed to be my life," I said.

We were sitting in a circle and a woman named Pat was talking about her childhood. Her mother had joined a satanic cult, she said.

"My little sister. They killed her. They killed her and they made me carry the body. I watched as they raped her. Her lifeless body. They made me carry it."

She broke down in heavy sobs.

I wrote down everything she said in my journal, incredulous.

"Satanic cults aren't real," I wrote.

There had been that scandal when I was a kid—I remembered it from the news—accusations of satanic ritual abuse that turned out to be false memories implanted by faulty hypnosis. I wanted to shout, *She's making it all up!*

But what if she wasn't? What if it had happened?

"I watched as they raped her," Pat said again. She sounded convincing. I didn't feel anything beyond a low-level horror.

Rape and rape and rape. We all talked about rape.

"We are all survivors," Melissa said.

After four days, I cracked. I called my mother.

"I can't be here anymore," I sobbed into the phone. "This is worse than being out there. This is worse than anything."

Her voice was soothing. "Okay, honey," she said. "We'll bring you home."

I flew back to Portland, dazed from the things I'd heard and seen at River Oaks. I didn't say much about it. It was too strange—a fever dream I'd had in the summer swamp.

Now that I was out, it seemed absurd that I would go to Vassar and equally absurd that I would not. I was almost eighteen, a high school graduate; there was nothing for me to do in Portland,

and my father had moved into Jennifer's one-bedroom, where there wasn't enough room for me to live. I hadn't gotten sober, but I wasn't sure I absolutely needed to, either; I couldn't possibly do more treatment after spending time in three programs over the course of one long summer.

But that was what my mother suggested, pleading with me over dinner one evening. "You can stay here," she said. "I'll help you. Maybe you can do an intensive outpatient program. Get a part-time job. Work retail."

I grimaced. *That* wasn't in the cards. And the more I thought about it, the more college seemed like a better idea than it had at any point over the last year. I would be away from my parents, independent. I could make new friends. Get a fresh start. *Vassar.* It sounded glamorous; it was one of the best liberal arts colleges in the country.

I told my father that was my plan. He sounded frustrated.

"I'll pay the equivalent of state-school tuition," he said. "That's as much as I can invest in this."

"Fine," I said. "I'll take out loans for the rest." I had no idea how I would do this, but it seemed like the right thing to say.

My last weekend in Portland before returning to New York, I drove out to Mount Saint Helens with two girlfriends. We roasted marshmallows over a fire and slept together in sleeping bags in an oversize tent. We swam in a lake, laughing, dunking one another under the water. I showed them how to make a fire with my bow drill, and we smoked pot out of a beat-up old pipe, blowing rings and watching the stars.

On the second day, we ate psychedelic mushrooms and hiked through the woods to a site nearby where there were caves.

"Is it a good idea to go spelunking when we're tripping?" my friend giggled.

"Definitely not," I said, and we erupted into peals of laughter.

Everything was green and gold, the light in the trees making shadows on the ground.

How could I give this up? I thought wondrously. *Drugs are so special, so beautiful.*

I stumbled upon a perfectly cylindrical hole in the ground, about six feet deep—the perfect size for me. Resting one hand in the soil, pinching it between my fingers, bending my knees, I jumped down into it.

It was dark and cool. I lit a cigarette. I looked up at the girls, who looked down at me, marveling. I heard a click as one of them snapped a picture.

"I don't know how I'm going to get out of this hole I'm in," I said. Suddenly, I was weeping. "I feel like I've been here forever."

Landing back at the airport in New York, I caught a taxi to Manhattan. It felt strange to get in, as I had so many times, and tell the driver to take me to Jennifer's apartment rather than my father's.

The doorman stopped me as I entered her building. I gave my father's name, then Jennifer's. He called up, looking at me suspiciously. The lobby of her building was grand and old-fashioned, a relic from an old New York that didn't exist anymore, crown molding and a vaguely musty odor.

"You can go up," he said. I rolled my eyes, irritated.

Upstairs, my father greeted me warmly. I once-overed Jennifer's apartment: it hadn't fully registered that this was the place to which I'd be returning. In the corner of the living room was a large golden birdcage, its door ominously opened. A tan sofa had a pair of sheets and a faded quilt folded on its cushions. The bathroom was through the bedroom; I'd have to pass by their bed anytime I had to use it, I realized. Almost immediately, I felt claustrophobic. Then, I heard the beating of wings as Jennifer's bird torpedoed through the air toward me, swerving just to avoid crashing into my head.

"Fucking bird," I muttered.

I went to dinner with Daphne and a large group of friends at a trendy sushi restaurant. It felt so odd to be back in the same places with the same people: I hadn't been back in New York since those men had pulled me out of bed in the middle of the night.

A mutual friend from wilderness had told me that Laurel had been working for an escort service in north Newark, turning tricks again. I texted her: "I'm back in the city."

"Where are you?" Laurel wrote back. "I want to see you."

"Dinner," I wrote. Then she called. I picked up at the table, to my friends' annoyance.

"Laurel?" I said.

"I'll get in a taxi right now," she said. "Just tell me where you are."

"You're taking a cab from Jersey?" I said.

"I can't wait to see you," she said.

I hung up the phone.

"Laurel has a lot of problems," I said to the group.

"No wonder you're friends," Daphne said.

She arrived halfway through dinner, exiting a cab in a revealing top, carrying a cheap black patent leather purse. She stood on the street looking lost. I watched her for a moment through the window, then went to bring her inside. She was stretched thin. Her features were collapsing into one another, like she was a watercolor painting. She ordered more sake for the table and pulled a wad of crumpled twenties from her purse.

"I have money," she slurred.

"We don't pay yet," Daphne said.

After dinner, we went out on the street to smoke. Laurel leaned on the hood of a parked car, clutching her stomach, sick from something.

Daphne kissed me on the cheek as she got in a cab heading uptown.

"You need to get sober, Sam," she said. "This is getting ridiculous. What the fuck are you doing with these people?"

"I'm fucking seventeen, Daphne," I said. "So is she. We're just—we're going through it right now. You know?"

She shrugged and got in the cab. Laurel sidled up next to me and whispered in my ear.

"Let's get some coke and go to a hotel," she said. "I wanna party."

In bed that night, Laurel lay next to me, her body pushed up close against mine. I could feel her chest rise and fall as she breathed. The drugs still pumped through me. I felt strong.

Inexplicably, I had an erection.

She turned to face me and I stiffened against her. I kissed her and began to unbutton her pants.

"Are you sure?" she asked.

"I've never done it with a woman," I said. I hadn't.

Once I was inside her, it started to feel instinctively wrong. She moaned theatrically. I came quickly, feeling grateful that I would never have to do it again.

Then, immediately, a wave of sickening regret surged through me, regret for treating someone as damaged as Laurel like a piece of meat. For doing to her what so many men with hungry eyes and wedding bands whom I'd met at gay bars in Chelsea all through high school had done to me. That cotton-mouthed hangover feeling to which I'd grown so accustomed, waking up next to a stranger at a midtown hotel, knowing perfectly well that I was an experiment he'd rather soon forget.

The next morning, we went out to breakfast at the diner on the corner. She ordered eggs, and we didn't talk about the night before. I paid the tab.

"It's the least I can do," I said.

She called a car service to take her back to New Jersey, and as she got into the town car, she looked at me.

"I'm so happy," she said. "I'm so happy this happened." Her
face split into a smile. "I'll see you really soon, okay?"

That night I sent messages to a guy I'd met the previous spring:
a Broadway producer with a spacious apartment on Central Park
West. He was silver-haired and a little portly. I had felt terrified
walking through his lobby, I remembered, because a friend from
school lived in that same building—what if she saw me and asked
what I was doing there? But I didn't care anymore. I could hardly
remember the person to whom things like that had mattered.

He invited me over, so I went, already drunk, getting nause-
ated in the backseat of a taxi. When he opened the apartment
door, I could already hear the groans of pornography. He shut the
door behind me. A pile of cocaine sat on a silver mirror.

"Have some candy," he said.

I did a line.

"More," he said.

I did another.

He kissed me on the mouth, biting my lip. "Good job, baby."

I followed him into his bedroom. There were two boys already
there, lying on his bed: naked and hairless. Porn was playing on
the television there, too. It was too much visual data, too much
sex to take in at once.

One of the boys, I realized suddenly, was in the video playing
on the television; I followed the tattoo on his hip from the screen
to the bed and back again.

"Why are you still wearing clothes?" the producer said. He sounded exasperated. "Strip." He wiped his gums.

I peeled off my shirt, then pants, then underwear. He looked at me appraisingly, as though I were a show horse. "You're cuter than the last time," he said.

Both of the boys on the bed laughed. "That's a shitty compliment, Richard," one of them said, sniffling. I felt vivid—like I had been living in monochrome and suddenly found myself in color. *Richard.* That was his name.

"Richard," I said. He turned to face me. I whispered in his ear. "I want five hundred for the night."

"My boys get whatever they want," he said. He shoved my head down. "So do I."

Nine

*W*hile I'd been in Portland, I'd been invited to join an online group of incoming Vassar freshmen; I had traded a series of flip messages with a girl named Annalise von Tegerfelden. Her photo showed her in a leotard, posing in a spectacular arabesque. She'd written that her interests were "ballet and Klonopin," which I loved.

"Write me when you're back in the city," she said. "We'll have drinks." When I did, she extended a prompt invitation.

"I'm so bored tonight," she said, as familiar as if we had been friends for years. "Just come over."

Her family's apartment was in a town house in the East Seventies, near Lexington, luxuriously grubby—shelves crowded with old books, a velvet sofa. Annalise wore a little black dress, her long dark hair pooling on her shoulders. She was sharp-featured and tiny, with a ballerina's build—she had spent two postgrad years dancing in a Parisian ballet company, she said. She was already a little tipsy, an opened bottle of red wine on a chest in the living room. "Mother and Father are at the house in the country," she said, a high-pitched bubble of a laugh erupting from her chest. She told me about her weekend—a threesome with two male models she'd met at a club downtown. Annalise specialized in male models, specifically European ones; later, she would take to sending me emails with the subject line, "This is what I've been doing all day," with a photo of a bare torso attached.

I told her about backpacking through Utah, the rehab in Tennessee, the psych ward in New Orleans.

"And when was all this?" she asked, pouring herself more wine. She had the rarefied delivery of someone much older, a Park Avenue divorcée in training, with a high, brittle voice and a laugh that continued past the point when everyone else had stopped laughing. (She was, in fact, already nearly twenty-one—old for a freshman—compounded by a worldliness that I assumed was born simply of being a Swiss banking heiress and a pedigreed party girl, as she was.)

"I just got out a week ago," I said.

She clutched her chest in a performance of dismay. "Darling! You must be wound so tight," she said. "Do you want a Klonopin?" She nodded, reinforcing her own ingenuity. "You should take a Klonopin."

"That sounds right," I said. She retrieved a prescription bottle from her purse and handed me a tablet.

The room shifted out of focus, then back into high-definition. She poured more wine, then put an old record on vinyl, a warm crackling, and we danced through the apartment.

"What do you think Vassar is going to be like?" I asked.

"Probably dreadful," she laughed. "Lots of kids from suburbs who are, like, so *excited* to be out on their own for the first time." I loved the implication—that we were different, that we were special.

"Let's try to have a good time," I said. "We can come back to the city as much as we want."

"Thank God for that." She sniffed. "There's a party at Marquee next weekend that I *don't* intend to miss."

"You're fabulous, Annalise von Tegerfelden," I burbled at the end of the night. "You're so fabulous."

She kissed me on both cheeks and put me in a cab.

That weekend, I met Annalise at her parents' apartment once more and followed her to Lexington, where we hailed a taxi.

In the cab, Annalise retrieved a water bottle full of vodka from her purse. "We're going to want to be drunk for this, right?" she said, releasing that high, peculiar laugh.

"Yeah," I said, taking a swig. We were headed to an apartment in Tribeca that had been rented out for a reception to welcome New York City–area incoming freshmen to the college. We got out on Washington, wandering the quiet cobblestoned streets.

"Where *are* we?" Annalise asked.

"Isn't that Leroy over there?" I said.

"Who?" Annalise said. "You know I don't go below Fourteenth Street. At least not sober." I didn't yet know this, but it was good to keep in mind. And indeed, while the shots I'd taken in the cab had left me feeling woozy, they only seemed to prime Annalise for the afternoon ahead. She walked more confidently now in her stilettos. She wore white jeans and a floral top that

made her hair look even darker and shinier, and her ass wiggled as
she moved, like the street was her catwalk.

At the event, well-heeled freshmen milled around; many
of them seemed to know one another. Annalise and I smoked
cigarettes on the terrace. We had come too late and missed the
remarks, the food, and any sort of camaraderie.

"Isn't there a bar?" Annalise said, scowling. "I want a glass of
Riesling."

"Everyone here is underage," I said.

"Should we kill ourselves?"

"Probably."

Annalise shrugged. "Well, at least we dropped by to let everyone know who we are, and that we're cool."

I nodded. At that moment, this seemed like the most important thing we could have done.

My father drove me up to Vassar in Jennifer's car, unloading my
things in suitcases and boxes. After I'd moved to New York, then
had most of my things put in storage when he'd moved out of the
apartment on the West Side, my worldly possessions had been
pared down to a surprisingly lean array of clothes and books.

My brother's roommate and best friend at college had a
younger brother who was also matriculating at Vassar that same
year; his name was Nate. We sent messages to each other in
August and decided to request each other as roommates, although
we hadn't met.

I arrived first. Our room was in the historic main building in the center of campus, in a tower up a winding flight of stairs. It felt like a boarding school dream. Big windows looked out onto landscaped grounds, and the floorboards creaked. If it was grand, it was also pretty utilitarian—a thin twin mattress, a desk and a dresser on each side.

We went to Bed Bath & Beyond somewhere in the Hudson Valley and I roamed the aisles idly. It was inconceivable that I would be living here for the next four years. There were so many other families shopping there, too—the air was thick with it, the excitement, the optimism. I felt so old and tired and used up.

My father, trying to make the most of a bad situation, offered opinions on patterns for bedsheets, but the light had disappeared out of his eyes. I asked for more things—more pillows, more things to hang on the walls—but he shook his head no.

Maybe he suspected that I would try to return those items and keep the cash. He wasn't wrong.

Nate's parents were in the room when we got back, along with Nate; my father had met them before, when taking my brother to school. They were all there, Nate's brothers and both of his parents, brimming with good cheer. They marked such a sharp contrast to my father and me.

It wasn't what I had imagined in my happiest moments, nor was it how I had feared it could be at its very worst—it was an anticlimax, a rite of passage that felt more like a resignation to a decision we both already knew was probably a mistake.

Nate was friendly. On some level, it registered quickly that

I'd be able to walk all over him, although I already felt guilty for that thought.

I walked my father back to his car, parked on the far edge of campus. The sun had gone down. He hugged me.

"Good luck, Sam," he said. There was a tightness in his jaw and an expression on his face that was unfamiliar. It almost seemed like he was worried he might never see me again.

For the life of me, I couldn't understand why.

"I'll be fine, Dad," I said.

"I'm pretty sure there's, like, a lot going on this week," Annalise said the following morning. We were sharing a cigarette outside my dorm, Annalise in comically large sunglasses, both of us clutching oversize coffees. Parents still moving in their kids glared at us.

"Like what?" I asked.

"I don't know—there's a barbecue, I think?"

I side-eyed her. "Do *you* want to go to that?"

"Of course not," she said, bristling. It was automatic: *obviously* we weren't doing this. I checked the time. I had a meeting with an academic adviser at 3:00 p.m. and it was only eleven—that left more than enough time to get high. "I'll meet up with you later," I said.

On my way back to my dorm, my resident adviser, whom I'd met while moving in the previous day, stopped me in the hallway. "Sam," she said. I'd already forgotten her name.

"Hey, you," I said by way of greeting.

"There's a fun barbecue in the quad," she said. "Don't you want to get to know people?"

"Of course!" I said. "I just have to do something first. I'll be right there." I flashed her a smile.

In my bedroom, I packed a bowl and hit it quickly, then fished around in my bag. I'd gone to a new doctor just before leaving the city, bringing the empty prescription bottles from May that I had saved as proof that I'd been prescribed these drugs before; he'd happily written me new prescriptions for Adderall, Xanax, and Ambien—plus, I had a few painkillers I'd found in Jennifer's apartment. I took a Xanax and opened my laptop.

When I woke up it was dark outside. I was under the covers fully dressed, sweating, confused.

It wasn't until I turned on the lights, waking up Nate, that I remembered where I was. *Oh. Right. College.*

The next night at convocation, we gathered in a beautiful old church to hear remarks from the administration, but I couldn't focus. Annalise found me and sat down next to me.

"This is boring," she whispered.

"I know."

"I already drank all the wine I brought from the city," she said.

"How?"

She looked pained. "It's been a *really* stressful day," she said. She took a Klonopin.

"We need to go buy alcohol," I said.

"Have you met anyone who has a car?" she asked. "Should we call a taxi to take us to the liquor store? Do they *have* car services out here?"

A boy in the pew ahead of us turned around, extending a hand.

"You guys have IDs?"

Annalise and I looked at each other. "Obviously," she said.

And soon we were speeding off into the town of Poughkeepsie in his Mercedes. He was a slick kid from New Jersey; he didn't seem like a fit for Vassar. Then again, neither did we.

He drove too fast and kept looking over at Annalise's lithe body as she twisted and twirled in the passenger seat to the beat of pounding electro. I smoked a cigarette out the window in the backseat, luxuriating in the moment.

College! I thought.

Annalise and I prowled through the liquor store, pulling bottles and stacking them in our basket. He had given us his credit card.

"Buy whatever you want," he said.

Swiping it at the register, Annalise looked at me.

"I can't believe it took this long to find somebody who wanted to fuck me," she said. She grinned. "This is going to be a great year."

———

I settled in quickly, but not well. Annalise was a dangerous friend to have, and she no doubt felt the same about me—we took the train back to the city most weekends, about ninety minutes each way, partying at clubs downtown and crashing wherever we could. I wouldn't have thought to tell my father that I was in town.

I registered for classes: A freshman seminar in memoir, where I wrote a piece about Dean, twice as many pages as had been assigned. We went around the room and read our work aloud, and I could feel my classmates' eyes boring into me as I read on and on and on—they could see right through me. By the end, my face was flushed from embarrassment; I had imagined that they would laugh and gasp, but instead their faces were expressionless except for some vague irritation at my overlong piece.

I dropped the class.

A course in linguistics, where I met an upperclassman who lived in the town houses on the other side of campus. Somehow, I figured out that she knew where to get cocaine, and we began doing it together after class each Thursday.

A philosophy class, where kids growing out their mustaches pontificated on Sartre. "The kind of people who want to take a freshman philosophy class are not my kind of people," I said to Annalise.

"I don't think our kind of people are in Poughkeepsie," she said.

A modern dance class, which I only went to when I was high.

It never occurred to me that I was really there to study. I turned in all my assignments late. On weeknights, I got high in my room and studied the effects of strange mixes of pills: *What would sixty milligrams of Adderall do if I took it with four milligrams of Klonopin?*

"Can you snort Klonopin?" Annalise asked me. "I don't know why I never thought to do it before."

"No," I said. "It doesn't permeate the mucus membrane very well. Better to just take it orally."

"Bottoms up," she said, and we each swallowed a pill with a glass of rosé.

Through my weed dealer, I met a girl who sold painkillers out of her room in the town houses across campus; she had two enormous bottles of Dilaudid and morphine.

"My dad's a surgeon," she said with a wicked smile.

I started off buying two or three at a time. The Dilaudid, in pale blue tablets, was good to snort; the morphine had to be taken orally, but it hit harder if it was crushed and dissolved in a beverage. I liked to put it in an energy drink, or a cold glass bottle of chocolate milk, which they sold in the bookstore.

I sipped it as I walked around campus: a strange, nostalgic delight.

One weekend in mid-September, Annalise and I took the train back to the city, declaring that we were done with the Hudson Valley.

"Fuck Vassar," I said proudly as we walked to the train station in Poughkeepsie.

"Yeah," she said. "Fuck Vassar."

In the city, we went to Ronan's house. I arrived with a mélange of pills, uppers and benzos and painkillers, and we drank gin-and-tonics, and we must have called for coke at some point because magically, one minute, it was there.

In flashes, little glimmers of memory across a period of hours, I remember Annalise dancing, half naked, her breasts shaking to the rhythm of Swedish pop blasting on the stereo. At some point I must have texted Robert, the guy I had smoked meth with the fall before, because when the sun was rising I was stumbling out of his apartment, electrified, my jaw stiff and that sour chemical taste in my mouth. Then I found another guy, a handsome banker in the West Village who had posted an ad online saying that he wanted to go "skiing."

Somehow I made it down to his apartment, and there was a platter of cocaine that looked mountainous, sparkling lustrous white, and I thought how wonderful it was that we wouldn't run out for hours, days even.

I was in bed with him, this stranger, when I got the first call, from Jennifer. I silenced the ringer and let it go to voice mail. She called several more times over the following hour, leaving messages, which I ignored.

I didn't know what she wanted, but it seemed unlikely that it was more important than what I was doing.

The calls began to irritate me, and eventually I picked up my phone to listen to Jennifer's messages. Her voice was grave and rough from crying.

"Sam. Your dad—he's had a heart attack. We're taking him to Mount Sinai. You need to get here as soon as you can."

"Sam. Where are you?"

"Sam. We're at the hospital. Call me as soon as you get this message."

"Sam. Call me, Sam."

I hung up the phone and tossed it onto the floor.

"My dad just had a heart attack," I said, to nobody; it wasn't really directed at the stranger in bed next to me.

I couldn't feel anything. Nothing except perhaps a minor annoyance, a sense of being inconvenienced, the absurdity of what poor timing this was.

"Shit," the guy said. "Do you need to, like, go?"

"No. It's fine."

"Are you sure you shouldn't—"

"It's fine," I said curtly. "I'm gonna do another line."

How could I leave? It seemed that as long as I stayed there, in that anesthetic inertia, the morbid reality of what was going on just a few miles north wouldn't become real, wouldn't end this bender on a sour note. I pulled the stranger close into me and kissed him, frozen-mouthed, the sound of our teeth clicking against each other, and I pretended like nothing had happened.

And that was where I stayed for the rest of the day, while my phone kept buzzing on the floor, over and over again, just loud enough to hear.

We ran out of drugs sooner than I'd expected—it was odd how that always seemed to happen—and so I left. Standing outside on Christopher Street, in the blearily sore-throated daze of the sec-

ond day of a cocaine run—this was, I was sure, the worst feeling
in the entire world—it occurred to me that there was nowhere I
wanted to go. Fear paralyzed me. It had been six hours since Jennifer had first called.

I went back uptown to Ronan's house to clean myself up, but
once I got there, I just settled on the stoop outside. For the next
hour or so, I remained there, staring out numbly, speechlessly.
The sun was shining; it was hurting my eyes; I was coming down
hard; I felt like a vampire.

Annalise came outside and sat down next to me on the stoop,
hugging her knees. "You need to go," she said. "You need to be
with your family. What if he dies, Sam? What if he's already gone?"

Strange feelings were beginning to claw at me and there was
nothing to stuff them down with, no more drugs left to take, no
more booze in the fridge. Thinking about showing up trashed at
the hospital, I resolved I really couldn't move.

"I can't go," I said. "I can't."

And then, with the wearied, self-pitying gravity that I had
mastered, I took a cab across town to Mount Sinai.

I walked slowly into the hospital. In his room, my father was
hooked up to wires and tubes, looking small and so frail in that
paper gown. My father, who had always seemed to me a statue of
well-tailored confidence, now looked so broken—and as numb as
I felt in that postcomedown melancholia, my breath still stuck in
my throat when I saw him lying there.

Jennifer's face was red from crying. As I leaned down to hug
my dad, it occurred to me that I probably reeked of liquor and sex,

and my nose was running—and I prayed, *Please, God, let that just be snot instead of another nosebleed*—so I pulled away rapidly, wiping my nose anxiously, coughing as though I were suffering from a head cold. When I looked back at my father, his face was contorted in a mask of concern and pain. Was it for him or for me? I stood by his bed while monitors beeped and halogen lightbulbs hummed, and I tried not to dull a flurry of competing thoughts. How strange that this extraordinary human drama had been unfurling in my absence. How strange to confront these emotions now when my day had started off so ordinary in its mundane debauchery.

"Sam," Jennifer said, "are you okay?"

"I'm fine," I said. "I'll be fine."

On the street, I joined the smokers outside the hospital door. A few nurses in scrubs, a few people who just looked tired. I glimpsed my reflection in the mirror. I looked tired, too.

Soon I'd be eighteen. It wasn't fun anymore, the way I lived my life—it was just exhausting. I was getting too old for this, I knew, but I couldn't conceive of a way to stop it.

I went back to Ronan's house. He and Annalise seemed concerned, but I didn't know what to say.

I drank myself to sleep and passed out in Ronan's brother's room for what felt like a hundred years. I had to wake up early to go see my father in the hospital. I *had* to.

But the following morning, I realized that I was out of cash, somehow—I couldn't remember where it had all gone. I walked to an ATM with Annalise and tried to take out a cash advance with the emergency credit card my father had given me, but it had been canceled. All I had was my return train ticket to Pough-keepsie and my meal card. I didn't even have money left on a MetroCard.

"I can't go," I said. "How am I going to get across town?"

Annalise didn't have any cash, either. We had to get to the train station at 125th Street. "Some cabs take credit cards, right?" she said.

"Yes!" I said. "They have those readers in the back. We just have to find one."

We wandered up and down West End, trying to hail a taxi; the drivers rolled down their windows, Annalise shrieked, "Do you take American Express?" and then, quickly, they would speed away. We went into a subway station and bought a MetroCard on her credit card, then took the subway up to 125th Street, where we waited for the crosstown bus to take us to catch the train. It felt like an odyssey.

On the train back to Vassar, I put on my headphones and disappeared into the ebb of the music, trying not to think about my father alone in the hospital.

When I returned to campus, I had an email from him. "I'm in a different room—way nicer!" it read. "Learning about my heart, drugs, diet, exercise, doctors. A good, intense education. Feeling totally fine—ready to get out of here, but probably not allowed until tomorrow or Wednesday."

I wrote back: "I'm glad to hear you're feeling better. I love you."

He replied quickly. "Thanks, Sam," he wrote. "What happened to you on Sunday? I thought you were coming to see me."

It hurt too much to respond, so I closed my computer. I crushed a tablet of morphine with my gilded razor and dissolved it into a bottle of chocolate milk.

———

At a party, I met a slender-hipped boy named Patrick; I took him back to my dorm room and pushed him up against the wall, thrusting into him.

I swallowed Ecstasy with a stoner dude and his curvy girlfriend and we triple-kissed, dissolving into a mass of limbs.

There were two handsome boys named Jamie and Thomas who had begun dating just when school started. I flirted with both of them; eventually I decided it was Thomas, who was sturdily built and blond, whom I wanted more than Jamie, who was slim and dark-featured. But Thomas was smart enough to steer clear of me. I hated this, so one night at a different party, I got drunk with Jamie; we ended up making out in front of his dorm.

They broke up, and I slept with Thomas a few weeks later, getting what I wanted.

One night I fell asleep drinking and watching a movie on my laptop. I woke up choking on a thick, bitter bile. Disoriented, I turned on my side, tucked my knees into my chest, and hurled. When I woke up in the morning my computer was caked in vomit.

"Shit," I said. "*Shit.*"

I rushed down to the bathroom in my underwear, trying to

clean it off with paper towels. But it had dried overnight, sticking in the keys. Several didn't work—they just wouldn't punch.

"It's fine," I said to Nate, not that he had asked. "I can just copy-paste *G*'s and *H*'s until I get it fixed." But instead, after snorting an enormous pile of Adderall a day later, it struck me as a good idea to pry off all the keys on the keyboard, one by one, and clean underneath them.

But since I didn't have any tweezers, I just worked with my fingers; eventually, I pried all the keys off, only to find I couldn't get them back on. I saved them in a drawer, thinking eventually I would fix it, but instead I just tapped on the rubberized nubs beneath the keys, which made it nearly impossible to type.

"It's fine," I said again to Nate. "I'll just write all my papers in the library." (I hadn't yet written any papers, and I'd never yet set foot in the library.)

Wisely, Nate started spending less and less time in the room. One afternoon, while I was blowing off class, cheerfully chopping up lines of Dilaudid on my desk to snort, he entered the room, with three or four classmates in tow. They all stopped when they saw me with a card and piles of cornflower blue powder on the desk.

"Hey," Nate said awkwardly.

"Oh, sorry!" I said. I was already loopy from Adderall and Xanax. "Don't mind me. I'll be out in just a minute." I snorted the powder in several quick breaths as they stood in the doorway, agape.

Annalise was descending into chaos, too, even if her spiral wasn't quite as impressive as mine. One weekend she brought to campus a Ford model, chiseled and stupefied; I recognized him from fashion magazines. We railed lines in my room and then they disappeared into the bathroom, groping each other in a fever.

"It's a good thing I'm flexible," she said to me the next day, nursing a hangover.

Although she, too, was a freshman, she'd been roomed with a sensible upperclassman after petitioning the housing board ("I'm so much older than these kids"—she sighed—"in more ways than one") but then had learned that the neighboring room was vacant. She moved in unofficially, claiming squatters' rights, then invited another girl we'd met, Claire, to live with her. Claire was from the city, too, and she was a game foil to Annalise's madness. They quickly became known for having noisy threesomes in the dormitory shower. High on amphetamines, they covered the walls of the room in tinfoil—a project that took days, if not weeks—turning the space into a dizzying, metallic fractal cube.

Annalise was less experienced with drugs than I was. Though we partied a lot together, I was always taking more before she came over, and then more still after she left. One night she returned to my dorm hours after leaving it. Her face was streaked with tears.

"I'm having the worst comedown ever," she sobbed. "I can't do coke anymore. I can't feel like this. I'm having such a panic attack."

"Did you take a Klonopin?"

"Of course I took a Klonopin," she said. "I took four Klonopin. I called my psychiatrist and he isn't answering."

"It's four a.m.," I said. Across the room, Nate rolled over.

"I want to leave school and go study in Paris," Annalise whined. "I don't belong here."

"You probably shouldn't be making major life decisions right now," I said. "Maybe, like, wait until your panic attack is over."

Annalise looked at me, lost. "You're so good at this," she said. "How did you get so smart?"

I celebrated my eighteenth birthday in the city by getting drunk at my favorite East Village bar and making out with the bartender, Ivan, in the bathroom. A friend gave me a gram of cocaine with a card attached.

"Birthday blow for the birthday boy," it said.

I blinked, and it was gone.

I was on a rampage. If pressed I wouldn't have been able to explain why I was behaving this way—so recklessly, on a warpath to self-destruction. I woke up every morning with a tunnel vision that I found perplexing but didn't think to question. The only goal was to get high and change the way I felt, which was lonely and afraid. I wasn't turning in homework or going to classes. In the brief moments when I was sober, I was wracked with guilt, but the drugs made the guilt evaporate, making it even less likely that I could rectify the academic mess I was making.

Quickly, I ran out of pills; I went to the doctor on campus and told him that all of my medications had been stolen out of my bag on a weekend trip back to the city.

He wrote me new ones.

I walked two miles to a pharmacy across town to fill them, afraid that the chain closest to school would flag how recently I'd filled the same prescriptions.

Eventually, I told the girl with the painkillers that I would just take the rest of her morphine.

"You want it all?" she said, looking at me like I was an addict for the first time.

"Back pain," I said, handing her all the cash I had.

My mother had been planning a visit to the East Coast for several months; she told me she would come up to Vassar for the scheduled family weekend.

"I'm looking forward to seeing you," I said to her on the phone. She was traveling the following day.

"Are you doing okay, honey?" she asked. Her voice was pinched, a little tenser than normal.

"I'm fine!" I said. It sounded like somebody else's words were coming out of my mouth.

That night, I met an older guy who lived in a neighboring town. I told him I was a student and that I couldn't host. "I'll pick you up," he said.

I was too drunk by the time I made it downstairs; we fucked in the back of his van, me with my pants around my ankles, wearing a white dress shirt and an expensive blazer. Halfway through, I started to feel queasy. Before I could stop myself, I had vomited onto his back. He yowled like an animal, squirming to get away from me, and pulled open the door. Disgusted with myself, laughing through the sick, I tumbled out of the door, my pants still down, landing hard on the concrete and skinning my knee. I flattened on the ground, laughing hysterically, as I heard him speed away, then crawled back to my dorm room, the lapel of my blazer splattered with vomit.

Once I had sobered up, I washed it in the bathroom of my dormitory in the middle of the night, but it still smelled. I wrapped it in a plastic bag, tied it up tightly, and dropped it on the floor of my closet, thinking I would take it to the dry cleaner at some point. (I never did.) I sprawled on the bed, packing a bowl.

There weren't enough pills in the world to take this feeling away—empty and ashamed. *What day is it?* I took an Ambien, then another, then two Xanax.

It was 5:00 a.m. Nate was lightly snoring across the room. I crawled up onto the desk, perching on the windowsill, and smoked a cigarette, looking out over the half-lit campus, empty of students.

Was it too late for me to turn it around? If I could make it through this semester, I could take the next one off—maybe go back to treatment. Maybe I would go back to the wilderness, as an adult now. I could be a counselor. I would quit everything, cold turkey, and lead a band of delinquent teenagers up through forests of bone-white trees. We would be wild and strong. My lungs and head and skin wouldn't hurt all the time. They would love me. Maybe I would fall in love there, with a swarthy guy who smelled like musk and pine, a guy with rough hands like mitts, calloused from tending fires. He would hold me under some gigantic Utah sky crocheted with constellations as a fire died at our feet. I wouldn't feel so alone all the time.

And then, just as quickly, I realized how absurd that was. I was worthless, broken, defective. I didn't have anything to give anyone. They wouldn't take me there. I was soft, inadequate. I would never stop doing what I was doing. I was selfish, entitled, manipulative, addicted. A vampire feeding on the few people who hadn't left me yet. Everything good had withered inside me.

Who could love me this way?

I felt my breath slowing as I teetered out the open window, like in a moment I would hurtle to the ground.

I stubbed out the cigarette and crawled into bed, praying that I would never wake up.

Sunlight sliced through the open window.

My face was mashed into the pillow, a crust of dried saliva gluing my lip to the fabric. Everything smelled like vomit and stale smoke. My phone was ringing. I looked over at it.

Thirty missed calls.

All from my mother.

I picked up.

"Sam, where are you?" She sounded angry, and afraid. "You were supposed to meet me at nine."

It was 3:00 p.m.

"I'm sick," I croaked.

"I took the *red-eye*," she said, the anger turning into pain. "I've been here *all day*."

I said nothing.

"Where are you?"

"In my room."

"What dorm are you in, even?"

"Main," I said. "I'll—I'll meet you in fifteen minutes. Mom—" What could I possibly say? "I'm really sorry."

I splashed some cold water on my face and threw on a hoodie.

Outside, the sun was shining. Instantly, I was too warm in my sweatshirt.

Of course! It was visiting parents' weekend. Everyone was out. Students I recognized from classes I'd stopped attending, flanked by their smiling nuclear families. They looked healthy and happy. I hated them all.

I found my mother in the quad, sitting on a bench in a long, stylish overcoat. Her face was lined with more creases than I remembered. She'd been crying, I could tell, and had fixed her makeup badly.

"Oh, honey," she said as I sat down next to her.

I'd formulated an excuse—something about how I'd gotten food poisoning the night before and had been sick all night, then overslept—and delivered it evenly. My hands were shaking, so I shoved them in my pockets.

She nodded, pacific, unwilling to challenge the obvious lie.

"I'm very sorry that happened to you," she said deliberately. I could see her trying to ground herself. Slogans from twelve-step meetings ran through my head like a tape. There was a wrapped gift next to her—for my birthday, I realized.

How old had I just turned? Eighteen? I had been lying about my age so long to all the guys I met online that I could hardly remember. My mouth was so dry.

Why didn't I think to brush my teeth? Disgusting. I was so disgusting.

I pointed to the box. "What's that?"

"Oh," she said, looking down at it like she had forgotten it, like the futility of the gesture pained her now. "I brought you a few things you might need." She handed it to me and I tore off the paper, grateful for the distraction. It was a small mercy to have something to do with my hands.

Inside was a cardboard box filled with little curlicues of tissue paper, redolent of childhood birthdays. There were sachets of expensive tea, a pound of artisanal coffee that she had brought from Portland. Cough drops and packets of vitamins. A bar of chocolate. A miniature flashlight. Wedged in the tissue was a glossy square photograph. I picked it out and cupped it in my hand, recognizing it as my class picture from the first grade.

In it, I was grinning a gap-toothed smile, my hair still blond from the summer sun.

"You know you're still my little boy, right?" she said. I blinked back tears. I imagined her standing at the checkout aisle at the supermarket. Telling the cashier she was making a care package for her son, who had just started college. Assessing her purchases to determine whether she was bringing me everything I needed.

"I just . . ." Her voice cracked. "I've been walking around this campus all day alone, watching all these kids with their families, and I didn't know if . . ."

"Stop," I said. "Please stop."

". . . I didn't know if you were alive or dead."

"I'm fine, Mom. I just got sick, that's all."

She looked at me with something like helplessness and began to cry. I couldn't remember the last time she had even bothered to look at me with skepticism, that she had bothered to challenge a clear delusion or an outright lie.

"I really don't want anything bad to happen to you," she said. "I know there's nothing I can do. You're an adult now. You've already been through treatment—more than once, I guess. It's up to you now." She squeezed my hand. "I just miss my little kid."

"I'm still right here," I said. My head hurt.

Maybe if I clutch my stomach and run to the bathroom she'll believe the lie.

She searched my face for recognition.

"If you say so," she said. I wanted to tell her how sorry I was, but I didn't know how.

She looked around at the throngs of families. Their happiness gleamed. "God, it's like a fucking catalog here," she said. "All they need is the station wagon and the golden retriever."

I laughed despite myself, snorting back tears.

"I know," I said. "I don't know why I have to be the most fucked-up person everywhere I go." I sighed heavily. "Even rehab."

"Are you sure this is the right place for you?" she said carefully. "Maybe you would do better in a school in a city, with people who have had—I don't know—more diverse life experiences. The people here look so—*suburban.*"

I thought of Annalise; I didn't even know if her parents had come. Probably not. A few days earlier, her mother had sent her a withering email criticizing her course schedule. Annalise had given a dramatic reading of it in my dorm room, a joint smoldering in her mouth. "For God's sake, Annalise, *do something right for once in your life!*" it ended, and we had wept from laughter at the histrionics of it. I didn't want to give up on college.

"What are you saying?" I said, suddenly defensive. The switch had been flipped: I felt the old coldness taking me over once more. My mother, yet again, trying to make my decisions for me; it felt so audacious. How *dare* my parents involve themselves? They hadn't been there when I needed them. It was too late now. She was right, of course—it had never been the right place for me—but my denial ran too deep for me to admit it, and so I lashed out.

"Are you telling me you think I should drop out, or transfer? Do you think I'm not good enough for this place?"

"No, honey," she said. "That's not what I'm telling you at all."

"I'm doing just fine here," I said. "I mean, sure, there's still some unresolved stuff that I need to work on, but . . . it's not like there's anything *pressing.* Just continuing to unpack the baggage from, you know, my family of origin scattering across the fucking country because my parents' marriage completely fucking collapsed." I knew what I was doing, but I was powerless to stop it.

This shut her down, as I had known it would. She stared off at all the other families, silent, sad.

But it didn't feel good to assert my dominance anymore, to snatch back the power I always accused her of trying to wrest from me. There was just an enormous dark emptiness inside me that stretched out for thousands of miles.

I looked down at the things she had brought me. I wanted to put my arm around her shoulder and tell her I was sorry, but I didn't know how. So I stared off at those other families, too. I would have traded anything to be them, even for a moment.

"It's out of my hands," she said. "I just hope you know what you're doing."

I met another guy online who lived in Poughkeepsie, but I'd learned my lesson; I took a taxi to his apartment and stayed there for an entire weekend, this time taking molly. More guys came over, with more drugs. I blinked in and out of consciousness. There were heavy drapes, an old couch. A muscular chest. There was music playing and I was laughing. I felt light and happy.

I must have had plans with Annalise because when I got back to campus on Sunday, she pounded on my door.

"You didn't answer your phone all weekend," she snapped. "Did you go to the city without me?"

"I was with a guy," I said.

Why was everyone *interrogating* me all the time?

She crawled up onto my bed, reaching for my pipe and weed. "What guy? Somebody on campus? You could have told me! I stayed *here* all weekend when I could have been fucking a model in the bathroom of Bungalow because *we* were supposed to go to a party on campus."

"I'm sorry!" I said.

"Who is he?" she asked. In fairness, I could barely remember, but I was ashamed, too, to tell her that I'd met some older townie.

"Can you interview me about who I'm sleeping with another time?" I said. "I was rolling all weekend and my serotonin is, like, super depleted."

"Why are you so mysterious?" Annalise said. She looked genuinely hurt. "We were supposed to be in this together."

"I'm sorry," I said. "I'm just so tired."

"Come over," she said. "You can help me finish tinfoiling the walls. I have a great bottle of prosecco."

I shook my head. "I just want to go to bed, I think," I said.

"You're *always* in bed," she said. "When was the last time you went to class?"

Class. Right. Somehow I was still scraping by. I was hardly ever there and hadn't turned in most of my assignments, but it didn't seem like my truancy had caught anyone's attention yet.

"I'm going this week," I said. "I promise."

And I did go to class—after crushing up pills of Adderall and Dilaudid together. "It's a Seven Sisters speedball!" I exclaimed to

Annalise. I snorted them in big blue lines, which made me just euphoric and energized enough to be productive. I caught up on a few assignments and even tidied up my side of the room.

As long as I had enough pills to get me through each day, I thought, this would be fine. Every day, I was ingesting a little bit more—another Adderall here, another morphine there, one more Xanax, an extra Ambien—and smoking pot most nights, but I tried to stay away from alcohol, which seemed to be a nasty potentiator.

I was nearly through October. If I could just get to December, I thought, I would be fine. Then I could figure out my next moves.

Each day felt like a victory in miniature. I took less Adderall so I could sell it, and spent the cash on painkillers.

I used my fake ID to buy alcohol for others, charging a modest fee.

I scraped by.

The biggest party of the year so far was a dance on Halloween. Annalise was a "slutty nun"; I was a prep school dropout, an unlit cigarette clenched between my teeth, a blue blazer, and shredded khakis. ("You're so fucking lazy," Annalise said. "Talk about typecasting.") We had picked up a few hits of Ecstasy for the occasion, and also some blow, and several bottles of vodka, which were stored in my room for safekeeping until the big event.

I started the day with some Adderall to get myself out of bed, then a few lines of Dilaudid.

Then a hit of morphine for good measure.

More Adderall.

I packed a bowl and smoked it. The pregame was in my room; people started to come over. My nerves were acting up.

I took a Xanax.

Annalise gave me two Klonopin.

I took an Ambien to get that surreal, floating feeling I liked so much.

Things got fuzzier, but I still didn't feel *good*—just sort of fatigued. I could have taken a standardized test.

We started doing blow.

We cut it with Ritalin to make it last longer.

We smoked again.

Annalise and I took the E. I waited for the roll to kick in. But it didn't. It was almost time to head out and I was still basically sober.

I cataloged everything I had ingested—how was this *possible*? I wanted euphoria. Barring that, obliteration.

So I started pouring shots of vodka, chased with a fruity alcoholic drink. My stomach was empty—it had been so long since I'd eaten a square meal. It went to my head.

I blacked out.

The beeping of a heart monitor. The pinch of an IV in my arm. I was in a hospital bed, paper sheets prickling my skin.

Oh no, I thought. *Not this again.*

A doctor murmuring. I couldn't understand what he was saying, so I just nodded.

Then, a taxi, winding through the back roads of the Hudson Valley. I shook my head, my vision flickering.

Then, back at my dorm, standing in front of the vending machine, I was so desperately hungry. The emptiness inside me had never been quite so enormous. A self-disgust that made me feel like my throat was closing. There was a twenty-dollar bill in my pocket; I slid it into the machine and started pressing buttons. Potato chips. Chocolate chip cookies. Sour gummy candy. Chocolate bars. Strawberry milk. I carried it in my arms up to my dorm, but the door was locked. I slid down in the hallway outside my room and started opening the snacks, tearing into them, rapacious, sucking synthetic cheddar dust from my fingers. I ate until my stomach was engorged and my mouth was sticky with mucus. I looked down at the contours of my body with complete loathing.

If I'd had a knife, I would have sliced myself open and emptied the contents of my gut out onto the floor.

You monster. You disgusting pig.

I could feel it starting to rise in my throat. Leaving the hallway littered with trash, I sprinted to the bathroom. Shoving two fingers into my mouth, I retched and hurled, shaking and gripping the edges of the toilet.

Stripping off my clothes, I walked into the shower. I lathered up with soap, washing the scum and shame away. I picked up a glass bottle of expensive facial cleanser, but my grip was so feeble, it slipped through my hands and shattered on the floor, sending wet soapy shards flying everywhere, slicing my feet. I yelped and dropped to the ground reflexively, cutting my legs and thighs. I didn't care.

Hot water poured down on my head as rivulets of bloody, soapy water swirled down the drain, staining the white tile pink. The anguish that had been building for two months bubbled up in my throat.

Something inside me ruptured. I began to sob—a deep, heavy, hacking cry. I shuddered and wept on the floor. *God*, I thought, *where are you now?* I thought about that moment alone in the wilderness with the fire, just me and the darkness and a little bit of light. I had felt so close to something—even just for a moment.

But that feeling was gone. There was no fire left. Dully, I considered the likelihood that the next overdose would be the one to take me out.

Annalise came over later that day. I was in bed, despondent. My head was pounding and my legs were covered in bandages.

"You're a mess," she said matter-of-factly.

"I know."

"Do you remember anything about what happened last night?"

I shook my head no.

"Do you want to know?"

I nodded.

"Well, first you threw up on some girl in the elevator," she said. "Then, at the dance, you were obviously super fucked up, so the security guard was trying to get you out—but you didn't want to leave, so you were, like, fighting her. And then you ran out. And she started chasing you. And this huge crowd started gathering, watching, and it was getting way unruly. So they pulled the fire alarm to evacuate the entire building and carried you out on a stretcher while everyone watched."

I stared blankly at her. "No, I didn't," I said. How could I have? I had no memory of any of it.

"You *really* did," she said.

"So everyone saw?"

"Yeah."

It was almost too much to take in. So far, my self-destruction had been mostly private; the idea that this showdown had been so public was more than I could stand.

"I have to leave school," I said. "I can't show my face here."

"It'll blow over," Annalise said, but even she sounded unsure.

"No," I said. "It won't." I paused. "I'm such a fucking disaster."

"I know, darling," she said. "But you're such a *lovable* disaster."

"There aren't that many people left who would agree with you."

She stroked my head. "It'll feel better tomorrow."

I began to cry. "I don't think this is going to work. Staying here, I mean."

Annalise looked frustrated. "You can't leave. What am I going to do without you? Everyone here is so"—she searched for the right word—"boring." She bit her lip. "Maybe you just need a little getaway. Canyon Ranch."

I shook my head. "I need to go back to rehab. Everything is so fucked up."

She considered this. "Well, that could work, too, I guess."

"I really need it to stick," I said. "I can't do this anymore."

She brightened. "I'll help you pick a really chic rehab."

I called my mother to tell her that I had decided to go back to treatment. She sounded relieved. But when I called my father, he was angry. "You can't finish out the semester?" he said, exasperated.

"I really can't, Dad," I cried. "I would if I could. But I really don't think I can. Things have just gotten really bad here." The walls of my dorm room were closing in around me. "I'm really sick."

"I'm so disappointed," he said. I wasn't even self-aware enough to realize that he had been right not to pay for college—that I was just as much of a liability as he'd expected.

Later, he sent me an email. Attached was a spreadsheet outlining my projected expenses for my stay in treatment, then an approximate budget for living independently after I left. He had checked with my student insurance to find my deductible for mental health treatment.

"I suggest that you pay the first $10,000 for your stay yourself," read the message, "then work with insurance companies to pay the rest." I stared at the screen, then pulled out a tab of Dilaudid to snort. It was my last one.

The message was clear: he was finished with cleaning up after me, finished trying to manage this expensive waste I had become.

I was broke—I didn't have enough for a pack of cigarettes. I'd taken out loans to pay for the failed experiment that my higher education was turning out to be. I couldn't take on more, but I couldn't stay where I was. I felt so trapped.

"He doesn't get it," my mother said when I called her. "You're sick. Would he be telling you to pay for it yourself if you had cancer? Or even if you were schizophrenic? Or had attempted suicide? He thinks it's a moral failure. It's not. It's a mental health issue." But it felt like a moral failure.

I could readily acknowledge that something strange happened to my body when I put drugs and alcohol in it—I couldn't *help* myself, I *needed* to be in an altered state all the time—but I was also certain that I was a fundamentally terrible person. Full of revulsion for who I had become, and yet helpless to behave any differently.

My mother called me back the next day. "I'll help you," she said grimly. "Just go get sober."

I told the administration that I was having a mental health crisis and had to leave school early. They didn't put up much of a fight—nor should they have.

Annalise and I found a program in Arizona. "Oh, Naomi Campbell went here!" Annalise exclaimed. "And they have an on-site acupuncturist!"

I booked a flight.

I spent my last days at Vassar smoking weed in my dorm

room and crying for hours at a time. I was going through opiate withdrawal, but I couldn't afford the pills anymore, so instead I got so stoned that I couldn't feel anything.

I rationed out my Xanax and Adderall carefully so I wouldn't run out before leaving.

Annalise knew the glamorous part was over—that it was silly to keep reaffirming how fabulous we were—but she kept it going just the same. When she came over, it was as if I were leaving on a luxurious holiday. She helped me pack up my things, deciding what I should take with me and what to put in storage.

"Do I need a green Dior trench coat in rehab?" I said.

"I mean, what's your rehab *look*?"

I thought about it. "Urban safari," I said.

She nodded briskly. "Pack it."

"It's funny," I said. "I came here to make a big impression, and now all I want is to be forgotten."

"You're unforgettable," she said, kissing me on both cheeks.

But preparing to leave was painful. I didn't say good-bye to most of my friends. I just wanted to slip quietly away into the night.

My father picked me up at Vassar the night before my flight. His face was stony as I carried boxes downstairs. Perhaps he was afraid for me, or maybe he was just incredulous that I'd managed to do this again. But I couldn't see what he saw, the pattern of embarrassing mistakes and unfulfilled commitments that was starting to become so predictable. I only saw the sharp-edged specifics of each little catastrophe, clinging to this insistent belief that it could have been different if only the world had been kinder to me. I would have told anyone who would listen that the blame lay with the university that should have kept a closer eye on me, the parents who should have loved me more fiercely, the friends who were such a bad influence, the rehabs that failed to fix me. Just so long as I didn't have to admit that it was all my fault.

We drove back to the city in silence.

The following day, my father and I went to the storage unit in East Harlem where my things from high school were being kept, and I dropped off my things from college.

I hadn't expected to be doing that so soon.

Alone in the storage locker, I pulled open a cardboard box with my name on it. My high school yearbook was inside. Letters from Dean. Homework assignments I had saved for some reason—I couldn't say why. All these relics of a person I had been. I wasn't him anymore, but I wasn't myself, either. I felt like a ghost.

A few hours before I left for the airport, Annalise texted me. "Did you leave yet? I'm in the city."

"Come over," I said.

She met me downstairs in front of Jennifer's building.

"People are already asking where you went," Annalise said. "There's a rumor that you got kicked out."

I smiled. "That makes me sound a lot edgier than I actually am," I said.

"Want me to keep it going?"

"Definitely."

I hesitated. I'd been self-conscious of anyone seeing Jennifer's apartment after I had projected this image of Upper East Side glamour; the rather humble reality of crashing on a couch in my father's girlfriend's Yorkville one-bedroom wasn't something I was eager to share. But it also felt wrong, somehow, to keep maintaining that illusion with the truest friend I had.

"Do you want to come up?" I asked.

"Sure," she said.

Upstairs, I saw it afresh through her eyes: the worn floorboards, the oversize birdcage, the kitchen in need of updating. But she didn't say anything, and I was grateful to her for that—for seeing who I truly was, not who I had pretended to be to delight her. She had always seen through it, anyway.

I gave her my little glass pipe. "I guess I don't need this anymore," I said. "Take good care of it."

"I'm going to drop this and break it in five minutes," she said.

I walked her out and we embraced on the street.

"Don't stay too long," she said. "I can't do this without you."

"Trust me," I said. "I'll be right back."

Ten

I sent postcards from rehab.

The emblazoned logo of the facility. Glossy card stock splashed with images of terra-cotta stonework, the leafy eyelashes of palm trees, the impossible cerulean rippling of the swimming pool.

This, I thought, *is how getting sober should be.*

The first Sunday I was there, there was a grief group. No one I'd known had ever died, I realized, but I had almost died—twice. Did that count?

Kathleen, a model from Los Angeles, talked about the abortion that she'd had when she was seventeen, how she had grieved the loss of the baby she never knew. Bernard shared about losing his father to cancer.

I said: "I'm grieving the loss of the person I thought I was supposed to be."

I began to talk about Princeton, about my dreams, about how it had all fallen apart. Midsentence, I looked over at Kathleen, who had an expression on her face that looked like contempt.

Later, smoking a cigarette outside, I approached her. "Did I say something to offend you?" I asked.

"You just think you had it so fucking rough," she said. "You don't know what it's like to lose anything."

"That's not fair," I said.

"Everyone here thinks you're fucking ridiculous," she said. "We talked about it in group today. It's not about where you went to school or who you partied with. Nobody here gives a shit. Some of us are trying to get sober so we can survive."

"I am, too," I said. How dare she? She didn't know me. She didn't know my pain.

Kathleen extinguished her cigarette.

"Well," she said, "start acting like it."

The Arizona desert was still by night, a quiet so deafening that it assumed a sort of magnitude, a weight in the air. I left my room at five o'clock in the morning, moving swiftly through the darkened space, trying not to fumble, not flicking on the institutional lights of the bathroom as I changed into swim trunks and a T-shirt. My roommates' still-sleeping forms in their beds. The door clicked quietly behind me and I stood there for a moment, looking out at the dark emptiness of the night.

I walked quickly down the footpath that led around the perimeter of the property, silent save the slapping of my flip-flops against the ground. It was so cold, neck-prickle cold, the brisk slap of the wind lifting the hairs on my calves. I curved up past the nurse's station and clicked open the gate enclosing the swimming pool, trying to make out the shapes in the dark, when I saw someone seated by the edge of the water. I squinted. A tawny head, sturdy frame.

"Jane," I said.

Jane raised a hand in greeting, kicking her feet, making ripples that interrupted the glassy surface of the water.

"Hi, Sam," she said.

I liked Jane, although I hadn't gotten to know her well in the two weeks I'd been back in treatment. She was a registered nurse who had become addicted to opiates after struggling with alcoholism her whole life; in her midforties, with close-cropped blond-gray hair and a sympathetic, maternal air. We didn't have our main process group together, but I saw her in twelve-step meetings and specialized groups. I always felt like if I'd gotten separated from my mother in a grocery store as a small child and I'd seen Jane, I would have asked her for help.

She was comforting, trustworthy.

"I haven't seen you here this early before," she said.

"I couldn't sleep," I said, taking a seat on the bench across from her.

She smiled. "I have a hard time sleeping, too. It's too quiet here." She stretched her arms up, feline. "So I wait until it's almost sunrise, and then I come out here to do my morning meditation. Starts my day off right. The gate's supposed to be locked, but it never is."

Jane pointed up to the sky, where tendrils of purple and orange were starting to snake out from the horizon.

"Good timing," she said. I nodded.

"You've been here longer than I have, right?" I said. "When are you being discharged?"

She shrugged. "Probably next week."

"Are you going home or to aftercare?"

She twisted her hands so her palms were facing up. *Who knows.* "I'll do whatever they tell me to do," she said. "I'm not in a rush."

"I wish I felt that way," I said.

"How old are you?"

"Eighteen," I said.

Jane laughed. "You have so much time," she said. "You're so lucky. All the pain you're sparing yourself. The years I've wasted. Decades, even. Smart to nip it in the bud now before it gets any worse."

I shook my head. This line of conversation was infuriating. "People keep telling me that," I said. "They use that word, 'lucky.' As though it's some gift that I have to be sober for the rest of my life."

"It is," Jane said. "You'll feel differently about it when you're older. I promise."

I hated that, too, but didn't want to tell her so. I wanted her to like me.

She looked around thoughtfully. "It's neat that they put rehabs in the desert," she said. "It's a good use of a waste of space."

"That's how an ex-boyfriend used to describe fucking me," I said.

She looked at me quizzically.

"Never mind," I mumbled. "Dumb joke."

"You like to make people uncomfortable, don't you?" she said. "Set their teeth on edge a little bit? Push their boundaries?"

"If I get to be crazy, I don't have to be vulnerable," I said.

"Yeah." She took a deep breath. "That works with other people. But when you get out here and it's just you and the sky, none of that matters." She looked at me, her expression affectionate but a little sad. "God doesn't care about your rapier wit."

"I've always seen God as having more of a fondness for tragedy, anyway," I said.

Jane smiled and flexed her arms, tucking her legs under her and rising to her feet. I stood up, too, and suddenly the cold hit me all over again, the dizzying strangeness of this winter morning in the desert so far from home.

"Should we jump in?" she asked.

"I'm cold," I said stupidly, although it wasn't really about that: I was self-conscious about my body. That was why I'd gone out there in the first place, in the hopes of swimming alone, being able to take off my shirt without that arms-crossed discomfort of former fat kids who get lean by adulthood but always remain convinced, on some level, that their bodies are disgusting.

"I bet it's warmer in there," she said. My insecurity must have been palpable because her face softened.

"How long are you going to stay afraid of everything?" she asked. It was the kind of question that people asked often in rehabs, an inquiry that would sound transgressively rude coming from a relative stranger in any other context, but was commonplace in the emotionally unbounded domain of treatment.

I stripped off my shirt and kicked away my flip-flops, moving around the circumference of the pool until we were standing side by side.

She reached for my hand and, for whatever reason, I gave it to her. She squeezed it tightly. It felt so odd, standing here half naked in the frigid sunrise with this woman I didn't know, the thrilling intimacy of it, like seatmates on a long flight bonded together by a plane crash.

"One," Jane said. "Two. Three." And I felt my knees flexing and hers did, too, and it felt like a long moment that I spent suspended in the air, waiting for the impact, and then the water hit me and I sank to the bottom, pressing my knees close to my chest, feeling the shock of that freeze, my limbs tingling. It wasn't warm.

And then I opened my eyes underwater and looked up at the morning through the rippled lens of the pool, a darkness that was now daubed with color like an impressionist painting, the expanse of a sky that was beginning to split open.

My therapist in rehab recommended an aftercare program—an intensive outpatient rehab to transition patients back into the real world after inpatient treatment—in Cambridge, Massachusetts. I knew Boston from visiting my paternal grandmother there throughout my childhood, so I went happily, and sober.

I was sure that I could approximate the experience of staying sober behind the walls of a rehab—where my only responsibility was to feel my feelings and articulate them for people who were paid to listen—in a new city, with all of the pressures and responsibilities of an adult life I'd never had to experience before beating at my back. I could do it, I thought. I had to.

This proved arrogant.

It's funny that, even though I moved to Boston sober, I remember less from those first few months there than I do from the years I spent under the influence. A few images are electrifying in their vivid clarity: the sun-dappled trance of a New England winter, my feet crunching on the grass, the ruddy brick brownstones along Commonwealth Avenue as expressive as faces.

But it gets muddier quickly. Memory distorts, glazing the surfaces of my small studio apartment in Cambridge in a crimson varnish. I remember that the curtains I hung on the windows were a deep cherry, and so the winter light that beamed through the glass cast a psychedelic red pall throughout the apartment, coloring the clean minimalist lines of the chain-store furniture and the unadorned white walls in a scarlet glow.

Now it seems ironic that in my first grown-up apartment, I had unwittingly created a regressive womb-like space where I could hide from the very adult responsibilities I had moved to Boston to embrace. Life in that apartment was a delirious waking dream of spinning wheels and broken promises.

If I could do it all over again, I would do things differently.

Quickly, I found a job managing a small boutique on Newbury Street, and I rented a remodeled studio apartment in Cambridge, on Massachusetts Avenue just north of Porter Square, with spit-slick hardwood floors and stainless-steel appliances and walls of pristine windows that looked out onto the road, one window framing a red neon sign that read LIQUOR in front of the beverage retailer across the street. The sign flashed incessantly through the night (I imagined the word tattooed across my forehead in neon light as I slept), and my buzzer didn't work and, incredibly, I failed to notice before signing the lease that there was no oven in the kitchen (not that I would have cooked).

But these were trivial concerns, of no real significance when the block was shady and tree-lined and I could walk to the subway in ten minutes. I had an apartment to come home to, an apartment that I could keep clean and tidy, and it was mine, even if I couldn't really afford it, and given the turbulent shape of the past few years, which felt even more peripatetic in retrospect than it had while I was living it, it seemed that nothing could be more important than finding a stable living environment.

At work, there were opportunities for career growth, I was told. Could I see myself being a corporate trainer? How on earth should I know, at age eighteen? I wondered. And with my first paycheck I bought linens and silverware and a flat-screen television from a department store in the Prudential Center.

I called Annalise and told her, "I like it here, I think I might stay for a while," but not even I really believed this was true.

———

Boston—stoic, inhospitable Boston. Boston, I discovered, was a city of paradoxes, a metropolitan college town full of athletic nerds, a liberal enclave with doggedly Puritanical blue laws.

There, the people were polite but never nice. I had always thought of Boston as New York's inferior cousin, and my first few weeks there confirmed this suspicion. I was drawn to it then because I thought that Boston was more like New York than most other places, but not enough like New York for me to behave the way I had in New York.

I went to Boston for a fresh start, to escape the ugly wreckage of my past—in recovery circles, this is called "pulling a geographic"—not realizing that nobody came to Boston to work a low-paying job in retail management, especially not at my age. Everyone I met was either a native or a student, and I resented both camps. Each morning, I walked to the Red Line and took the train into work in my grandfather's silk-lined herringbone topcoat, glaring at the other commuters behind haughty aviator sunglasses, and when I spoke I was painfully conscious of my short *A* and rhotic pronunciation, conscious of the fact that I was eighteen (which to me, then, felt very old) and that I had left college to go to rehab and, frankly, had no idea if I was ever going to find my way back to higher education.

The men who cruised me on the street weren't stylish like they were in New York. In Boston, they wore baseball caps and hoodies, more boyish swagger than urbane charm, and even while some piece of me yearned for the high gloss of men with manicured eyebrows and European-cut suits, there was something appealing about the effortless masculinity of the men I met in Boston. An old family friend who was in graduate school at Boston University told me that she kept meeting eligible men at bars but couldn't go home with them; she said she could never respect a man who lived in Boston. I pointed out that she, too, lived in Boston, but I think that was the point.

The program my therapist had recommended treated drug addicts and patients with eating disorders in a brownstone not far from the Harvard campus; I liked the eating disordered women the most, since much of the reason I'd abused so much Adderall was to stay thin, and I felt like I had more in common with them, mostly privileged white girls from the suburbs, than with the hardened addicts who lived at the halfway house.

Twice a week at the center, I sat with eight or ten girls for three hours in a windowless room where first we talked about eating dinner, and then we ate dinner, and then we talked about having just eaten dinner. Some of the girls were wasted, with the brittle frailty of the terminally ill, but others were robust; people, even mental health practitioners, tend to lump patients with disordered eating under one umbrella, even though anorexics and bulimics couldn't be more different. I learned that whereas anorexics tend to be neurotic, tightly wound, and perfectionistic, bulimics are impulsive, gregarious, and spontaneous, and while the bodies of anorexics are externally enervated—that is, they *look* like people with eating disorders—the bodies of bulimics deteriorate from the inside out, so bulimics never get as skinny as they want to be. Yet as their bodies are deprived of nutrition, their organs begin to shut down, until one day they simply drop dead from organ failure. This, to me, seemed like the cruelest irony of all—to die from malnutrition while still overweight.

A therapist once told me that the hardest sickness to treat is the sickness that masquerades as health, and I would think of this as we smoked cigarettes in the alley adjacent to the center, the fat girls who wore too much makeup and the skinny girls who didn't wear enough and me, all of us dying.

Because it *was* about dying—I knew that it was. I could see my past behavior with enough clarity to at least know that.

It wasn't about euphoria; it hadn't been for a long time. It didn't feel that way, at least. After all, I had been filling prescriptions for hundreds of amphetamines a month, using so much cocaine that I left bloody chunks of flesh wadded in Kleenex roses, deliberately ingesting double the fatal dosage on a bottle of promethazine syrup just to see what would happen.

There had been so many stints in rehab. It all stuck together in my mind, a hazy blur of self-fulfilling sickness. Clearheaded and sober, I still didn't know why I did any of these things, things that I often did not want to do, feeling only that I must be carrying a fatal parasite, a brain tumor, or some satanic energy that wanted me dead and would stop at nothing until I had fatally self-destructed.

In the twelve-step meetings I went to, they called this "your disease," and my disease seemed hungry for chaos. I was stringing together some tenuous sobriety, but it didn't matter that the party was already over: I still felt insane about everything—the smallest social slight, someone's bad behavior at work, a call with my father gone wrong. It helped that I looked perfectly sane—that I could put on my good suit and dress shoes that kept me sliding through the icy streets of Boston, digging my heels into the ground and pleading with a God I didn't know if I believed in that I wouldn't slip and fall on my way to work.

But the fact remained that even though I was stone-cold sober, I was just as crazy that winter in Boston, as I slipped through the icy streets of Back Bay, as I had been in New York after three consecutive days without sleep, the metallic freeze of ketamine burning in my septum, waking up midflight while I was falling down a staircase in Grand Central Terminal.

<hr/>

Shortly after I arrived in Boston, I began working with a sponsor, Charlie, a part-time art dealer with genteel good looks. I met him at a twelve-step meeting in Harvard Square; he told his story of growing up in a tony beach community in Maryland, where he delivered kilos of cocaine via speedboat for a high-powered drug cartel. This was so glamorous, I thought. This would be the right person to help me learn how to survive sober.

I discovered after I asked him to sponsor me that Charlie was addicted to laxatives, which kept his body lean but lent him a sort of pasty, veiny dermal sheen that I found simultaneously compelling and repulsive, and although I couldn't really trust the instruction of a sponsor with an active eating disorder, I didn't have the heart to fire him.

Charlie gave terrible advice, but provided me with a passive sounding board for my poor decision-making. When I called him and said, "Charlie, I'm going to go see this quack doctor in Chinatown who gives you B12 shots in your ass and prescribes phentermine, no questions asked," he asked me for the address so he could come, too, and when I told him, "Charlie, this guy I dated who once threw me down a flight of stairs is in town and wants to have dinner," he recommended a fashionable new Asian fusion restaurant.

Yet if I had been asked what I wanted on a grand, existential plane, I probably would have said that all I wanted was to love and be loved. I couldn't say why I thought any of the things that I was doing would bring me love, but I was so lonely, terribly lonely.

Maybe drug addicts are just people who feel loneliness with the acuteness of a bad fever. I was quick to fall in love with any man who made me think that maybe we could have the sort of love that I always wanted. A quiet, domestic love that would provide me with the satisfaction that a thousand one-night stands never could. But that was also the kind of quiet, domestic love that I believed, even if I would never vocalize this note of internalized homophobia, gay men simply weren't allowed to have—but that wouldn't stop me from trying.

I met James for the first time on a cold day, which must have been in December. He sent me a message on an online dating site; I remember looking at his pictures and thinking how handsome he was. He looked like a leading man from a bygone era, in his early forties, his face warm and creased with age, hair just beginning to go gray. Strong, almost heroic. The text of his profile read: "Smart is sexy."

It is, I thought. *And* I'm *smart, right?*

We met at the old movie theater in Coolidge Corner to see a documentary that I found dull and that James seemed to enjoy, and afterward in the parking lot we stood by his car and he kissed me. His hands were large and his five o'clock shadow rubbed against my face, and it was freezing and people were staring and I felt lucky. In my head, I was already remodeling the master bathroom in the house on Cape Cod that we would buy together, selecting a palette of cool hues, slate blue tile and a bamboo bath mat, and I was putting fresh flowers in the kitchen that he wasn't noticing, and he was forgetting our anniversary, and we were going to sleep without having sex, and even if I grew to loathe waking up beside him in the morning I would never leave him, even as our marital bliss waned to nothing.

As I rode the Red Line back to my apartment I was warm and contented, thinking maybe I might not die alone in a studio apartment in Cambridge, unloved and unlovable. A week later, we made plans to meet again. At 7:00 p.m. I texted, then called.

He never responded.

Anxious, I left messages, wrote him emails, checked the news and the obituaries, suspecting there had been a tragic accident, but I found nothing. At home, I sat in my desk chair rocking back and forth (*literally* rocking back and forth in a desk chair, growing crazier by the minute, as the LIQUOR sign branded my chest with ambient red light), wondering how it was possible that my perfect domestic future with this perfect man could have been shattered so quickly—how I had already managed to destroy it, as I did everything I touched.

James never called. Months later, after I had left Boston, I sent him an email that read, "Thought of you today. Don't know why."

"I think of you every day," he wrote back.

"Liar," I said.

Maybe he saw in me the same sickness that I saw in myself— it was hard to miss—but the exquisite agony of that rejection was paralytic, reinforcing some privately held belief that I was fundamentally damaged or defective.

True intimacy was a distant point on the horizon, too evanescent to count on.

I relapsed on a bright, clear day in March, not intending to use any drugs, but not intending not to, either.

I had been sober for a few months, but I felt sure that it didn't matter anymore whether I was crazy and sober or crazy and on drugs. In many respects, I was right.

I met a man online named Greg. In his pictures, he had mean eyes and a thin, villainous smile and a muscular chest. He invited me to a shuttered, dilapidated home in Dorchester. When I entered the house, Greg was in the adjacent room, lying naked on a mattress on the floor, a freebase pipe in his left hand, a propane lighter in the other, a bare bulb overhead. He offered me some crystal meth and I said no, I didn't care for any, but thank you. In the kitchen, there was another man, John, who was mixing a quart of electric-blue Gatorade with drops from a small brown vial of GHB. He offered me a hit. It did not occur to me that I was supposed to be sober, that I had been for months; I just said yes. The solution was soapy and acidic; it burned in my throat. Then, I was on the mattress. Someone was kissing my stomach. Everything was dark. And then I was in the bathroom, vomiting in the toilet, with Greg, whose mean eyes had gone kind. He walked me to the T station on Dorchester Avenue and told me that he had been sober once, too, that he was going back to treatment soon.

"Good luck in rehab," I said.

A day passed. I had voice mails from my employer telling me not to bother coming in, that this was the last straw, that they would mail me my final check.

My rent was due over the coming weekend.

My parents wouldn't bail me out this time: I was on my own.

I sat on the floor of my apartment and studied my flat-screen television, not wanting to sell it. I thought of Laurel.

I opened my computer and added myself to an online escorting site.

The first man who responded to my ad was a young, attractive advertising executive named Jason. He invited me over to his high-rise in Kendall and we took Ambien and had clinical, dispassionate sex. He paid me $300 and told me that he wanted to see me again, and the next night, he picked me up in his car and we drove into Back Bay for dinner, where, lubricated by red wine and his affections, I could feel myself becoming more radiant and charming than I had ever been before, fawning over him, reaching across the table to touch his hand, collapsing into his gaze.

This was it, I thought, the romance I'd craved; I hadn't expected it to come like this.

When he dropped me off later, I told him that I really liked him. He tried to give me money. I wouldn't take it. His face soured.

"I think you're confused," he said. "Why would I want to have a relationship with you that's anything more than transactional?" His words were like a slap.

I sprinted up the stairs into my building and collapsed onto my bed, sobbing from this validation of my worthlessness. I called a friend from rehab and wept into the phone.

"What's wrong? What's wrong?" she kept asking, and I didn't know how to explain what I had done.

This is where my memories begin to splinter, which must mean that it was the end.

The first night was with a man in the South End, and he wanted to smoke meth. "Party," that's what the gay users simply call it, just "party," but what that actually means is smoking meth, except they call it "tina" for some reason. Whatever snobbish disdain I had held for this particular drug, which I'd done only a handful of times and usually guiltily, just seemed so tiresome and

so irrelevant now, like such a pointless vestige of a person who I
hadn't been for a long time, and so we smoked his tina and took
his GHB, which they call liquid Ecstasy because it's a clear soluble
liquid that tastes the way antibacterial soap smells but makes you
swirl in a euphoric daze, and we sprawled in each other's bodies
in the living room in the dark while he was telling me to shut the
fuck up because his husband was puttering around in the kitchen
illuminated by a beam from the track lighting overhead, pouring
himself a glass of wine while I lay on the floor with this stranger
who had a husband who was there in the kitchen, wondering if I
was invisible.

Then a night, maybe the next night, with a drug dealer in a
Range Rover who had a gun in the glove compartment, and he
picked me up and there were security cameras in his bedroom,
and I sucked his dick to the thunderous beat of house music while
men were laughing in the hallway, glasses clinking, my heart palpitating, watching my grainy image on closed-circuit television
with wide-open eyes, and then I was in that empty apartment
with no furniture that belonged to the tweaker who just wanted
one more hit, one more hit, and I told him that I was leaving and
he grabbed my coat and his eyes were desperate and red-rimmed
and he told me that he would do anything, anything, and there
was porn playing on a broken television where men were wearing black latex masks and it wasn't sexy, and then I was in a
house somewhere in Dorchester, and a guy I didn't know stuck
a syringe into the base of my groin (I'm a nurse, he said, I know
how to do this, don't worry, I won't fuck it up, because you keep

going limp and I need to fuck and this is better than Viagra, you'll stay hard for hours). And I started carrying a crack pipe in my coat pocket and little bags of crystal in my wallet and taking cabs where I would listen to glitchy techno on my headphones and tap my head against the window to the beat until the cabbie looked at me funny, and there were men in the South End and the North End and Beacon Hill and Fenway and Jamaica Plain and Allston and Newton and Waltham, men in apartments and houses, men in the city and in the suburbs, a man in a boutique hotel with art deco fixtures in Cambridge who looked so straitlaced and corporate as he pulled the wedding band from his finger and set it on the nightstand (*you piece of shit*) and then he lit a joint (*marijuana! I'd forgotten you existed*), and I drank a bottle of cough syrup in the bathroom and would have been so ashamed if he knew that I was Robo-tripping (how puerile, how humiliating, even though 450 milligrams of dextromethorphan hydrobromide was almost as good as a half lick of ketamine, it's still a dissociative anesthetic, *don't tell anyone*) and from between his legs his stomach was like an undulating plain of sand dunes, rippling as he inhaled and exhaled, and I felt like the air was tickling me. At a different hotel, this one on the Charles River, the hallways were long and circular, and I followed them around for what felt like hours before finding the right room, and the man had scars on his face and he ripped off the condom and I didn't care, and after it was over I asked him if I fucked like someone who had been sexually abused and laughed too loudly and he gave me a big tip. I came home after a week, or ten days, without having slept at all, and I had $2,000 in cash stuffed haphazardly in various pockets and a quarter ounce of meth and thirty-six new voice mails and the skin around my lips was red and broken and crusting, my hands were charred and bleeding, and I went into work to pick up my things, snorting a fat bump of ketamine out of the strip of skin between my thumb and index finger, dripping with perspiration and cracking up at my boss's baffled face (not even horrified, just confused, as though I were some sort of mirage that only she could see), elbowing my way into the stockroom to pick up a sweater and a commuter mug and collapsing on the floor, and everyone staring (*what's wrong with him?*), and no matter what I put on that rash around my mouth it just seemed to grow and spread like an indelible stain until I imagined that it had spread all over my body. Then, in my apartment, a guy with a sunken torso asked me if I wanted to slam, and he had clean needles and I had a teener (*that's all we need*) and I remember marveling at his medical precision as he melted the flakes of blue-white crystal in a spoon with a propane lighter and loaded a syringe with it, a small, narrow syringe, not cartoonish and dirty like I'd imagined but glistening and harmless as a shot that I really needed (*it's time for your medicine*), and then he tied a belt around my arm, and told me to take a deep breath because I wasn't going to be breathing for a long time, and we couldn't find a vein until finally we found one (and we were both laughing, how strange to be laughing in a moment like that), and he said, "Are you ready for the cough?" and I said "What cough?" and as he plunged the needle into my arm I remember a heat spreading through me starting from my chest and oscillating out to my appendages and digits and then I coughed just like he said, one short, hot cough, and I was in a fever for days and I don't remember anything except getting out of the shower to hear the fire alarm shrieking and the four men (what were their names?) who had been in my apartment were gone, two freebase pipes left smoldering on the ground, leaving black residue on the hardwood floor, and the lights were on and I hadn't seen sunlight in what felt like an eternity, and the room was full of red light. Crystal meth tore my body apart like nothing else ever had, especially when it was injected directly into my veins; it forced its way out of my skin in acneic sores and I could taste that hot chemical smell in my mouth, all the time. My cuticles were shredded and bloody, a bright, dark pink, the color of exposed gums at the dentist, the color of asbestos insulation in attics, a Crayola crayon color, and they bled constantly, and my arms were pocked with track marks. It was like this for two months, maybe three, and it felt like a week and also like a lifetime, and by two months into this run I was someone completely different and I did not know myself anymore, and frequently I thought of a man I heard speak in a meeting once, whose voice was strong and sonorous until it cracked midsyllable and he began to cry and said, "Meth took *everything* from me," and it was sad but I didn't know what he meant, imagined that he meant things like a house and a car and a family, didn't know that he was talking about something intangible but necessary, something that he could never get back.

Even thousands of miles away, my mother always knew when I was on drugs, and she called me, her voice grave, begging me to please get help.

There were no words to explain that I had fallen too far, that I didn't have the strength to ever get sober again, that I didn't know how to moderate and I didn't know how to quit, that even when I promised myself that I wouldn't pick up I ended up slamming crystal, that I had lost the power of choice, that it was too hard and I had given up, that I was going to shoot meth until I died, that I hoped that would be soon—and what was most fascinating (to me) was that I felt none of this with the self-aggrandizing theatricality of how I'd felt even a few months earlier but rather, with a slightly rueful resignation, as detached as if the circumstances of my life were a distant tragedy occurring to strangers somewhere very far away.

Charlie sent me emails telling me to just *go to a fucking meeting already* and also I should probably get tested for hepatitis C (among other things), and I ignored him because I knew with utter conviction that I could not stop.

I could not stop.

My father told me in an email that he was getting me a plane ticket to San Francisco, where he had moved to from New York, and I could stay with him and detox there if I wanted to get clean. The date of the flight approached, but I had already decided that I wasn't going; I couldn't leave my apartment anymore for *any* reason, let alone to travel across the country.

Reduced to a cliché of tweaker paranoia, I peeked out the windows at the speeding cars on Massachusetts Avenue and played German trance music at deafening volumes so the secret listeners couldn't hear (I considered them a viable threat) and scrubbed the hardwood floors with lemon polish twice a day. (*Are those fucking paparazzi outside again?* And I laughed alone in my shiny apartment.) In the hours before the flight I slammed again (telling myself, as I always did, that it would be the last time, and also making sure I had enough left to do it again later), and I began throwing clothes into suitcases, emptying the cabinets full of dishes and silverware into black trash bags, the symphony of shattering glass, and my hands were bleeding again, smoking cigarettes, freebasing meth, deciding that I wasn't going, and then packing again, unable to leave but unable to stay.

Ninety minutes before my flight, I called a john who lived nearby in Somerville and asked him to come drive me to the airport, and before I could tell him not to bother he said sure, that he would be there in fifteen minutes. (His name was Rick and he told me once while he was fucking me that he wished I were Korean because he really preferred Asian guys; I did not know what to say to him then, and I would not know what to say to him if I saw him today, but I owe him a tremendous debt.) And when his car pulled up I left my furniture and television, food that I never ate still sitting in the refrigerator with all the labels facing out and conservative New England overcoats still hanging neatly in the wardrobe on walnut hangers spaced exactly one-inch apart (I'd measured while high on meth one night), and I got into

his car and he told me I looked like shit and we drove to Boston
Logan and I knew that I wasn't going to make it—there was no
way I was going to make it on this flight, it was all a joke, and like
an idiot I had thrown away my freebase pipe and now I was going
to have to go all the way to that fucking head shop by the Fens to
buy another pipe or maybe I could steal one from Ian, that slam-
pig in Charlestown, if I could lure him over to my place by telling him I had picked up good shit—and I was sprinting through
security, panting, drenched in sweat. And at the gate I knew that
once I boarded this plane, I could never go back to this life; that
if I went to San Francisco, I would need to detox and count days
of sobriety and start over, and in a flash, as I handed the flight
attendant my ragged boarding pass, I relived the most joyful
moments of my storied career in addiction, daytime drunks on
Upper East Side rooftops with friends I thought I'd have forever,
sex on Ecstasy with a boy I once loved profoundly, and the sheer
ecstatic euphoria of the first time I shot meth, like a thousand
orgasms collapsing into one breathless instant of pure happiness,
and I wasn't ready for it to end and I buckled my seat belt and I
did not believe that I would survive. And my mouth was bleeding and I spilled the ice water that the flight attendant brought
me and babies screamed and my ears were ringing and there were
spiders crawling under my skin and the muscular grinding of the
wheels against the concrete made me shake and in the cramped
lavatory I crumpled to my knees and I prayed.

Please, God, if you are out there please help me to do this because
I can't and if you won't do it for me because I know this is all my fault

and I haven't earned your grace then don't do it for me, God, do it for anyone who loves me, even if nobody does.

My father met me at the airport in San Francisco, and his expression was cold and blank when he saw my staggering gait, my ravaged face, my bleary bloodshot eyes, that abraded skin around my lips, my jaw locking my mouth in an underbite, and he didn't touch me. In the car I wanted to tell him about the epic battle between good and evil that had been waging in my body for months, about how far I had fallen, about how afraid I had been, about how I was certain that I had lost everything. That I had worked so hard in the pursuit of some greatness that was always just beyond my grasp, and in doing so, I'd managed to wreck my entire life, a life that had only just begun.

But instead I began to cry and said "Daddy," and I kept waiting for him to look at me while searing beams of headlight blinded me and happy people smiled on billboards and he just kept his gaze fixed on the road, driving on into the night.

The next day, before the sun rose, I walked to an early-morning twelve-step meeting in the Castro. My legs ached. I was dumbfounded that I was alive, that I had survived the night. The spring air was balmy and fragrant.

I told the people in the meeting my name, and I said I was an alcoholic and a drug addict.

"This is it," I said, sobbing to a complete stranger. "It's over. I'm done. I will never go back there, as long as I live. I will never do this again. I will do whatever it takes. It will never be like that again."

"Take it one day at a time," she said soothingly. "That's how this works."

"No," I said. "You don't understand. You don't know the things I've been through. You don't know the things I've done. This is the end."

"What if you don't say it's the end?" she said. "What if it's just the beginning of something new?"

The people there gave me their phone numbers and told me to call anytime, day or night.

And I kept my jacket on so they couldn't see my arms, which were so bitten with track marks and abscesses that it was a week before I could raise them above my head.

Eleven

I was nineteen when I got sober. At the time it felt very old, like I had passed my expiration date a hundred times. In the beginning, I carried myself with the weariness of someone who had survived a war.

After a month with my father and Jennifer in San Francisco, counting days of sobriety, I returned to Portland to stay at my mother's house in the woods. I had no plan, no lofty goals. Maybe I would get a low-pressure job somewhere nearby, I thought. Maybe that would be as big as my life ever got again.

I enrolled in classes at the local university, where I spent my days. At night, I went to twelve-step meetings and stayed up all night with the other sober kids I met. We rolled through the starry streets in beat-up old cars that stank of stale cigarettes, pounding energy drinks and talking shit.

In the mornings, I prayed on my knees that God would keep me clean and sober for one more day.

I collected a thirty-day coin, then a sixty-day, then a ninety-day.

My mother would wake me up in the morning with a cup of sweet coffee. She cried often out of sheer relief, and for once, I did not mind her sentimentality.

"You're a miracle," she said.

All of my new friends were sleeping with one another, but I was afraid to date. "You can't drink with a dick in your mouth," one of them joked, which always made me laugh.

But I was sober, and that meant I had lost my edge, my verve, the confidence that would surge up when I was intoxicated. There were still so many pieces of me that were damaged. I couldn't fathom that anyone could take me as I was, after all the things I had done.

A few months after I got sober, I asked my new sponsor, Brian, why nobody ever talked about slamming crystal in meetings. It was hardly an underground thing, I said; surely I had shot up with half the gay dudes in Boston.

"It's not that nobody does it," he said. "It's just that nobody makes it back."

Brian taught me what to say when people ask me why I don't drink alcohol: I tell them that I'm allergic, and if they ask what happens when I *do* drink, I tell them that I break out in crystal meth. It's a shame that most people have too much decorum to ask, so I don't get to use that line very often.

And it was with Brian that I sat on the balcony of my home, surrounded by a dense canopy of coniferous trees, and wrote down a list of the qualities that I had always wanted in my ideal partner: a man whose intelligence was surpassed only by his kindness, a man who would accept me no matter how grievous my mistakes had been. Once the list was compete, we lit the sheet of paper on fire, watching it turn to ash, sending smoke signals up to God or the ocean that I might someday be loved.

Then came Michael.

I met him at a coffee shop in downtown Portland for our first real date. I was self-conscious, but so was he. We talked about all the things you aren't supposed to talk about on a first date—religion, politics, previous relationships—and we talked about how we were talking about those. How taboo that was supposed to be, but how natural it felt.

He rode his bicycle there, and wore a sporty windbreaker that felt so quintessentially Portland, and I remember thinking about how I used to date men in suits, how those days had to be all gone now that I'd escaped to the damp Pacific Northwest, with its grand old western red cedars and its quiet nights, its restaurants where drinks were always served out of mason jars.

Michael was taller than I was, which was unusual. He was broad-featured and athletic, handsome in an old-fashioned, slightly goofy way. Graying at the temples, which I liked. Although he was thirty-seven, and very much an adult, he did not remind me of my father, and I was grateful for that.

Later, when Kat's mother met him, she took to calling him Super-H. He looked like a superhero, she said.

Michael took me back to his house, a two-story Victorian in a gentrifying neighborhood, not far from where Jerick had lived. Then crackheads had ambled the streets, frightening me; now the sidewalks were clotted with little restaurants with rustic decor and prix fixe menus, cocktails made with muddled huckleberries, cocktails I didn't drink. We lay on a brown leather couch that smelled like tobacco and the woods, and my pulse throbbed in my ears when he kissed me. We ate hors d'oeuvres naked in the kitchen. We made love. He read me his favorite passages from his favorite books. We talked about Tobias Wolff, Frank Conroy, Vivian Gornick.

He was an English teacher, after all.

It was a big house for a single man, but he wasn't single, I learned, not really—or at least, he hadn't been, because it was the house he had shared with his wife and son. The marriage was over, he said; it had been for a long time, but the divorce was slow. The house was on the market. He had custody of his son some evenings and every other weekend. He'd gotten sober for his son, he said.

I was certain that I could not handle meeting him, this child that was a product of a marriage that predated me. This tousle-headed, apple-cheeked kid in photographs on his dresser. I imagined his laughter streaking the walls, his footsteps on the hardwood floors, haunting as a horror-movie ghost. I put my hand on Michael's heart, and it felt unimaginable that he could have made another person.

We spent the weekend together in that house, and when I left, I was so hysterically full of feeling that I wept in my car. I smoked a cigarette anxiously. My breaths were short and panicked.

"Is this how it feels?" I asked my sponsor. "Is this how it's supposed to feel? Is this just what being human is like?"

I stayed with Michael for nearly a year.

Michael and I had been together for about six months when my father came to Portland from San Francisco; he was in town on business, and it happened to coincide with my birthday. We were not on good terms, but we were not on bad terms, either, and I appreciated that he was there at all. My older brother, who was now in graduate school in central Oregon, came up for the day. The three of us had breakfast and then drove out to the coast. I was wearing a maroon sweater that hugged my arms too tightly. The sand and ocean were all washed-out gray, a saltwater taffy dream. My father took a picture of my brother and me standing on the beach, and in the photograph, I am squinting at the light.

I look like a little boy, but more than anything, I look like my father's son.

That night, the four of us went to dinner—Michael, my brother, my father, and me—at a restaurant in Portland with an outdoor garden. It was a clear, bright autumn evening, and the sun was going down. Michael was nervous, and he didn't say much, but I loved him for being there, even though things had grown difficult between us by then.

Those lusty nights and indolent espresso mornings had yielded so quickly to a temperate, sexless familiarity, but he had been drinking in secret and lying about it, and that terrified me. The alcohol was hot and sweet on his breath—how badly it made me crave a drink, even as I loathed him for his recidivism and resented his willingness to anesthetize the often-excruciating clarity of sobriety. That was something that I wished I could do, too.

But he was sober at dinner, and my father was graceful and inclusive, considering that Michael was closer in age to my father than he was to me.

I held Michael's hand under the table. His leg was shaking. I put my palm on it, felt the smooth texture of his jeans on his knee, the vibrations of his muscles, the anxiety that rippled through his body.

I loved that he cared enough to be afraid.

Later, I asked my father, "What did you think of Michael?" There was silence on the other end of the telephone.

"I don't know," my father said. "He seemed like a good guy." Perhaps it was too strange, that situation, for him to take in much more than the age disparity. I told myself it didn't matter.

A week later, in the interest of reciprocity, after Michael told me for the hundredth time that it would mean a lot to him, I went to meet his son, at a pizza place.

I tried to connect, tried to bond over school and dinosaurs. He mostly ignored me, which I didn't mind.

I never knew how to talk to children, even when I was one. It was all overwhelming, to be that age, with my boyfriend who was twice my age and his son who was half my age, and I felt in that moment that there were so many roles I had never learned how to play: How could I possibly be a stepfather? I was no defter at playing a father than I had ever been at playing a son, no better at playing an adult than I had ever been at playing a child.

Michael had all of the qualities I had listed in my inventory, and some flaws, too; some grievous ones, even. I was too young to be able to interrogate our age difference fully—what it meant that we desired each other. I told myself that there was little chance that I could align my interests with those of an age peer; or, more arrogantly, that I was too mature, had too much life experience to be with someone my own age. But the simple truth was that I loved Michael for who he was, his strong arms and quick wit, and because, since I had told him once, shortly after we met, that I had an insatiable need for validation, he sent me a short email every morning telling me something that he loved about me. Something new, every day, for months on end.

From the outside it might have looked creepy, but it didn't feel abnormal when we were together. At moments I wondered whether this was just the same old dysfunction, but when he looked at me, the lines of his face would soften, and I knew that it was real.

Those emails stopped after he started drinking again. We began to fight, bitterly. "I would never do anything to jeopardize your sobriety," he said.

"I know that," I said. "But the risk isn't worth it. And neither are you."

I couldn't quite bring myself to leave him just yet, even though I knew the relationship was going to fail because of it. The ship was flooding—I could see it—and there was only room on the life raft for me. And it was strange, too, to be in pain because someone else couldn't stay sober, and mostly when I cried as

Michael was driving home, not knowing whether he was drunk or not—whether he might crash and kill himself or someone else—I thought of my parents. I finally tasted one drop in the ocean of pain and fear they must have felt all those years.

But what I could never tell him was something more com-plicated—that there were other times, too, when we were having sex, that I would close my eyes and pretend that he was a stranger, that the breath on my face belonged to a man who wouldn't think to ask me my name, who would just leave cash or drugs on the nightstand.

I would imagine that familiar heaviness in my arms, the fever burning in my chest, the acrid taste of chemicals in my mouth, and I would tell Michael that I loved him, not even sure if that was the right name for the emotion that, sometimes, just felt like a resignation to the way things were now, and a longing for a life I had left behind. And when I saw zombie gays on the street with locked jaws and fidgety hands and red-rimmed eyes and instantly knew their secret, I envied them, and hated myself for it, and something, too, swelled inside me when I saw young people stag-gering out of bars.

As time passed and my life began to change, soon there were happy hours and corporate retreats and birthday parties and lonely evenings—all those markers of adult life that felt so funny with-out alcohol. I weathered them sober and sometimes even gladly, but even at my best I never felt quite normal. Maybe "normal," I thought, wasn't the point.

I reminded myself that I was lucky to be sober, lucky to be

healthy, lucky to be alive. *Lucky.* That was the word, wasn't it? But it was remarkable to me that I bore no mark of Cain—that my features hadn't changed, that my history wasn't written all over my face. When people told me that I had my whole life ahead of me, I said I was just grateful to have survived the whole life behind me.

"You never have to go back there." I heard people say this in meetings about their addictions, and it always confounded me. There was so much of me that had never really left. There was so much of me that I had lost there that I knew I could never get back.

At night, lying in bed with Michael, I had strange, vivid dreams where everything sparkled—a gilded razor, a mound of shimmering powder, a golden handgun that gleamed in the light. When I turned to look at my reflection in the mirror, there was glitter streaming from my nostrils, clinging to my lips, dripping from my chin.

But then I would awaken to find sunshine pouring through the window, and I would turn to feel it on my face. After spending so much time in the darkness, my eyes had adjusted. It got easier over time, but there were still mornings where it was the most frightening thing—to step out, blinking, into the sunlight.

Eventually, I moved back to New York. Michael stayed behind in Portland. After a few years, we lost touch.

Yet there was one moment at that dinner with my father and my brother and Michael when I was caught somewhere between a child and an adult—grown-up enough to get things right from time to time but still young enough not to know that wouldn't always be enough. Where the amber glow of that affection felt like all the nourishment I could have ever craved, where the world and all the people in it spilled over with so much possibility, and it felt likely, not just possible but *likely*, that things would be different for me.

Fathers and sons and brothers, all of us tall and strong and failing.

But all of us trying.

Acknowledgments

Thank you to my passionate and diligent agents, Andrew Stuart and Jason Richman, my tireless manager, Jon Klane, and my patient and wise editorial team, Mitchell Ivers and Natasha Simons. I am most grateful, too, for the early mentorship and support of thoughtful teachers and editors Debra Gwartney, Tom Bissell, Anna David, Josh Kendall, and Sarah Hepola, who helped me to tell my story better.

To dear friends, trusted readers, sharp-eyed colleagues, and everyone who carried me through the writing of this book in ways both big and small: Kelly Stone, Bradley Stern, Kendall Storey, Eden Sher, Allyn Morse, Debby Ryan, Stacy Waronker, Matthew Scott Montgomery, Jessica Newham, Kipton Love Davis, Bethany Skeen, Cady Groves, Ryan O'Connell, Esperé Nelson, Daisy Bell Mellors, Nile Kohli, Dan D'Addario, Kelly Conniff, and George Henry.

And to my family, who bore with me through my darkest years and through this revisiting of it, I am most fortunate that you love me anyway.